ŚAṄKARA—NO-OTHER
(*A Tribute to Ādi Śaṅkarācārya*)

ŚAṄKARA—NO-OTHER
(*A Tribute to Ādi Śaṅkarācārya*)

Raghunandan Trikannad

Ocean Books Pvt. Ltd.
ISO 9001:2015 Publishers

Published by
Ocean Books (P) Ltd.
4/19 Asaf Ali Road,
New Delhi-110 002 (INDIA)
e-mail: info@oceanbooks.in

ISBN 978-81-8430-561-6
ŚAṄKARA—NO-OTHER (***A Tribute to Ādi Śaṅkarācārya***)
by Raghunandan Trikannad

Edition
2025

Price
₹ 500.00 (Rupees Five Hundred only)

Printed at
Shree Sai Printers, Sahibabad

Contents

Foreword

It was a most delightful and enlightening experience to go through the contemplations of Sri Raghunandan Trikannad, on the life and message of Bhagawan Śri Śaṅkara Bhagavadpāda. Śri Śaṅkara was undoubtedly unparalleled. Rightly, the author has given the title ***Śaṅkara—No-Other***. It is not easy to recapitulate the highly spiritual significance of the events that made up the life of the greatest Indian in recorded history through our limited vision. Yet many have tried to approach Śaṅkara bringing more and more enlightening insights which marked that exemplary life.

Who was Śaṅkara?

Was Śaṅkara really born? Where was he born? When was he born? As we bow down to his Eternal spirit, these questions have no relevance. What is of importance to us is that Śaṅkara WAS, Śaṅkara IS and Śaṅkara WILL BE. Deep as the ocean, lofty as Himalayas, expansive as Sky, ancient yet young, profound in wisdom but silent, beyond this phenomenal world, yet One with it—not even the thousand tongued *Anaṅta* can adequately describe the manifestation of Divinity that Śaṅkara was.

The age was ripe for one to appear to fulfill the prophecy: "I will come whenever virtue subsides". It was the South that was to receive the blessings and the home of the pious Nambūdiri couple Śivaguru and Arya Devi in the cozy village of Kalady became the chosen place for the manifestation. The events that marked Śaṅkara's short life can easily be summed up. But, who can comment on the wonderful commentary that he was of

Truth, of Self-existent Knowledge and of Life Eternal. For thirty-two years this star of unusual effulgence lit up our sky before it disappeared in the folds of Time.

In his own inimitable style, Sri Raghunandan has recapitulated the events in Śaṅkara's life, each one revealing the grandeur of the Advaita philosophy of which Śaṅkara was a living example.

This world of fleeting sensual pleasures could not hold him even as a young child. Like the renowned Nachiketa, he too left the beaten track of worldly enjoyments and took to the lonely path of renunciation and contemplation to reach the most difficult of destinations, the citadel of Truth. It is to Śaṅkara's everlasting glory that even at that age, following the Upaniṣadic teachings and techniques of intricate analysis, reasoning, negation and 'self'-annihilation, he could realise the truth within him and attain oneness with it. No wonder, that this child monk of unsurpassed grace and wisdom brought a new dignity to the order of Sanyāsis.

The depth of understanding and the rare brilliance of erudition with which Śaṅkara examined and studied various doctrines and philosophies by itself became an act of polishing and purifying them and when commented by this embodiment of Truth, who was none other than the incomparable Dakshinamurthy, they revealed a new meaning and significance. Truth confined in texts, expressed through rituals, idolized in temples, practised by priests, propagated by teachers, lived in daily life by common people, all of them acquired a new ethereal glow at his divine touch. The words of transcendental wisdom that emanated from this knower of Brahman — the most powerful vibrations of Advaita, ruthlessly demolished the parasitic growth of perversions and superstitions on the ancient Sanātana Dharma into which now flowed the life giving sap of Truth again bringing it to blossom. Śaṅkara did not stop with intellectual exercises alone, he entered the temples, rectified the mistakes in their rituals and ceremonies, transforming them again into centers of power and faith. The idols therein literally came to life at his call, when in absolute identification of the

Eternal All pervading self, he breathed unto them the essence of his own eternal life. The glories he sang of the temple deities are marvels of transcendental poetical beauty.

All these have been brought out in a simple touching manner by the author transporting us into the presence of Śaṅkara and his disciples, enlivening each of these incidents. We become one of them as our doubts also get cleared through dialogues of Ācārya. Mystical incidents have been logically scrutinized and straightened out so that the reader can effortlessly visualise and absorb the significance of them even from this far-off time.

What is Advaita, the crest jewel of human thought, India's unparalleled gift to humanity, in which alone, as rivers merge in the ocean all the human efforts can finally find their ultimate destination and fulfillment.

Advaita can be understood in an over simplified way by understanding three of its major concepts:

1. The Ultimate Reality is One only, the *Nirguṇa* Brahman, indescribable, yet realisable by the human mind in this very life.
2. Out of this Brahman, like a web from the spider has come out the phenomenal world of pluralities, in it, but not of it. This world is taken as the reality by the ignorant due to the play of *Māyā*, the deluding power of intellect and its 'creative misinterpretation'.
3. The third concept is that of '*Avidyā*' or ignorance. This ignorance is different from the usual lack of knowledge we speak about in that it is conditioned by *Māyā* which prevents man from recognizing his true nature or reality within him and makes him behave as a non-entity suffering from the pangs of day-to-day life. The life as is known and lived by us today is the combined effect of *Māyā* and *Avidyā*. So long as we remain in their grip, like a dreamer in a dream we experience the joys and miseries of the dream. To rescue the dreamer from his dream experiences, the only way is to end the dream. That is, to wake him up. Similarly,

to end the miseries in the life and gain Bliss, *Avidyā* must end, and man must wake up to his True Reality within. Knower of Brahman verily becomes the Brahman.

There was no cult or creed in India which could stand up to the challenges of this perfect thinking and analytical reasoning. All erroneous and false practices and pretentious teachings crumbled before the mighty wave of Śaṅkara's Advaitic thoughts. He became "*Sarvajña*", the repository of the highest and most profound knowledge, reasoning, analysis and realisation. Like the mighty Himalayas and ever-gurgling Ganges, Śaṅkara also became the personification of the quintessence of the best which India had to offer to the world? That WAS Śaṅkara.

Today Śaṅkara IS the favourite of Western intellectuals! What is so fascinating to modern thinkers, logicians and scientists is that his Advaita provides a system 'totally devoid of internal contradictions'. To have been the master of such a clear, precise and perfect system and that too at such young age is what makes Śaṅkara supremely adorable and acceptable to one and all. No wonder that all *Sādhakas*, like the present author, wants to pay his homage to this gigantic intellect trying to understand him in their own way.

As material science moves nearer to the Ultimate Truth, the importance of human mind and consciousness in the scheme of things is also becoming clearer. Advaita with its daring pronouncement "*Tattwamasi*" stands today as the only logical conclusion for all the varied scientific enquiries, because only it can provide, to quote author Isenberg: "A complete philosophical and conceptual framework within which the findings of advanced modern physical science can be placed without stress or tear." So long as there was a gap in the scientific understanding and matter and energy were thought of as two separate entities, Advaita's monism was not acceptable for the Western scientists. The tables are turned now. Recent discoveries in the field of science are repeatedly proving that matter and energy are the obverse and reverse of the same 'something'. What could that 'something' be, other than Divine Consciousness of which man is the rightful heir? This omniscient, omnipotent Universal Truth which India has proclaimed thousands of years ago is at last entering into the understanding of the best of scientific brains in the West. This all-pervading unerringly applicable and realisable monistic truth is what Śaṅkara started searching, as a child escaping from the jaws of the crocodile's illusion and having realised it spared no pains to share it with the entire world.

Today, baffled with the results of their far-reaching theoretical and experimental analyses when scientists are groping in darkness, it is Śaṅkara with his light of Advaita who is lighting their paths. As science is approaching nearer and nearer to Truth, the material in it is undergoing dissolution and the spirit is taking over. As the material scientific search finally establishes (if at all) its contact with the ultimate, self-existent Truth, Brahman of Vedāntin or by whatever name It may be called and merges with It, there is bound to be the emergence of a new light 'as though a thousand suns have together lit up the sky.'[1]

That would be when India will again regain her supremacy in world thought. Advaita would have proved its worth as a system of thought par excellence. Wherever and whenever the human mind cuts asunder its shackles of ignorance and in a spirit of adventure soars high into realms unknown, through perfectly analytical and rational contemplation to reach for TRUTH there WILL BE manifestation of the spirit of Śaṅkara again and again.

Śri Raghunandan's narration of the complex phenomenon of Śaṅkara and his life's message is in such an easy style to follow that allows us to slip into the intimate congregation of the Guru and Śiṣyas and allows us to be a part of it and share the valuable insights offered by the master, which help us to refresh and redefine our knowledge of the various principles and their societal significance in the light of Advaita. One great achievement of the author is that Śaṅkara is not projected as a stern and uncompromising Guru but a most benevolent and

---

1. दिवि सूर्यसहस्रस्य भवेद्युगपदुत्थिता ।
यदिभाः सदृशी सा स्याद्भासस्तस्य महात्मनः ॥ श्रीमद्भगवद्गीता 11.12 ॥

understanding 'mother' from whom Advaita has poured out in poetical, musical and life giving cascades of pure knowledge. As a bonus, the reader gets to look into the original verses and quotations in Sanskrit from the scriptures as well as the commentaries of the Master.

Glory to the land—which gave birth to ŚAṄKARA! Glory to the culture that fashioned his genius! Glory to that Eternal, Immortal Spirit, which manifested as ŚAṄKARA. Blessed would be the reader who would read through this narration and recapture the glory of Śaṅkara. Twice blessed is the reviewer who could recapitulate the spiritual blossoming of the human soul of Śaṅkara. Thrice blessed is the mind, which could visualize Śaṅkara's inimitable life and share it once again with the discerning, for establishing the infallibility of Advaita.

Dr. M. Lakshmi Kumari

Vivekananda Kendra
Vedic Vision Foundation
Kodungallur, Kerala

With a doctorate in Botany from the University of Madras, Dr. M. Lakshmikumari served as a Professor of Botany in Sri Padmavathy Women's College, Tirupati, and was later awarded a post-doctoral fellowship at Ukrainian Academy of Sciences, Kiev, USSR, where she spacialised in Microbiology and subsequently joined as a Scientist at Indian Agricultural Research Institute, New Delhi. Having an innate urge to serve the cause of Swami Vivekananda, she dedicated her life to service, and got closely associated with Vivekananda Kendra at Delhi as its Vice Chairperson and later became the All India President of the organization. Widely travelled, she spearheaded the Vivekananda Bhārat Parikrama for all the 347 days in its marathon journey of 22,000 kms. In 1993—a century after Swami Vivekananda's historic visit to the United States, she addressed three major Parliaments of World Religions at Washington, Chicago and Calcutta. Presently, Dr. Lakshmikumari is the President of Vivekananda Kendra Vedic Vision Foundation at Kodungallur.

Preface

On the eve of his departure from Britain, an English friend had asked Swami Vivekananda as to whether he would like his motherland now, after four years' experience of luxurious, glorious, and powerful West. Swamiji had responded in his inimitable manner: "India I loved before I came away. Now the very dust of India has become holy to me, the very air is now sacred; it is now a holy land, the place of pilgrimage, the *Tīrtha*." It was given to Swami Vivekananda to restore the glory and grandeur of our country in the eyes of the West, which saw only blind superstitious faith, poverty and callousness, and a total lack of civilization! While describing Hinduism, he took his listeners beyond the normally accepted religion, and in its place introduced *Vedānta* as the *future of all religions*! The reason for this bold declaration is that, *Vedānta* deals with the inner growth of human beings.

Śaṅkara Bhagavadpāda was instrumental in reviving our culture more than a thousand and two hundred years back. Śaṅkarācārya for some, has become synonymous with terse, logical and complex philosophy of *Advaita*; or with *Brahmanism*—a word coined by Western philosophers, and a notion that he is relevant to only a particular caste; or with the ascetic way of life that promotes escapism. This book tries to present *Ācārya* Śaṅkara as a prodigy discovering his mission; as a person who learnt from many persons and situations, after coming in direct contact with the masses and classes of the society; as a prophet who had the foresight to select the eligible persons for his mission; as a forerunner who included all persons at every stage of growth in his teachings; and as a synthesizer of hand, heart and head; and most of all as an inspiration for scaling that *Peak* which lies within each one of us. Sister Nivedita observes that "In devotion he was like Saint Fransis of Assisi; in intellect he was like Abelard; in dynamism and freedom, he was like Martin Luther; in imagination and efficiency, he was like Ignatius Loyola. In fact, he was all these characteristics united and exemplified in one person."

Intellect ruled the elite during Śaṅkara's time and Sanskrit was a preferred language. And he used it very effectively to describe the Truth and how to *see It*. Truth is always simple, and to understand it one has to be simple. Our intellect which is attached to complexity imagines that the Truth *has to be complex* else it cannot be the Truth! Many persons have expressed this fact through their life and teachings. The author learnt this from *The Gospel of Sri Ramakrishna* by 'M', the dialogues of Paramahaṅsa with his disciples and devotees; and also from the writings and discourses of Swami Ranganāthānanda, Swami Chinmayānanda, and Swami Akhaṇḍānanda Saraswati, on *Upaniṣads* and *Prakaraṇa Graṅthas* of Ādi Śaṅkarācārya. He was inspired by his visits to Ramanashramam at Tiruvannamalai (Tamil Nadu)—where peace and silence are almost *physical*, he had glimpses of the Self.

The Foreword by Dr. M. Lakshmikumari, President Vivekananda Kendra Vedic Vision Foundation Kodungallur Kerala, has added value to the book. Author gratefully acknowledges the encouragement and support from Sri Lakshmi Niwasji Jhunjhunwala, Chairman Emeritus LNJ Bhilwara Group and Chairman Ramarpan Educational Society.

This book is a verbal tribute to Śri Śaṅkara Bhagavadpāda, who has done so much for our great culture and to the ancient spiritual tradition that continues and will continue to be relevant to human growth from millennia to eternity.

Śaṅkara Jayanti

Śankara (Prologue)

There have been many *complete men* who are alert, sensitive, understanding, responsible, and spontaneous individuals who *care*, and whom we can emulate and start our pilgrimage towards fulfillment of human life, in the past and also in the present guiding us through their exemplary lives. Two such men stand tall over many and who have been the beacons of our grand culture. Kṛṣṇa Dvaipāyana who came to be known as Veda Vyāsa for not only editing our four Vedas, but also for protecting and preserving their sonic as well as verbal quality; for writing *Vedānta* or *Brahma Sūtras*, *Mahābhārata* and *Śrīmadbhāgavatam*. It was he who revived our great culture more than five millennia back when factions representing different ideas were at loggerheads. Going around the vast country he lovingly corrected the stray, and organised the kings to establish peace and prosperity. However, as always, the law of Entropy prevailed and our culture or the values for which it stood, fell.

Four thousand years after Kṛṣṇa Dvaipāyana Vyāsa, only eight years old Śaṅkara—who was to be called later as *Ādi Śaṅkarācārya*, realised his responsibility of contributing his share for the revival of our culture. In him we find an efficient performer of actions that are socially and individually healthy. He possessed an extremely alert, analytic and open mind ready to learn and experiment with new ideas. Action is the basis of life. It was given to Śaṅkara to bring out the *Song of the Lord—Śrīmadbhagavadgītā* out of *Mahābhārata* of Veda Vyāsa and to establish its present status of a *Śāstra*. He experimented with the ideas contained in *Śrīmadbhagavadgītā* in all his activities. He went around our large undivided country thrice to be with diverse people, learn from them and also mend their ways towards more fulfilling life.

Śaṅkara was bestowed with a sensitive heart that could accommodate the whole universe. No one was a stranger to him, as he had become the friend of the universe *after befriending his Self*! His *Stotras* are the hearty outpourings of his infinite love on the deities which are nothing but the human qualities with form. They give a glimpse into his ecstasy, as Śaṅkara had that sensitivity to behold beauty and bliss in every situation and location. He inspired the society to be the proud custodian of a grand culture which accepts every faith as a true individual and unique *perspective*. He was ready to sacrifice his very life even if it could benefit one individual as he lived that love for love's sake.

Śaṅkarācārya clarified the essential truth contained in the *Upaniṣads*—the foundations of our culture through his commentaries based on his experiential understanding. He further demonstrated that the truth *can and is to be lived and not just discussed or debated*. His *Prakaraṇa Granthas* are verbal documents which offer practical hints to the seekers at all stages of their pilgrimage to fulfillment. All his writings declare his mastery over language.

Śaṅkara Bhagavadpāda emanated his power and taught through his life, by demonstrating to mankind that life has a meaning and purpose; that there is an indestructible *Reality* of an incomparable beauty, a life of *perfect peace and bliss within the heart of all beings*. His life is an inspiration to all those who value life and its interdependence with all creation.

Volition (Hands)

Footsteps in Quest (Map)

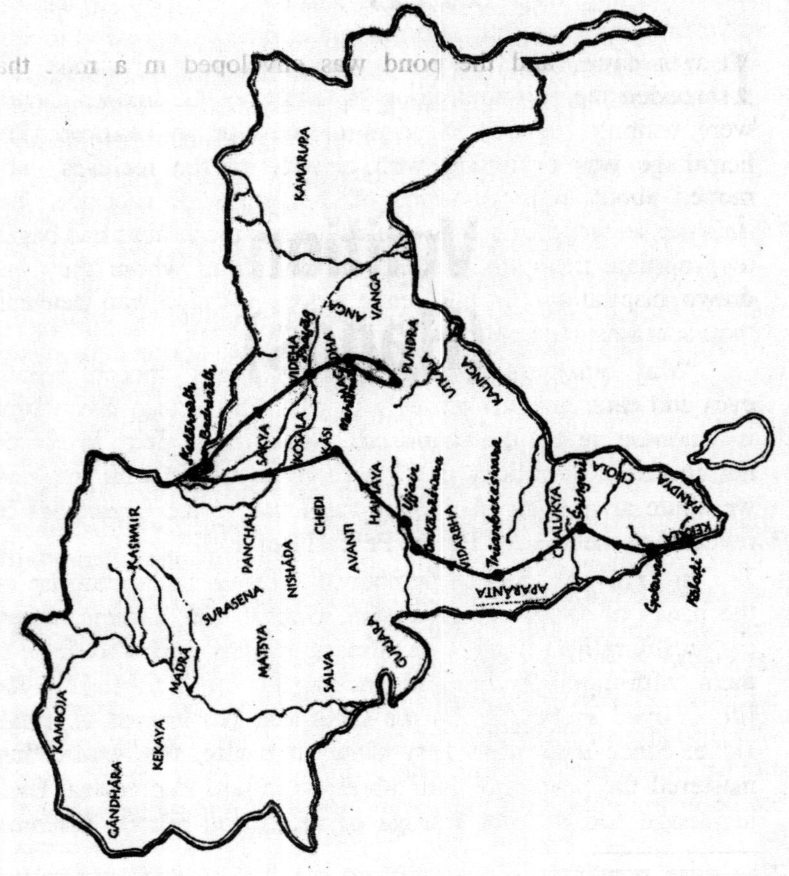

1
Trying Times

It was dawn, and the pond was enveloped in a mist that shrouded the surroundings with mystery. The lotuses therein were waiting for the first rays of the Sun to blossom. The hermitage was brimming with activity of the recluses, who moved about in preparations of the daily fire sacrifice. The *Ācāryas* seating themselves around the sacrificial altar had begun to propitiate the gods they adored and from whom they had drawn inspiration. As the gentle smoke spiraled into heavens, their sonorous voices sang:

"May quietness descend upon my limbs, speech, breath, eyes and ears; may all senses wax clear and strong. Everything is *Brahman*, reveal the *Upaniṣads*. Never may I deny *Brahman*, nor *Brahman* ever deny me. I with Him and He with me, may we abide always together. May the Truth of the *Upaniṣads* be revealed to me? AUM! Peace! Peace!! Peace!!!"[2]

In *Āryāvarta,* a large number of *Āśramas* had sprung up on the banks of the rivers *Saraswati*, *Gangā*, and *Yamunā*, where the presiding *Ṛṣis* lived in saintliness, inspiring all who came to them, with moral fervour and teaching the art of noble life. The life as lived and taught by the sages was not limited to rituals alone. Since they were very close to nature, the *Āryans* had mastered the power of their observation and expression. Each hermitage had its own lineage of sages and related *Mantras*.

---

2. आप्यायन्तु ममाङ्गानिवाक्प्राणश्चक्षुः श्रोत्रमथो बलमिन्द्रियाणि च सर्वाणि । सर्वं ब्रह्मौपनिषदं माऽहं ब्रह्मनिराकुर्यां मा मा ब्रह्मनिराकरोदनिराकरणमस्तु अनिराकरणं मेऽस्तु ।तदात्मनि निरते य उपनिषत्सु धर्मास्ते मयि सन्तु ते मयि सन्तु ॥ ॐ शान्तिः शान्तिः शान्तिः ॥ साम वेदः ॥

But they all pointed towards the same Reality—One without the other.

"Wise call Him *Iṅdra*, *Mitra*, *Agni*, *Varuṇa*, that heavenly *Garutmān* the golden-winged (Sun). To that One, sages give many a name; they call Him *Agni*, *Yama* and *Mātariśvan*."[3]

"As light, He dwells in the luminous sky; As *Vasu* (air) He dwells in the mid space; As *Hotṛ* (fire) He exists on the sacrificial alter; As guest He dwells in the house; As Supreme Entity He exists; As *Ṛta* (the rhythm and right) He exists everywhere; He shines in the sky, in water, in light, in mountains and in Truth."[4]

"He who is the Father of us all, the procreator, the great Providence, He who knows the whole Universe, He is One, yet assumes many names of Gods; About Him all people of the world become desirous to know."[5]

"That which is wisdom, intelligence, and steadfastness; that which is the inner Immortal Light within creatures; that without which no action can be performed; may that help my mind, to will what is auspicious."[6]

"Born of you, mortals go about you; you bear bipeds, you quadrupeds. Yours, O Earth, are these five human races, for whom mortals, the rising Sun spreads with its rays the light immortal. Let all those creatures together yield fruit to us; the honey of speech, O Earth, do you assign to me."[7]

This mastery of expression had not been in any way easy, amidst the ever changing and challenging limitations—the fury and turbulence of nature with its elements, the pressure

---

3. इन्द्रं मित्रं वरुणं अग्निं आहुः अथो दिव्यः स सुऽपर्णः गरुत्मान् ।
एकं सत् विप्राः बहुधा वदन्ति अग्निं यमं मातरिश्वानमाहुः ॥ ऋग्वेदः 1:134:43 ॥
4. हंसः शुचिऽसत् वसुरन्तरिक्षऽसत् होता वेदिऽसत् अतिथिः दुरोणऽसत् नृऽसत् वरऽसत् ऋतऽसत् व्योमऽसत् अप्ऽजाःगोऽजाः ऋतऽजाः अद्रिऽजाः ऋतम् ॥ ऋग्वेदः 4:40:5 ॥
5. सः नः पिता जनिता यः विऽधाता धामानि वेद भुवनानि विश्वा यः देवानां नामऽधाः एकः एवं मं संऽप्रश्नं भुवना यंति अन्या ॥
॥ ऋग्वेदः 10:92:3 ॥
6. यत्प्रज्ञानमुत चेतो धृतिश्च यज्ज्योतिरन्तरमृतं प्रजासु । यस्मान्न ऋते किन्चन कर्म क्रियते तन्मे मनः शिवसंकल्पमस्तु ॥ यजुर्वेदः 34:3 ॥
7. त्वज्जातास्त्वयि चरन्ति मर्त्यास्त्वं बिभर्षि द्विपदस्त्वं चतुष्पदः ।त्वेमे पृथिवि पञ्च मानवा येभ्यो ज्योतिरमृतं मर्तेभ्य उद्यन्तसूर्यो रश्मिभिरातनोति ॥
त नः प्रजाः सं दुह्रतां वाचो मधु पृथिवि धेहि मह्यम् ॥ अथर्व वेदः 12:15,16 ॥

of physiological needs and the ever-existent psychological weaknesses of greed, lust, fear, anger, jealousy and infatuation. They had successfully recorded their observations—through pithy and yet poetic verses in a language known as *Girvāṇiḥ* or Speech of the Divine—they called such collections as the *Vedas* or the Word, which had all branches of knowledge including the language, psychology and other related subjects as well as the secular sciences, which helped man in his growth.

Though it was just the dawn of thought and man was only beginning to think elsewhere, the Indian psyche could dwell on such thoughts on Unity, is really awe inspiring. The *Mantras* or the verses were *perceived* by the sages in their inspired states of meditation. Such inspired persons were addressed as *Ṛṣis* or *Mantradṛṣṭas*—the seers of the *Mantras*. These verses were transferred from the preceptors to their disciples in a long oral tradition. But then, the technique of meditative understanding the *Mantras* was lost to the mechanical repetition. In spite of the fact that the verses declared the lofty states of unity and harmony, their spirit got lost. It is said that in nature there is neither completely white, nor black! With all such lofty flights of the soaring Indian spirit, the feet were firmly chained to the ground—the chains being the self-created differentiation of *mine* and *not-mine*. While the society soaked in the ritual of fire sacrifices that were designed for the seekers of welfare in the worlds *hereafter*, the priests indulged in comparisons of one another's scriptures. The priest-class was split in two distinct sections, the *Trayī,* one that believed that there were only three recognised *Vedas*—*Ṛg*, *Yajur* and *Sāma*, as they claimed that the *Atharva* included secular sciences like medicine, state craft and sorcery. The other advocated the inclusion of *Atharva* as one more *Veda*. This schism wasted so much energy of the sages, that the content and spirit of their lofty verses was gradually lost. It is very natural that at such times when the society is divided and is in disharmony, the negative forces do not miss the opportunity to push the wedge deeper!

During such points of time, the providence plays a prank to awaken men by throwing challenges at them. It had appointed

Sahasrārjuna as its spearhead in its campaign of awakening the *Ṛṣis* and to goad them towards action. Whenever the sleep is disturbed, there is bound to be destruction. In his efforts to unite the different schools of thoughts, *Muni* Parāśara—grandson of *Muni* Vasiṣṭha, travelled along the banks of the Gaṅgā, Yamunā, and Saraswatī. His method of bringing them together was unique. His *Tapas* was intense, consistent, and impeccable, which could be felt by all those whom he met. His amicable and sweet nature made him acceptable to them. *Muni* Parāśara never resorted to pointing out the flaws in either their rituals, or recitation. All he did was to set an example through correct rituals and recitation of the *Word*, which he had mastered. He used to move from one *Āśrama* to the other, goading the inmates to continue their *Tapas*, and inspired them to preserve the rich heritage of our country.

It was one of those few times when he was returning to his own *Āśrama*. He was shocked to see what had happened. It was as though the death had danced. All the huts had been gutted; sacrificial alters desecrated, inmates killed and women molested. This was too disturbing for the *Muni* and he sat on a rock in a state of deep agony and sorrow. It had taken him nearly two decades to set up this holy place, which had been destroyed within hours. His disciple Aśval came and coughed to inform his presence to the sage who was in a pensive mood. When the sage looked at him, Aśval announced the arrival of Sahasrārjuna with his forces, by indicating the dust thrown by the chariots, horses and men. Parāśara got up and walked towards the head of the procession, to the dismay of Aśval, who ran for cover in an effort to save himself.

At the head of the procession was a caparisoned chariot in which Sahasrārjuna sat, appreciating the destruction brought on by his forces. There was an arrogant smile on his face as he could see clearly in his mind the total annihilation of the *Āryans*. Parāśara decided to face the invader with an appeal to his conscience. Years ago he had met Arjuna, as a fierce young man proud of his strength, at his grandfather Sage Vasiṣṭha's *Āśrama*. Parāśara went forward, leaving his fate in the hands of the gods, to catch hold of the reins of Arjuna's horses and faced him. Drunk as he was of the power of hatred for *Āryans* Sahasrārjuna failed to see a genuine and affectionate appeal, he struck the *Ṛṣi* wounding him very seriously. Without even a glance towards his victim, he continued his journey of plunder, violence and rape. On the outskirts of what was once his *Āśrama*, where he had led his numerous disciples along the path of godliness, Paraśara lay unconscious. It appeared as though there was no possibility of any recovery. But the Providence had its own plan!

A little after sunrise, the boat of a fisherman Jaruth reached the bank where Parāśara lay wounded and unconscious. Jaruth lived on an islet in the Yamunā. Whenever he went for fishing, he used to pay a visit to the *Āśrama* to offer salutations to the sage. He had seen the *Āśrama* burning, and he had dared not to approach it. When after confirming that the vandals had left, he moored the boat, and he stepped out on to the bank along with his family. Among them was his fourteen-year-old daughter Matsyā. While her father and uncles were busy lighting a fire, Matsyā saw a man lying short distance away on the sandy shore. She ran towards him and realised that it was the venerable *Ṛṣi* whom she recognised. Scared but curious, she approached him to find that he was still, and bleeding from the corners of his mouth. Matsyā's heart wept at the sight of the kind sage lying in a pool of blood. Seeing her crying loudly, her mother Candodari came rushing to her daughter and realised that the *Ṛṣi* was alive. Calling out for her husband and other men, she managed to shift him to a hut in their islet, and nursed him back to health. All this while, it was Matsyā who looked after him with love and devotion. From the union of this *Ṛṣi* with a mission, and an innocent but adventurous fisher girl, was born Kṛṣṇa Dvaipāyana, who was to be known as Veda Vyāsa in future.

When Kṛṣṇa was of six years, he joined his father *Muni* Parāśara and in turn the great task of revival of Vedic tradition. *Muni* Parāśara had to be on the move constantly as he had the difficult mission of uniting the different *Āśramas* which followed various branches of the Word. Kṛṣṇa followed his father like a shadow and everyday for him was new as he always learnt something new. Extremely competent and sharp by nature, Dvaipāyana mastered the *Maṅtras* and went on increasing his boundaries of wisdom. He observed that his father corrected the ways of the inmates of different *Āśramas* by living the truths and not only through speech. When he came to know that the *Maṅtras* were found wanting in accent or intonation he would chant the correct version. The *Muni* insisted that unless all the *Āśramas* followed the identical code of conduct, the Word cannot be preserved for the posterity. Every night *Muni* Parāśara would talk to his son about his dream of making the *Āryāvarta* into a haven of austerity, of righteousness of Purity and Holiness. He would insist that the elimination of the schism between the *Atharva* School and the *Trayī* School was the primary step. But death sought *Muni* Parāśara before he could see the fulfillment of this dream.

The untimely death of his respected father did not discourage Kṛṣṇa Dvaipāyana from involving himself in this mission. He continued his journey through the length and breadth of the land, meeting people encouraging them to lead righteous lives according to the Vedas. Like Bhagīratha performing the feat of bringing the celestial Gangā on earth in the distant past, Dvaipāyana had the great task of standardising the order and accent of each *Maṅtra* and dividing them into four divisions *Ṛk*, *Yajus*, *Sāma* and *Atharva*. He prevailed upon the contemporary society to accept *Atharva* as a *Veda*. This he did by becoming a disciple of *Ṛṣi* Mahā Atharvaṇa Jābāli to master the *Atharva* lore and also taking the daughter of the great sage as his companion. Destiny chose him to be the key figure in the history of *Āryāvarta*.

Śantanu the Monarch of the Kuru dynasty was ailing and he was not responding to any treatment. Kṛṣṇa Dvaipāyana reached the kingdom and he treated the monarch using the technique he had learnt under Mahā Atharvaṇa Jābāli. He discovered to his pleasant surprise, that his dear mother Matsyā had become the empress Saraswati and royal consort of Śantanu. And thus the Providence had chosen to bring about the reunion of son and mother under strange circumstances. With Kurus as his allies the daunting task became lighter as all the *Āśramas* got the protection from the likes of Sahasrārjuna and peace reigned on *Āryāvarta*. Vyāsa plunged into the great task of organizing the Vedic *Mantras* into four divisions. He convinced the Kuru scholars about the need to unite all the available resources to begin the renaissance of our culture. Using the opportunity of reviving the *Dharmakṣetra*—the sacred ground he conducted the *Aśwamedha*—the horse sacrifice by choosing the *Ṛṣis* of all the four schools as the officiating priests. This was the beginning of a new age of understanding and mutual acceptance among the two schools.

Kṛṣṇa Dvaipāyana was primarily a learner and then only a teacher. He discovered amidst all the collection of the *Mantras* there was a definite pattern. *Trayī—Ṛk*, *Yajus* and *Sāma,* represent the *Karma* aspect of life, or the rituals that governed the healthy and righteous living. *Atharva*, the fourth deals with the day-to-day life covering the secular needs like treatment of ailments, warding off evil, and statecraft. Surprisingly, all the four *Vedas*, deal with philosophical thoughts through lofty verses. Vyāsa learnt the rituals and only after understanding their essence, introduced the contemplation and meditation on the *Mantras*, to the society by assigning one disciple each for preserving the great Indian oral tradition.

It was given to Dvaipāyana Vyāsa to revive many aspects of our culture. In each *Veda*, there was a ritualistic portion called the *Karma Kāṇḍa* and a contemplative and wisdom portion called the *Jñāna Kāṇḍa* contained in the *Upaniṣads*. Vyāsa had mastered both the portions but he took care to stress the importance of *Jñāna Kāṇḍa* without which *Karma Kāṇḍa* was just an empty gesture having no substance by writing a masterly spiritual scripture *Vedānta Sūtras*—the aphorisms on the essence of *Vedas* explaining the significance of *Upaniṣadic Mantras*. Kṛṣṇa Dvaipāyana Vyāsa became a living legend and had a great influence on the monarchy as well as the common society. He was on the constant move visiting the *Āśramas* on the river banks as well as mountains and inspired the officiating sages to lead exemplary lives for the common people.

He realised that the subtle truths enshrined in the *Vedas* was beyond the understanding of the masses and wrote *Mahābhārata* the story of Kuru dynasty for them. In this great Indian classic he incorporated the subtle truths in the story by weaving characters that were personifications of human strengths as well as weaknesses. As he had witnessed the history of the Kuru dynasty closely and had played an active role, he included himself as one of the characters in *Mahābhārata.* The main character in this epic drama is of Kṛṣṇa Vāsudeva—the son of Vāsudeva whose Divine presence is felt throughout. His life blissful in spite of all the possible personal problems, meditative in spite of intense activity, and his unconditional love amidst hatred and conspiracy against him, set an example of ideal life. The key portion of this voluminous work is *Śrmadbhagavadgīta*—the Song of the Lord. Necessarily, it is sung by Kṛṣṇa to Arjuna, one of the Pāṇdavas. The stage, on which this song is sung, is the battlefield of Kurukṣetra when the two armies are ready to fight! This *Śāstra*—scripture gives guidelines on sane and healthy living to every human being. It gives out methods and means of achieving peace amidst intense activity through efficient selfless action, of discovering love amidst all the emotions, and of establishing enlightenment and wisdom in the so-called ordinary life. The story of *Mahābhārata* continues to engage the active interest of common people.

Unfortunately, *Śrīmadbhagavadgītā* was lost to the common man in the interesting story of the Kuru dynasty which has web of intrigue and drama. Another great man had to bring it out of the main body of the book to give the status on its own after almost three millennia.

With a view of helping the society, Vyāsa introduced the concept of *Tīrtha*—a place of pilgrimage where the righteousness is lived, as a consequence of which enlightenment blossoms. *Tīrthas* are the places that would inspire the common mass of people to lead a life of righteousness. Vyāsa was one of those who gave that spiritual orientation to our culture. It was Vyāsa who inspired his son to organize the order of *Sanyāsis* who would not only pursue enlightenment but also guide the society for a healthy and harmonious life. These *Sanyāsis* would roam around the country following a strict moral code and austerity.

In later years, Dvaipāyana Vyāsa felt that he had not considered the most important faculty of emotions in his writings. A common man is basically an emotional being and has difficulty in understanding as well as living the highly subtle intellectual principles. *Śrīmadbhāgavatam* was the outcome of this thought, in which he stressed the need of love for love's sake through the episodes and examples of those who lived the Love of God. Though he took up the different incarnations of Viṣṇu, he stressed on the exemplary life of Kṛṣṇa Vāsudeva in this great book. In the ages that followed *Śrīmadbhāgavatam* became a kind of reference book on *Bhakti*. However, as in most of our scriptures, *Śrīmadbhāgavatam* has many *Jñāna* portions as well.

As it always happens with the passage of time, the values so carefully lived and preached by Dvaipāyana Vyāsa fell, due to the absence of persons living them to set example, or perhaps due to the old habit of human beings to dilute the values if they are unable to live up to them! Providence had to wait for the appropriate time to make preparations for the advent of another man who acted like the much-needed elixir for the revival of our grand culture. It was Ācārya Śaṅkara Bhagavadpāda who carried the flame to re-ignite the mission of the renewal of our great culture.

❒

2
Stirrings of the Master

As his eyes gazed at the wavelets dancing on the river *Pūrṇā* reflecting crimson red of dawn, a thought crossed his mind, that though there were millions of waves, they belonged to the same river. While there is only one sun, there were millions of reflections. He was also awestruck to see that though the colour of the sky kept changing with the movement of sun, the sky remained unchanged. This observation and the accompanying thoughts—not unlike waves in the river—were rising in the mind of Śaṅkara who was only eight years old. When he was about to plunge deeper into the thought, there was a call—soft, kind and loving. It was his mother, Āryāmbā who had been widowed recently. She was concerned about her only child, who did not behave like the other children of his age. She felt he was too serious and mature for his age. He appeared to be lost in thought whenever he had time. Instead of toys and play, he could sit quietly for hours, gazing at nothing in particular.

Āryāmbā remembered the birth of her son gratefully. Śivaguru—her husband and she, had been childless and had almost lost hopes of having any, in their advanced age, and yet as a last resort they had visited the great Śiva temple at Thrissur. In their sleep, they both had dreamt of having a son who would be different from others, and who would achieve fulfillment in his very life. She shuddered at the last part of the dream which predicted a short life for her child. But, presently, there he was, in front of her and just by looking at him, she felt fulfilled. Knowing that her son was different and divine, she was proud of him. And yet she wished that he was like other children, who were playful and not so serious! Calling him she would chide him—not very seriously—for not being like other boys of his age, but pamper him with her maternal love lest her admonition pained him!

Śaṅkara in turn loved and respected his mother. He realised that without his father, he was her sole support. He would not do anything that would cause pain to his mother. His nature of plunging totally in whatever he did, helped him in giving total attention to his mother, making her very happy whenever he was with her. Even when he was with his friends, Śaṅkara gave them company in frolic and play, but his friends knew that he was different from them! They loved to be in his company and not only enjoyed the play, but their conversation with him. It appeared as if he always had a much larger perspective than mere enjoyment. He goaded them to look around and learn about the conditions prevailing in the society. A child prodigy that he was, whatever he read or heard became part of his permanent memory. He would narrate the episodes from our mythology and history. They were not just stories to be enjoyed at bed time he would say, but had to be made a part of our daily life, to be lived. And that such attitude alone could help us preserve our grand heritage and culture.

Śaṅkara had become *Dvija*—twice born,[8] when he was just five years. This made him eligible for the study the *Śāstras* and peep into the wonders of our national psyche. At *Gurukul*, while absorbing whatever was heard, he would ascertain that he understood it thoroughly without any trace of doubt. The recluses under the guidance had to beg food as a part of discipline to develop *Vinaya*—humility. They had to beg from only five houses and had to be satisfied from whatever they obtained. It was on the twelfth day of the fortnight, when Śaṅkara stood in front of the house and uttered "*Bhawati Bhikṣāṅ Dehi!*", the lady of the house rushed to her kitchen and

8. After the initiation into "*Gāyatri Maṅtra*" is known as 'thread ceremony' man becomes a *Dvija*.

to her consternation found it empty. How could she possibly send the *Brahmacāri* empty handed? All she had was *Āmalaka*—gooseberry, soaked in salt water, what could she do? But sending the child empty handed was painful. Taking the gooseberry she rushed out!

The general practice at that time was that the people used to observe fast on the eleventh day of the fortnight, and break this fast on the twelfth day. Usually, meal used to be more sumptuous on those days. As she came out looking at the bright face of the *Brahmacāri* standing in front, her heart sank, how could she possibly give him just an *Āmalaka*? She hesitated and there were tears in her eyes. Śaṅkara requested her to give him whatever she had for him. When she reluctantly dropped the gooseberry into his bowl, sensitive Śaṅkara felt the pain in the lady due to penury, and a spontaneous hymn in praise of Goddess Lakṣmi poured out:

"Salutations to Thee, the embodiment of the Vedas which give fruit of good deeds;

Salutations to Thee Rati Devi the reservoir of fine qualities;

Salutations to Thee, Śakti—the embodiment of strength, whose abode is lotus;

Salutations to Thee Puṣti—who nourishes, the beloved of the Lord Puruṣottama.

Salutations to Mahādevi, whose face is like a lotus;

Salutations to Śrī Devi—the Goddess of wealth born in the Milky ocean;

Salutations to Lakṣmi who bestows joy like the moon and nectar born with her;

Salutations to the consort of Nārāyaṇa."[9]

This prayer coming out of the pure heart of child Śaṅkara, had such an effect that the poverty of that house was alleviated

---

9. श्रुत्यै नमोऽस्तु शुभकर्मफलप्रसूत्यै रत्यै नमोऽस्तु रमणीयगुणार्णवायै ।
शक्त्यै नमोऽस्तु शतपत्रनिकेतनायै पुष्ट्यै नमोऽस्तु पुरुषोत्तमवल्लभायै ॥
नमोऽस्तु नालीकनिभाननायै नमोऽस्तु दुग्धोदधिजन्मभूम्यै ।
नमोऽस्तु सोमामृतसोदरायै नमोऽस्तु नारायणवल्लभायै ॥
नमोऽस्तु हेमाम्बुजपीठिकायै नमोऽस्तु भूमण्डलनायिकायै ।
नमोऽस्तु देवादिदयापरायै नमोऽस्तु शाङ्र्गायुधवल्लभयै ॥ कनकधारास्तोत्रम् 11, 12, 13॥

so much so, that this hymn consisting of eighteen verses came to be recited by those who were in material poverty. Somehow Śaṅkara's attention was drawn towards prevailing conditions which he felt were due to the lack of understanding the age-old and tested truths and to the mute and blind following of customs and rituals. He felt himself responsible and wanted to contribute his mite to bring in a positive change in the society. Apparently, a young boy thinking of the society or the nation appears to be an exaggeration. But Śaṅkara was no ordinary boy, but a person with a mission.

During one of his discourses, the teacher mentioned about the need to develop *Samadṛṣṭi*—equal vision for achieving the fulfillment in life. When Śaṅkara sought clarification, the teacher said that it is that attitude which stops seeing the physical and psychological differences. And it is possible only when one takes to the life of *Sanyāsa*. The teacher explained that there are two ways of leading our life: *Pravṛtti*—involvement, and *Nivṛtti*—non-involvement. Normally, after the period of learning—*Brahmacarya*, we take to *Gṛhastāśrama*—house-holder's life. But those who wish to lead the life of non-involvement take to the life of *Sanyāsa* after *Brahmacarya*. The teacher added that there were very few who could take to this kind of life, and that such life was possible only under the guidance of an Enlightened Master like Goviṅda Bhagavadpāda. The seed was sown in the fertile field of Śaṅkara's mind which did not take much time to sprout and become a tree!

After spending only two years at *Gurukul*, his teacher told him that Śaṅkara had learnt whatever there was to learn from him and that now he had to find an Enlightened Master, who alone could guide him towards enlightenment. On his return from *Gurukul*, an incidence revealed Śaṅkara's capacity to organise people for a cause. Once when his mother failed to return after her bath, Śaṅkara rushed out to find her unconscious on way from the river. After bringing her home and treating her, he organised his friends and worked in such a way, that the river started flowing just in front of their house.

Śaṅkara, who was eight, felt the urgency to go in search of the Enlightened Master. When he approached his mother for permission to take leave of her for taking *Sanyāsa*, she flatly refused on grounds that he was her only support and she needed him always by her side! He too agreed as he was concerned about the welfare of his weak mother. But when there is a very strong will and a pure intention, the Providence always helps in moving towards goal. Śaṅkara was bathing in the river and his mother was observing her dear son. A crocodile caught hold of his leg and would not leave him. Āryāmbā panicked and was helplessly watching her son being slowly dragged into the river. Śaṅkara knowing that his end was near, requested her to give her permission to take *Sanyāsa* before death. He also said that if he took *Sanyāsa* it could be considered as death as he would enter into a new life and there was this likelihood of the crocodile sparing his life!

The mother's heart melted and she felt that with the permission, her dear son would at least be alive. And so, at the age of eight Śaṅkara took to *Sanyāsa* mentally, for dedicating his life to the cause of *Dharma* and for the protection of our sacred culture. While taking leave of his mother, Śaṅkara promised her that he would be by her side whenever she needed him, and that he would never forget or forsake her. As she tearfully bid farewell to her son, Āryāmbā remembered her dream of having an extraordinary son with a great mission in life, and also her husband's words that for a greater cause, one has to sacrifice one's selfish interests. She stood on the bank of Pūrṇā and gazed at the vanishing form of her dear son.

However, the memories of his childhood, his words of affection and respect, his devotion for the parents, his totally unselfish and pure love, and most of all, that guileless and all encompassing smile, remained in her heart and were to give her company for the rest of her life.

Śaṅkara started walking in the northern direction for he had been told that Paramahaṅsa Goviṅda Bhagavadpāda stayed on the banks of river Narmadā. He decided to take this walk as a pilgrimage in search of his Guru and also an opportunity to discover his great country. As he entered a village and sat on the edge of a pond, he saw an old man sitting nearby, murmuring something to himself. He appeared to be quite advanced in age almost nearing death. When Śaṅkara went near him, he heard the old man muttering about his coconuts not being sufficiently paid for! Looking into the eyes of the old man, Śaṅkara said that the time was ripe for him think about and to account for the actions he had performed throughout life! This apparently small suggestion coming from guileless child of eight years had a transforming effect on the old man, who got up as though woken up from sleep! He started laughing at his own foolishness. The work of the teacher in Śaṅkara had begun!

He had to pass through the mountain range named after Ṛṣi Ṣṛṅga—the place where the great sage had performed *Tapas*. It was noon and the sun being harsh he sat on the bank of River Tuṅga, to rest when he saw a very strange sight. A frog was being offered shade by a huge cobra with its hood spread! Śaṅkara thought for a while and remembered that in the presence of such persons who are established in non-violence even the enemies do not show their animosity.[10] It struck him that this would be an ideal place for a centre to spread spirituality. He started contemplating on the course of his future action. Foremost of all actions was that he had to be eligible to understand the intricacies of our spirituality by experiencing it and also understand the condition our population was in, and then alone take steps to introduce the corrective measures which had to be as easy to understand by the common masses as it was to practise them. Years later, he would revisit this place and establish Shringeri Śārada Pīṭham, which is on the banks of River Tuṅga, the centre to spread spirituality in the South. Even to this day, we can see a stone sculpture of a cobra protecting a frog under its hood on the spot.

Śaṅkara resumed his journey on foot towards North. He stayed in a temple of a village for the night. In a conversation with the priest of the temple, the story of *Mahābhārata* came up. Very knowledgeable that the priest was, he described the

---

10. अहिंसाप्रतिष्ठायां तत्सन्निधौ वैरत्यागः ॥ पातञ्जल योगदर्शनम् 2:35 ॥

different persons with their characters, as well as the greatness of Kṛṣṇa and his being the central figure in the whole story. Keen listener in Śaṅkara noticed that the priest made only a passing remark on dialogue between Kṛṣṇa and Arjuna, without going into any details. He remembered the dramatic dialogue on the battlefield in between the two armies ready to fight! Śaṅkara felt its relevance in everyday life. With these thoughts predominant in his mind, he entered forests on the slopes of Sahyādri Mountains.

It was noon, and he had just finished his *Mādhyānnikā* (*Sandhyāvandanam*)—the noon ritual which was obligatory for a *Dvija*, when a venerable sage—with dark complexion, silvery flowing hair and beard approach him. Śaṅkara offered his salutations and stood respectfully with his arms folded in front of his chest. The sage made a sign to sit near him.

"I am Kṛṣṇa Dvaipāyana Vyāsa, son of Sage Paraśara. A while back, you thought about the dialogue between Kṛṣṇa Vāsudeva and Arjuna. Your birth has been for a great purpose of synthesis of the secular and the spiritual. *Sādhu*—well done!! Your contemplation about the usefulness of the dialogue in everyone's life is true, for that was the very purpose of introducing it in the *Mahābhārata*. When you travel in search of your venerable Guru, learn to live the truths in the *Śrīmadbhagavadgītā*."

"Venerable Sir, the whole work appears to me as a book of synthesis among Action, Devotion and Wisdom; between *Pravṛtti*—the intense involvement in the effortful, efficient and cooperative action and *Nivṛtti*—the intense renunciation of selfish interests, which paves way for *Abhyudaya* the rising of the society as a whole. How should I proceed?" Śaṅkara asked.

"It was meant to clear all the conflict that appears to be a part of existence! This was when Arjuna was chosen to represent a common man. His doubts about the very cause of war; conflicts between violence involved in killing kinsmen and compassion and renunciation of kingdom and other values are all doubts which are common to all. Son, first of all you start applying the truths mentioned in the *Śrīmadbhagavadgītā* in your action, because your very life is filled with activity. I too realised the secret of action first and then alone tried to contribute something to the world." Venerable Vyāsa said compassionately.

"*Bhagawan*, I shall try my utmost, but you will have to guide me if I have any doubts."

"*Vijayī Bhava*—be victorious in all your endeavours!" So blessing the sage withdrew.

Śaṅkara was re-inspired to plunge into the mission he had chosen for himself after meeting and receiving the blessings from venerable Veda Vyāsa. The suggestion of the sage was so powerful that as he started walking joyously, he simultaneously started observing himself. He noticed that all his actions were for achieving something—*Phala* or fruit as it is mentioned in the *Śrīmadbhagavadgītā*; that the preoccupation on the fruit of action *during the action*, affects the efficiency of the action; that every action is to be taken as duty towards oneself and the other members of the society; that every action can be taken in as an offering to the Divine, thus purifying the mind as well as the action; and finally with a pure mind, one begins to see that it is not the individual who does the action but *it is the Divine which acts through the individual*. It struck him that when such action became spontaneous, he would be able to convey them to others through example.

Life and action are synonymous and normally as we understand life, life cannot exist without activity! Behind every action there is always an attitude which governs the action itself. If one is aware of the attitude, one is aware of the action itself. These truths are not obvious to the common masses as they are either deeply involved with their day-to-day problems of survival, or in their body and senses or with their selfish ambition. If one could understand the secret of action and act accordingly, not only could one act efficiently, in unison with others for the collective good, but *Abhyudaya* is a natural consequence. These realised truths were not only powerful thoughts but were not very difficult to practise in life.

In every village and town, Śaṅkara started interacting with people and peeped into their psyche. There appeared to be three types of persons— totally unconscious, selfishly conscious and totally conscious. He met the first two, but the third type was indeed very rare. The impediments in human growth as observed by Śaṅkara were in three dimensions: the physical in which he included senses; the mental restrains like languor, indulgence with senses, involvement and attachment thereof; and the intellectual limitations like lack of discrimination and openness of mind or resistance to accept anything new. He was careful to note that sometimes, even the experienced seekers fell short by getting diverted to the powers acquired during the search, losing their goal of Self-realization. He understood that the only way out of these impediments is by purifying the action for the purification of mind; purifying the tendencies by directing the emotions to the Divine; and *Vicāra*—the non-involved contemplation and self-observation.

Śaṅkara started understanding our real culture through his personal experience. He began with the most obvious—action. Activity is mandatory for existence, without it survival is not possible. He would *totally* involve himself in the activity at hand because the thought of the fruit of the particular action never crossed his mind *during* the action.[11] Consequently, his action was always complete. Such action was efficient and conserved his energy. For instance, when he walked, he would be aware only of the act of walking. Such action he realised brought about the *Cittaśuddhiḥ*—purification of mind, as the mind has the habit of completing the incomplete action!

As and when Śaṅkara became more and more aware, he realised that he was not only conscious in the waking state, but he was also conscious of the dreams and deep sleep. While he had learnt to be consciously aware during the wakeful state, he had less or even no control over his dreams or deep sleep! His quest for the unity behind diversity, and the changeless behind the evanescent and transient continued. Even as he travelled on

11. कर्मण्येवाधिकारस्ते मा फलेषुकदाचन ।
मा कर्मफलहेतुर्भूः मा ते सङ्गोऽस्त्वकर्मणि ॥ 2.47 ॥

foot covering large distances, his contemplation and meditation continued. He realised that while the body, senses, mind, intellect as well as the emotions kept changing, his *real Self* just witnessed, without any involvement. His continuous search for the substratum of consciousness was on.

Those who came in touch with him could not make out that Śaṅkara was so deeply involved with his search, because his behavior was more than normal. Some of the persons inspired by his sense of purpose and the lofty mission for the nation even tried to follow him, but Śaṅkara politely asked them to wait for the right moment, when he would definitely take their help in reviving our grand culture.

It was with such state of mind that Śaṅkara was steadily approaching his Preceptor, ready, willing and receptive to receive the benediction for enlightenment and blessings for the work ahead. The lamp of Śaṅkara was getting ready for the flame from Goviṅda Bhagavadpāda, to usher light of spirituality to the world.

❐

3
At the Feet of the Preceptor

Whenever there is pure and unselfish intension, congenial circumstances get created for achieving great goals. It is as though the whole of existence is waiting for such a soul to appear on earth. This happens even in the so-called ordinary lives, unknown to us help comes to us as if from nowhere, and our problems which had appeared overwhelming just dissolve. In our preoccupation we do not take notice of it. Times of Śaṅkara were troubled, with lack of proper direction on one side and life characterized by self-interest on the other. He came in contact with the intellectuals who were involved in hair-splitting arguments, ordinary people steeped in rituals invoking gods to bestow them heavenly *afterlife* while they totally ignored the present that was right in front, and also the simple innocent mass of people being exploited by the intellectuals as well as the priests by using fear and greed as their weapons. Our country has always had the tradition of persons involved in seeking *Mukti*—salvation. Śaṅkara noticed that they had become totally exclusive, without any toleration for others who were following different paths, forgetting that all those paths lead the pilgrims towards the same goal of Self-understanding!

All those people whom he had met could never ignore him—either they loved him or hated him for what he was—pure, committed to our culture and a wonder boy with a mission! The exploiters hated his fearless questioning, and the mass of people loved as they recognised their own innocence, and his guileless intension to understand and offer help to them.

While interacting with people, he came face-to-face with their woes and feelings that continued to give him the first hand knowledge. Śaṅkara had started living the essence of the *Śrīmadbhagavadgītā.* On examining the day-to-day experiences, he found that they leave impressions on us *only* when we get indulged (through body and senses), or involved with the feelings resulting from the experiences.

"O Son of Kuṅti, the contacts between the senses and their respective objects, which give rise to the feelings of heat and cold, pleasure and pain, etc., are transitory and fleeting; therefore Arjuna just forbear them. Arjuna, the wise man whom pain and pleasure are alike (as they are transitory and fleeting), and who is not tormented by these contacts, becomes eligible for immortality (as he becomes aware of the changeless and eternal Principle within.)"[12]

These verses give the technique of meditative action, which suggests us to look deeper and become aware of something which is *Pure Witness*. A sudden insight flashed across his consciousness: *what he was going through could not be called an experience, because everything—including the ego, intellect, mind, senses and body—were activities and were being witnessed*!

But it was just a flash; he had to be certain that it was not the figment of his imagination. However, Śaṅkara was full of joy which filled him with new vigour and energy. Wherever he went, he observed the innocence and spontaneity of the simple people who were basically emotional. They could neither understand nor practise any contemplation or meditation. They had to be given something else. Śaṅkara became aware of the daunting task that lay before him. The conviction in our grand heritage and its innate potential to meet any challenge in the face was so strong that his knowing smile only displayed that it was not

12. As other verses, these too have various levels of understanding!
मात्रास्पर्शास्तु कौन्तेयशीतोष्णसुखदुःखदाः । आगमापायिनोऽनित्यास्तांतितीक्षस्व भारत ॥ 2:14 ॥
यं हि न व्यथयन्त्येते पुरुषं पुरुषर्षभ । समदुःखसुखं धीरं सोऽमृतत्वाय कल्पते ॥ 2:15 ॥

really a crisis, but only a *task* which could be completed through effort. His very birth was for the purpose of accomplishing this mission of revival of our grand culture. The age-old cultural heritage saw in this child, the determination writ on his face, eyes and gait, the prospect of its own resurrection and smiled!

Śaṅkara knew that the *Mahābhārata* which had been called as the *fifth Veda*, had solutions to most of the problems ailing the society. He remembered that *Maharṣi* Vyāsa had taken care to include all possible permutations and combinations of human nature—from animal to Divine—as well as situations which are representative of existence. The guiding questions in the mind of Śaṅkara were "How this task would be handled by Lord Kṛṣṇa? What would *He* do under the circumstances?" Invariably, he would get an insight through a verse from the *Śrīmadbhagavadgītā*.

He was nearing the banks of River Narmadā. The monsoon had set in, with dark clouds spread throughout the sky. In the Viṅdhya Mountains, it had already started raining, and the river was in deluge, so was the mental state of Śaṅkara. He had been preparing for this meeting, since the day he had heard of Goviṅda Bhagavadpāda from his respected teacher. It had been a really a long walk from Kālaḍi, the place of his birth. Omkāreśwar on the bank of River Narmadā is one of the twelve *Jyotirlingas*—the symbol of Śiva, the Great God, and is a very popular place of pilgrimage. The devotees were seeking what was most needed by them from the Deity. Śaṅkara felt that all the devotees were like the children approaching their father with their individual demands, and their action was justified because they were making a plea to their own father! This intimacy with the innumerable gods and goddesses was so natural that the so-called ordinary emotions could be used to purify the mind, because they are directed to something very lofty and infinite.

In Omkāreśwar, he enquired about Master Goviṅda Bhagavadpāda. But no one had even heard of him! Śaṅkara was not surprised. His Master belonged to a class of great Persons who remained incognito while inspiring and guiding the world through silence.[13] Moreover, he was aware that to find one's Preceptor involved a lot of effort. But he had the advantage of knowing about his *Guru* and his great lineage, starting from Nārāyaṇa—Viṣṇu and Brahma—the Creator.[14] He started walking in the forest and became aware of a peculiar attraction in one particular direction which led him deeper into the Vindhya forest slopes. When he was quite far from any settlement, he found a few scattered huts wherein lived recluses who were deeply involved with spiritual practices including Vedāṅtic contemplation. They happily welcomed Śaṅkara to their fold. While interacting with them he came to know that all of them were attracted to the place by some strong force which seemed to beckon them! Śaṅkara was convinced that his Guru had remained in solitude, but was in the vicinity and that he had to find him. One morning when Śaṅkara was returning to his hut after his bath in River Narmadā, his feet started taking him to a spot, not very far from the water's edge. The spiritual vibrations became very strong and his feet stopped in front of a hole about a cubit wide, so small that Śaṅkara felt that it could not possibly be enough for anyone to stay in. But his feeling of bliss convinced him that it must be here.

Having prostrated in front of the cave, Śaṅkara recited the verses in praise of Guru Goviṅda Bhagavadpāda. A voice was heard asking for his identity. Instead of giving his name and his lineage, he introduced himself as "That One—Auspicious and Pure", in ten verses.

---

13. "The greatest men in the world have passed away unknown. The Buddhas and the Christs that we know, are but second-rate heroes in comparison with the greatest men of whom the world knows nothing. Hundreds of these unknown heroes have lived in every country working silently. Silently, they live and silently they pass away; and in time their thoughts find expression in Buddhas and Christs, and it is these latter that become known to us." Swami Vivekananda (*Complete Works*, Vol. I, p. 105, Advaita Ashrama, Calcutta, 1997).

14. This is a prayer chanted all over the country to pay homage to the spiritual lineage of *Brahmavidyā*.

नारायणं पद्मभवं वसिष्ठं शक्तिं च तत्पुत्रपराशरं च ।व्यासं शुकं गौडपादं महान्तं गोविन्द योगीन्द्रमथास्य शिष्यम् ॥
श्री शंकराचार्यमथास्य पद्मपादं च हस्तामलकं च शिष्यम् ।तं तोटकं वार्तिककारमन्यानस्मद्गुरुन् सन्ततमानतोऽस्मि ॥

"I am neither earth nor water, nor fire, nor air,

Nor space, nor sense organ, nor am I the combination of all these.

For all these are transient, variable by nature, while the Self

Is proved by the unique experience of deep sleep.

I am that One, Auspicious and Pure, That alone remains.

"For me there is neither waking nor dream nor deep sleep,

Nor am I the one conditioned by the three states (*Viśva*, *Taijasa*, *Prājña*);

For all these of the nature of ignorance,

But am the fourth (*Turīyam*) and beyond these three.

I am That One, Auspicious and Pure, That alone remains.[15]

Listening to the verses potent with spiritual understanding, Guru Goviṅda Bhagavadpāda extended his feet out of the narrow mouth of the cave. Śaṅkara worshipped them, washing them with his tears of joy and surrendering his total being. The news of the presence of Paramahaṅsa Goviṅda Bhagavadpāda and the arrival of his worthy spiritual heir spread attracting many enlightened and experienced seekers to take advantage for their growth. Thus, it was that the spiritual forces united to meet face-to-face the challenge given to our culture by history.

Having accepted Śaṅkara into the great lineage of enlightened Masters, Goviṅda Guru began transferring the Wisdom he had received from *His* Preceptor Gauḍapādācārya. He was so pleased with his disciple who had such keen listening skills that he could recollect whatever was uttered only once. To test Śaṅkara, he started with *Māṇḍukya Upaṅiṣad* for which Ācārya Gauḍapāda had added *Kārikā* or the gloss. It is considered to be one of the briefest *Upaniṣads*, and yet the most profound. Śaṅkara not only understood the *Maṅtras* but could *be* in the very lofty states mentioned therein. As expected Goviṅda Guru was a hard task master, and tested

15. न भूमिर्न्नतोयं न तेजो न वायुः न खं नेन्द्रियं वा न तेषां समूहः ।
अनैकान्तिकत्वात् सुषुप्त्येकसिद्धः तनेकोऽवशिष्टः शिवः केवलोऽहम् ॥ दशश्लोकी 1 ॥
न जाग्रत् न मे स्वप्नको वा सुषुप्तिः न विश्वो न वा तैजसः प्राज्ञको वा ।
अविद्यात्मकत्वात् त्रयाणं तुरीयं तदेकोऽवशिष्टः शिवः केवलोऽहम् ॥ दशश्लोकी 8 ॥

the strength of his disciple from time to time. When asked to explain the whole scripture briefly, Śaṅkara spontaneously summed it up in just two verses:

"I bow to that Brahman, which after having experienced in the waking state the gross objects by pervading all human objectives and endeavours through a diffusion of manifestation of unchanging consciousness that pervades all that moves and moves not; which again having drunk in dream state, enjoying all the variety of objects created by desire, action and ignorance through *Māyā*; watched over by the purified intellect enjoys bliss in sleep again through *Māyā*; and which is counted as *the fourth* from the point of view *Māyā* the Supreme, Immortal and Birth-less.

"May that Fourth protect us which, after having identified with the universe, enjoys during the cosmic dream state experiences through Its own light the subtle objects remembered by Its own intellect; which, further in deep sleep or cosmic dissolution withdraws promptly all these into Itself; and which is ever free from all attributes, from every distinction and difference."[16]

The simple yet beautiful language and the gist contained in these verses were very pleasing to the ears and appealed the *Guru*'s heart. Goviṅda Guru appreciated the capacity of his young, illustrious disciple. These two verses were used as the invocation for the commentary he was to write on the *Māṇḍukya Upaniṣad* later on. This was followed by the other principal *Upaniṣads* when Śaṅkara absorbed the essence and lived the insights therein.

The dam of ancient wisdom gathered and held so far by Goviṅda Bhagavadpāda, burst open and poured on Śaṅkara who willingly and lovingly gathered it in his phenomenal and prodigious mind. The experienced seekers who had settled in

---

16. The gist of the whole *Upaniṣad* is enshrined in these two verses.

प्रज्ञानांशुप्रतानैः स्थिरचिरनिकरव्यापिभिर्व्याप्य लोकान् भुक्त्वा भोगान्रथविष्ठान्पुनरपि धिषणोद्भासितान्कामजन्यान् ॥
पीत्वा सर्वान्विशेषान्स्वपिति मधुरभुङ्मायया भोजयन्नो मायासंख्यातुरीयं परममृतमजं ब्रह्म यत्तन्नतोऽस्मि ॥ 1 ॥
यो विश्वात्मा विधिजविषयान्प्राश्य भोगान्स्थविष्ठान् पश्चाच्चान्यान्स्वमतिविभवाञ्जोतिषा स्वेन सूक्ष्मान् ॥
सवनितान्पुनरपि शनैः स्वात्मनि स्थपयित्वा हित्वा सर्वान्विशेषान्विगतगुणगणः पात्वसौ नस्तुरीयः ॥ 2 ॥

the nearby region started gathering and took advantage of the dialogue taking place. They were awestruck at the capacity of the mere boy in not only understanding the difficult concepts but in explaining them in a language which was sweet and simple. Goviṅda Bhavadpāda who had developed many advanced techniques was an established Yogi. Having found an ideal receptacle in Śaṅkara, transferred them to his beloved disciple.

As he was learning them Śaṅkara discovered that it was as though he was only *remembering* and *re-practising* them. It was as though his Master was only reminding him! Some of the *Vidyās* which took life times to learn became as easy to him as breathing! Goviṅda Guru was more than convinced that he had lived only to transfer his wisdom to posterity through Śaṅkara. Thus, it was that Goviṅda Bhagavadpāda became free of his debt to *his Guru* Gauḍapādācārya. In the later years, this phenomenon of the flood of wisdom was interpreted by his devotees and later the followers, as the flood in the River Narmadā and Śaṅkara controlling it with his *Kamaṇḍalu*—the water gourd which resembles a head, and saving his preceptor!

When the transfer was complete, the preceptor realised that Śaṅkara was more than ready to receive the final benediction from him. Goviṅda Guru initiated Śaṅkara into the *Advaita*—No Otherness, when he uttered the four great Statements—*Mahāvākya*s,[17] into the willing being. The *Mahāvākyas* are found in four Vedas in their Upaniṣadic portions. In spite of receiving the wealth of wisdom from the *Guru*, the disciple has a feeling of being separate from the Truth; that *he* is *other than* the Truth. This can be eliminated only by an enlightened *Guru*, who *breathes* these Statements into the *being* of the disciple.

---

17. The traditional *Upaniṣadic* practice involves listening to, and contemplation and meditation on these statements. A select few, who are ready, identify with *Advaita* by just listening to these from a *Realised Sage*. The chapter "From Intellect to Intuition" gives further details.

प्रज्ञानं ब्रह्म ॥ ऋग्वेदः ॥

अहं ब्रह्मास्मि ॥ यजुर्वेदः ॥

तत्त्वमसि ॥ साम वेदः ॥

अयमात्मा ब्रह्म ॥ अथर्व वेदः ॥

Śaṅkara transcended time, space and matter, he could not call it as an experience, because for experience one required the object, experience and the subject. In this all the three are merged and there is only *experiencing.* He could not really find words and nor did he try to, but *HE JUST WAS*! Having spent a few days in the *Advaita*, Śaṅkara came back to the so-called normal plane, because the one which he had been in was more normal than the one he had returned to! For he was presently experiencing the world through the inter-mediators like senses, mind, whereas *Advaita* is immediate and direct.

He prostrated in front of Goviṅda Guru in extreme gratefulness. There were tears in the eyes of Goviṅda Bhagavadpāda, tears of joy because a worthy disciple in Śaṅkara had been sent to him. He asked his beloved disciple to study the *Vedāṅta Sūtras* of Veda Vyāsa and to write a commentary based on his recent *Anubhava*—being the Inner Self. Obeying the command of his Master, Śaṅkara started immediately. He was pleasantly surprised to discover that the truths therein, matched with his own insights, and so he completed the task of writing very soon. When he read his completed work, it was genuinely appreciated by Guru Goviṅda. Śaṅkara had tried to answer the difficult doubt of *Vedāṅta,* that if we are struggling to seek whatever is *already within* and we only remember what we already are, what is the reason for our phenomenal forgetfulness? This was replied by introducing the concept of *Adhyāsa*. As usual, his simple language and the simplicity of the concept are exemplary.

The genuine appreciation from the person like Goviṅda Bhagavadpāda, did not affect the ego of Śaṅkara at all, as he was interested in fulfilling a far greater mission of the revival of our culture. Instead he wanted something that helped him in his mission. Seeing through the mind of his disciple, Goviṅda Guru asked him to write a commentary on *Viṣṇu Sahasranāma*, a portion of *Mahābhārata* which is chanted by Bhīṣma—the grand old man of Kurus. This action would open the heart of Śaṅkara, so that he could identify himself with the masses, understand their problems and try to solve them.

Viṣṇu Sahasranāma is a *Stotra*—adoration on one of the Trinity of gods, who is responsible for the sustenance of the universe. *Viṣṇu* means All-Pervasive—one who pervades the whole universe.[18] When he started meditating on this portion of *Mahābhārata,* Śaṅkara realised that this work helped him expand his consciousness for understanding the feelings of the common man involved with his day-to-day problems of survival. In his introduction, he writes, *Abhyudaya*—overall good of the society and *Niḥśreyas*—individual enlightenment as the goal of reciting this adoration. Though achieving this lofty goal by just reciting this *Stotra* appears exaggerated, if we observe that whenever we start, identifying with something vast, our so-called problems dwindle into insignificance; when we try to lend a helping hand to the unfortunate, there is a feeling of life well spent. Śaṅkara wanted our society to be self-sustaining, and self-propelled, where there is mutual understanding, sharing and help.

Śaṅkara started visiting the Omkāreśwar to feel and understand the aspirations of common mass of people. It was during these visits that the plan of action to spiritualise the ordinary the so-called mundane activity, and to introduce deeper practices in the worship of ideals through the idols. He was more than convinced that for those dwelling in the emotional level, contemplation of the truths given in the *Upaniṣads* was very difficult. But the truths could be brought to *their* level through the simple practices and chants. When he discussed this with his Guru, Śaṅkara was directed to study the *Tantra* and *Āgama Śāstras* describing the mind quietening techniques, which had to be improvised to suit the common people. Thus, it was that the seed was sown in his mind for a constructive step towards associating the nation as a whole in the great work of reviving our culture and the spiritual identity of our great nation.

Paramahaṅsa Goviṅda Bhagavadpāda had handed over the baton of responsibility of continuing the great spiritual heritage to Śaṅkara. Having fulfilled his part of the mission of preserving and transferring pristine *Vedāntic* wisdom, he dropped his body

---

18. यस्मद्विश्वमिदं सर्वं तस्य शक्त्या महात्मनः तस्मादेवोच्यते विष्णुः ।

like a well used and worn cloth, Śaṅkara and the other disciples immersed the body into River Narmadā. Śaṅkara felt as though his Guru was very much with him guiding his every step, feeling his preceptor as a continual presence which reassured him that he was not alone in his chosen mission but the whole existence stood behind him with its protective glance and its infinite hands ready to offer assistance. A *Maṅtra* from *Śvetāśvatārōpaniṣad* and a verse from the *Śrīmadbhagavadgītā* express this.

"The Existence rushes to offer all help unasked to those who, having united *Manas* with the gods (senses), directing the intellect towards Infinite Bliss and merging the consciousness in the Brilliance of Brahman."[19]

"Persons who, meditating on me as non-separate, worship me through everything they do, to them, who are thus zealously established in Reality, I provide what they need and preserve what they already have."[20]

As far as Śaṅkara was concerned, he had become a willing instrument of the Divine. Śaṅkara remained in the hermitage that had given him much wisdom and experience for a few more days. During this time, he went through the rare manuscripts on *Vedāṅta* to store them in his phenomenal memory and having understood their essence and made it part of *his being*. He was awestruck at the genius of our national psyche which directed every human effort and endeavour to the manifestation of the Divine within. He realised pleasantly that it was not necessary to study *all* such literature because they were *just different expressions of the same truth*.

According to the instructions given by his beloved *Guru,* he started his journey to Kāśi—the hallowed city of light, of Śiva and of learning. Covering small distances daily, interacting with those who came into his contact, Śaṅkara left a trail of light from his being to have the rendezvous with Viśvanāth—the Lord of the Universe, the presiding Deity of Kāśi!

❐

---

19. युक्त्वाय मनसा देवान्सुवर्यतो धिया दिवम् ।बृहज्ज्योतिः करिष्यतः सविता प्रसुवति तान् ॥ श्वेताश्वतारोपनिषद् 2:3 ॥

20. अनन्याश्चिन्तयन्तो मां ये जनाः पर्युपासते ।तेषां नित्याभियुक्तानां योगक्षेमं वहाम्यहम् ॥ श्रीमद्भगवद्गीता 7:22 ॥

4
Blossoming of the Master

Horizon blushed crimson as the sun withdrew for the night. Though for an onlooker, the Gaṅgā assumed the colour of the sky she flowed incessantly, towards her destination, Gaṅgāsāgar without identifying with the surroundings! Śaṅkara sat on the *Ghāt*. The gurgling sound, the mild breeze and the peaceful milieu had a meditative effect on his being. She had responded to the intense *Tapas* of King Bhagīratha, into the matted locks of Mahādeva and on to the earth. She symbolised *Tapas,* for on her banks many a sage had delved into the inner consciousness and discovered the nuggets of Truth within. It was Kāśi—the city of enlightenment, and he was filled with gratefulness that overflowed in the form of poetry:

"Sparkling, overflowing and waving Goddess Gaṅgā! You destroy all impurities and are a stairway to heaven. I who had been involved in the gross and sensual, have lost taste for desires, and am worshipping Kṛṣṇa on your banks. O Bhagavati Bless me!

"May the enchanting Gaṅgā, coming down the Mountain of mountains, uplifting the people who take a dip in Her waters, which roll from one shore to the other, removing fears of the world, imitating the snakes and like creepers adorn the head of Śiva, and sporting in the region of Kāśi, bring victory!"[21]

---

21. भगवति तव तीरे नीरमात्राशनोहं विगतविषयतृष्णः कृष्णमाराधयामि । सकलकलुषभंगे स्वर्गसोपानगंगे तरलतरतरंगे देवि गंगे प्रसीद ॥ गंगाष्टकम् 1 ॥
शैलेन्द्रात् अवतारिणी निजजले मज्जत् जनोत्तरिणी पारावारविहारिणी भवभयश्रेणी समुत्सारिणी ।
शेषाहेरनुकारिणी हरशिरोवल्लीदलाकारिणी काशीप्रान्तविहारिणी विजयते गंगा मनोहारिणी ॥ गंगाष्टकम् 6 ॥

Though the presiding deity of this holy city is Viśvanāth—Śiva the Lord of the Universe, Śaṅkara remembered Kṛṣṇa—his family Deity and who had been guiding all his actions. While Śiva is considered as the Master of *Tapas* in all forms, Kṛṣṇa had been inspiring him to take to the *life of Tapas* for his life mission! He saw many waiting for death, for it was and even to this day is considered that whoever breathes his last in this city gets liberated. He met persons deeply involved in the study of linguistics and scriptures; persons dedicating their lives for *Yoga* and other spiritual practices. Many of them had just begun practising without realising the consequences; some were at the intellectual level engaged in hair-splitting arguments; and a very few, whom Śaṅkara could recognise, were into the real spirituality. Śaṅkara tried to have a dialogue with them. Looking at Śaṅkara, many of them commented that he was too young for any discussion. But none of them could discourage him, on the contrary, he said that he was a seeker and had come to them to learn. Looking into those clear eyes reflecting his noble mission, they complied and realised to their consternation, that it was not he, but they had much to learn from him.

Slowly, people started gathering around Śaṅkara to listen to his experiential understanding of the scriptures. Soon the *Ghāts* in Vārāṇasi started reverberating with the *Mantras* from the *Upaniṣads* sung by *Ācārya* in his sweet resonating voice. The few practising seekers came to him quietly and clarified their doubts. Out of such persons was Sanandana, from southern part of the country. It was evening and he had followed the *Ācārya* to the temple of Annapūrṇa—the nourishing Mother of the universe, and found him reciting spontaneously and musically the *Stotra* on the Goddess:

"O Mother Annapūrṇeśvarī!—who gives eternal bliss, dispeller of fear and giver of boons and protection, who is the ocean of beauty bestowing purity by washing away all sins, who is verily the great Goddess, who purified the entire race of Himavān, who is the supreme ruler of Kāśīpura and receptacle of mercy—grant me alms.

"O Mother Annapūrṇeśvarī!—who is the giver of the bliss of Yoga, who causes the extinction of all enemies, who makes Her devotees follow *Dharma* steadfastly, who possesses the splendour of the moon, sun and fire, and is the protector of the three worlds, who is the dispenser of all prosperity, who gives proper reward to penance, who is the supreme ruler of Kāśīpura and the ocean of mercy—grant me alms.

"O Annapūrṇa, who is ever full with element that sustains life, and who is always full and never exhausting, O beloved of Śaṅkara—grant me such alms so that I become firmly established in wisdom and renunciation.

"Pārvatī Devi is my divine mother, Lord Parameśvara my father. My kith and kin are the devotees of Śiva, and all the three worlds are my own places."[22]

Sanandana had never heard such enraptured recitation and had never seen such full emotional rendering of any *Stotra*. He was surprised at the change of mood of the *Ācārya* from intellectual analysis and brilliant discoursing during the course of the day, to *Mahābhāva*—the state of emotional ecstasy. He had always felt that both head and heart are exclusive and a person who is emotional cannot be an intellectual and vice versa. But here was Śaṅkarācārya, who was different. He noticed ṭhat the chest of *Ācārya* was red, with the hair standing on end and tears of joy were flowing from the luminous eyes.

Sanandana was awestruck and fell at the great saint's feet, begging him to accept him as a disciple. *Ācārya* seeing through the sincerity, the receptivity and readiness for total dedication in Sanandana, accepted him into the inner circle. He became like Ānanda to Siddharth Gautama Buddha, who preserved the words of the Master for posterity through his phenomenal memory. Most of the *Stotra*s that was to be known to the world later are

---

22. नित्यानन्दकरी वराभयकरी सौन्दर्यरत्नाकरी निर्धूताखिलघोरपापनिकरी प्रत्यक्षमाहेश्वरी ।
प्रालेयाचलवंशपावनकरी काशीपुराधीश्वरी भिक्षां देहि कृपावलम्बकरी मातान्नपूर्णेश्वरी ॥ अन्नपूर्णाष्टकम् 1 ॥
योगानन्दकरी रिपुक्षयकरी धर्मैकनिष्ठाकरी चन्द्रार्कानलभासमानलहरी त्रैलोक्यरक्षाकरी ।
सर्वैश्वर्यकरी तपःफलकरी काशीपुराधीश्वरी भिक्षां देहि कृपावलम्बकरी मातान्नपूर्णेश्वरी ॥ अन्नपूर्णाष्टकम् 3 ॥
अन्नपूर्णे सदापूर्णे शंकरप्राणवल्लभे । ज्ञानवैराग्यसिद्ध्यर्थं भिक्षां देहि च पार्वति ॥ अन्नपूर्णाष्टकम् 11 ॥
माता मे पार्वतीदेवी पिता देवो महेश्वरः ।बान्धवाः शिवभक्ताश्च स्वदेशो भूवनत्रयम् ॥ अन्नपूर्णाष्टकम् 12 ॥

the fruits of his efforts. Sanandana was basically a devotee and hence emotional. His *Iṣṭadevata*—chosen deity was *Nṛsimha*—the fourth incarnation of Viṣṇu, in the form of half-human and half-lion. His intense penance had gifted him with a pure mind and sharp intellect due to which he could grasp the nuances of *Vedānta* without any difficulty.

Normally, most of the discourses on scriptures involved hair-splitting arguments based on linguistics and over a period the listeners would lose interest. But with Śaṅkarācārya it was different. His approach was to inspire the listeners to start living the truths laid down in our culture. Gradually, the persons taking advantage of the company of Śaṅkarācārya started swelling as he would relate the scriptures with day-to-day life. The difference being that these discourses were not just explanations but were insights into the wonderful world of mind and spirit. The listeners would invariably identify themselves with the examples and situations thus relate intimately with the truths heard from the mouth of the master. Many if not most of the listeners gained the confidence to begin the spiritual journey. The disciples—especially Sanandana, were very happy. But Śaṅkara felt that there was something still missing in his life. His intuition was right, as he was yet to learn the most important lesson in his life!

Perfected masters are the sacred instruments through which the Reality functions for maintaining the universal rhythm and to keep the field of the world healthy for the onward evolution. The Infinite Will can readily play itself through such men of total identification with Reality, and they alone are competent instruments for the Universal to accomplish the divine purpose. To artists, their instruments are the most prized possessions. The instruments are well cared for, trimmed, sharpened, cleaned and tuned up always, with diligent attention and soothing love. The Reality also never spares its chosen instruments. Śaṅkarācārya too was not spared from this cosmic law. He too had to be restrung and retuned from time to time.

Mist from the river surface rose towards heaven as if in veneration. Eastern horizon blushed in anticipation of Sun's arrival and the river reflected the red hue. Śaṅkarācārya approached the *Ghāt* with his disciples, and as he started descending the steps to approach the water front, a man with a pack of dogs was climbing up. The man appeared to be a hunter, thus an outcaste. Śaṅkara instinctively, asked the hunter to move and give way. This was the usual practice those days and such instruction was always obeyed with an apology. Instead, the hunter just looked into the eyes of Śaṅkara and asked:

"O best among the twice-born, what do you really mean when you say 'Move away, move away', do you wish to move matter from matter, or you mean consciousness from consciousness?" This Person was the real Teacher indeed, felt Śaṅkara and to the shock of his disciples, fell prostrate at the feet of the Hunter, who had killed the last beast of ignorance from his being. Śaṅkara realised that in spite of all his learning from his Guru and experience thereafter, he fell short as far as *living the Advaita* was concerned. With his throat choking in grateful emotion he sang in praise of the hunter. This came to be called as *Manīṣā Pañcakam*: "He who has realised that he is not the seen, but that he is the one Consciousness that illumines all experiences during the waking, dream and deep-sleep states, the one Consciousness that is the sole witness of the entire play of the universe, the one Consciousness which is the very spark in all forms—from Creator to the ant—he alone is my Guru, be he a hunter or a Brāhmaṇa. He who in his direct experience of the Immaculate Supreme Bliss, has come to the firm understanding that the entire universe is but an extensive play of Pure Consciousness, all projected by his *ignorance* expressed in the three *Guṇas*, while he himself is but Brahman—He alone is my Guru, be he a hunter or a Brāhmaṇa."[23]

During the fag end of nineteenth century, a wandering monk stayed in the palace grounds in a tent, at behest of Maharaja Ajit Singh of Khetri. He was invited to be at the musical concert of a

---

23. अन्नमयादन्नमयमथवा चैतन्यमेव चैतन्यात् । द्विजवर दूरीकर्तुं वाञ्छसि किं ब्रूहि गच्छ गच्छेति ॥ 1 ॥ जाग्रत्स्वप्नसुषुप्तिषु स्फुटतरा या संविदुज्जृम्भते या ब्रह्मादि पिपीलिकान्ततनुषु प्रोता जगत्साक्षिणी ।सैवहं न च दृश्यवस्त्विति दृढप्रज्ञापि यस्यास्ति चेत् चण्डालोऽस्तु स तु द्विजोऽस्तु गुरुरित्येषा मनीषा मम ॥ 3 ॥ ब्रह्मैवाहमिदं जगच्च सकलं चिन्मात्र विस्तारितं सर्वं चैतदविद्यया त्रिगुणयाऽशेषं मया कल्पितम् इत्थं यस्य दृढा मतिस्सुखतरे नित्ये परे निर्मले चण्डालोऽस्तु स तु द्विजोऽस्तु गुरुरित्येषा मनीषा मम ॥ 4 ॥

dancing girl. He refused with an excuse that being a *Sanyāsin* it was not proper. The dancing girl came to know about it. Feeling disappointed and sad she sang the following song of Saint Sūradāsa with all her emotion:

"Oh Lord, look not upon to my limitations,
Your name O Lord, is *Samadarasī*—the equal visioned
You alone can take me across.
One piece of iron is in the idol of the temple,
And the other, the knife in the hand of a butcher;
But when they touch the philosopher's stone,
Both alike turn to gold."[24]

The Swami was deeply moved. The woman and her song told him that he was forgetting something, that all is Brahman, and that the same divinity is at the substratum of all beings—even in this woman whom he had looked down upon! Speaking of this incident later, the Swami would say, "Hearing the song I thought, 'Is this my *Sanyāsa*? I am a *Sanyāsi*, and yet I have in me this distinction between myself and the woman!' That incident removed the scales from my eyes. Seeing that all are indeed the manifestation of the One, I could no longer condemn anybody." This *Sanyāsi* came to be known as Swami Vivekananda, who paved way for the spiritual as well as the social renaissance of our nation.

Normally, we attribute divinity and sometimes even thrust divinity on to the great men. Such incidents in their lives reassure us that they too are human like us, along with emotions and a limitation or two. They too have had encounters with their own limitations. But their greatness lies in the fact that they *totally accept their limitations taking on full responsibility and never try to justify them*! On the contrary, the very obstacles are converted into opportunities by them, thus inspiring the so-called ordinary to emulate them. It appeared the hunter episode had cleansed the *Ācārya* of his *Bheda Vāsanā*—the tendency to differentiate, and his state of *Advaita* became stable. His

24. प्रभुजी मेरो अवगुण चित न धरो ।समदरसी है नाम तिहारो चाहे तो पार करो ॥ इक लोहा पूजा में राखत इक घर बधिक पर्यो ।पारस गूण अवगुण नहिं चितवत कंचन करत खरो ॥ प्रभुजी मेरो अवगुण चित न धरो ।

disciple Sanandana who was like his shadow became pleasantly aware of this change. He felt convinced that his Master fulfilled the eligibility of being a real Preceptor, as—*Śrotriyam Brahmaniṣṭham*—the master of scriptures and established in *Brahman.*[25] *Ācārya* Śaṅkara felt that time was appropriate to go north towards Himalayas, to complete the writing work. He left with his companion disciples to *Badrikāśrama* for composing the commentaries. The journey on foot was to take him through various kingdoms en route, exposing him and his team to new people and newer experiences.

It was during this journey that the *Ācārya* decided to revive the concept of *Tīrtha* as envisioned by Veda Vyāsa. He felt that this age-old practice could be used to integrate the country spiritually, which was divided politically. After reaching Badrikāśrama, he recovered the idol of Lord Nārāyaṇa from Nārada Kuṇḍa in the River Alakanandā and re-installed it in a temple with due ceremony. He directed that a Nambūdiri Brāhmaṇa from Kerala should be appointed for conducting regular worship at the temple and also prescribed rules for the *Pūjā*. The king of Jyotirdhāma carried out the instructions. This tradition, which links the southernmost state of our nation with the northernmost one, has continued ever since and even now the *Rāwal* (priest) of Badrinath is a Nambūdiri Brāhmaṇa from Kerala.

As they were settling down to commence the difficult task of writing the commentaries, Sanandana approached the *Ā*cārya to seek clarification for his doubt:

"I have heard that you learnt the scriptures from Respected Govinda Bhagavadpāda, why did you not write while learning them? He would have seen the completed work and may be, would have suggested the necessary changes."

Śaṅkarācārya did not respond to the query immediately, but took time to gaze at the River Alakanandā and then looking into his disciple's eyes observed:

"I was so busy absorbing the details as well as the essence that I could not give any thought to the act of writing. But after

---

25. तद्विज्ञानार्थं स गुरुमेवाभिगच्छेत्सवित्पाणिः श्रोत्रियं ब्रह्मनिष्ठम् ॥मुण्डकोपनिषद् 2:12 ॥

the incident in Kāśi I am more than convinced that I was not ready to write at that time, as *Advaita was only at the verbal and intellectual level!* But now is the appropriate time, as I am living *Advaita*. Moreover, even if I had written at that time, *I would have wanted to change* what was written!"

"Why do you say so?" asked Sanandana in a very curious voice.

"We write from the level we are in—physical, sensual, volitional, emotional as well as spiritual.[26] Our scriptures were uttered or written spontaneously by those great persons in their transcendental State of Being. When you learn the scriptures from the realised Persons like Goviṅda Guru, you can get a *glimpse* into the Reality. But for achieving the stability in the State, you have to get rid of your limitations. For me it was the great shaking given by the Realised Hunter! Now I am ready to write them."

Badrikāśrama offered a wonderful ambience for spirituality. Neelkanth peak, River Alakanandā and the ethereal vibrations of millennia long penance of the sages stabilized the *Advaita* in the Ācārya. He would sit under a tree with his disciples to not only drink the beauty of nature but also from the scriptures he had chosen to comment upon! *Śrīmadbhagavadgītā* was brought out from the mind bewitching story of *Mahābhārata* by him, for the first time. The method of writing was singular. They would recite the verses led by the *Ācārya*, and then contemplate on the verses. The Master would then write and recite the commentary in the meditative state. It took nearly four years to complete the task of writing commentaries upon fifteen books.

It was during the time when the *Ācārya* was teaching the *Brahmasūtra Bhāśya* to his disciples an old Brāhmaṇa started attending the discourses. He would always sit quietly incognito so that his presence did not disturb the proceedings in any way. But Śaṅkarācārya noticed that it was no other than *Bhagawān* Veda Vyāsa. When the disciples dispersed to their respective

---

26. It is said that Sri Aurobindo revised his monumental work "*Savitri*" seven times, every time from a deeper and a more comprehensive level.

duties, Śaṅkara approached and fell prostrate at the feet of the sage, who blessed him by saying:

"I have realised that you are the most eligible person to interpret and comment on the *Brahmasūtra*. *Sādhu*—well done! Your thoughts on *Adhyāsa*[27] are especially refreshing and will prove helpful to many a *Jijñāsu*—seekers. I see that you have started moving the wheel of revival of *Dharma* and have attracted a band of dedicated disciples. Before leaving this sacred place of Badri, you will receive such help and guidance that will save a lot of your time, for you are only a brief visitor to this land of mortals! Whenever you require any kind of help, I shall be there for you! My blessings!!"

"I am the same Śaṅkara who had the privilege of meeting you and get your guidance. If you feel that the *Bhāśya* helps those approaching the *Vedānta Darśana* I consider that my life is blessed indeed. *Bhagawān*, your words have not only encouraged me to pursue the mission, but am confident that it shall be fulfilled. I am always eager and ready to learn whatever is helpful in our mission. I shall need your blessings all the time!"

One night when everyone in the commune was sleeping, the *Ācārya* felt a presence. As his eyes unfolded, he beheld a youth—bright and handsome, in his early teens, smilingly looking into Śaṅkara's face. Getting up, he prostrated seeking the blessings of the youth, who observed:

"I have something to share with you, and in turn pay my debt to my Gurus."

Śaṅkara said in all humility:

"If you feel that I have the eligibility to receive it I will gratefully accept it."

That night on, Śaṅkara learnt the art of *Akāśagamanam*—Tele-transportation. As he could control the mind completely, he learnt the art of *Saṃyama—Dhāraṇā, Dhyāna* and *Samādhi* together, very easily. He was asked to perform *Saṃyama* on the

27. This will be dealt in the chapter entitled "*No-Other*".

relationship of the body with *Ākāśa.*[28] It involved dissolving the particles of the body into space at one place and then re-assembling them at the destination. The physical body is made up of innumerable particles of matter held together by forces of cohesion, these forces being resident in *Ākāśa* the universal medium. One can merge the gross body with the elements into *Ākāśa*—space at a place, and *reclaim* the same in some other place. So travel does not involve any time but is instantaneous. The *Ācārya* would definitely need it and use it to fulfill the mission, but more than that he could *feel* the whole universe in his palpitating heart. In a way, it involved the expansion of consciousness to the universal level. He remembered gratefully his Guru Goviṅda Bhagavadpāda, who had directed him to comment on *Viṣṇu Sahasranāma* that had opened his heart, the experience was much the same, and only the intensity had increased. When the Luminous youth told him that his work was done, Śaṅkara asked him:

"Can I teach this *Vidyā* to the eligible persons?"

The youth smiled and said:

"This *Vidyā* is *yours*, you can give it to anyone you feel, is eligible. Moreover, unless you transfer it to someone you cannot be free of *Jñāna-ṛṇa*—the debt of wisdom!"

"May I know the name of the Guru, who taught me *Ākāśagamanam*?" asked Śaṅkara.

Pointing to his own body the youth said smilingly:

"You can call *this* by any name, but I am one, of the four Sanatkumāras[29] and our life is meant for the help of seekers. When anyone enlarges his heart to develop love and is in need of any help, we appear. Our blessings are always with you."

This meeting and the subsequent learning had reassured the *Ācārya* that the whole creation was with him and he was with the creation. Without either worry or concern in his mind and heart, he became a perfect instrument in the hands of Reality to work out the destiny of our culture!

---

28. कायाकाशयोः संबन्धसंयमाल्लघुतूलसमापत्तेश्चाकाशगमनम् ॥ पातञ्जल योगदर्शनम् 3:43 ॥
29. Sanaka, Sanātana, Sanandana, and Sanatkumara are the four *eternal children* guiding the seekers.

During discourses, the disciples noticed that Śaṅkarācārya would keep addressing Sanandana, as if it was exclusively for him. They were bitten by the scorpion of jealousy! Actually, he was the most eligible among them. One day, Sanandana was on the other side of River Alakanandā collecting firewood. The *Ācārya* called out for him, since the regular way would take long, he started walking without bothering that the water was deep. Wherever his step fell on the water surface, a lotus supported him, as though there was a pathway of lotuses!

"Wisdom flows equally to all but the most eligible are able to receive and contain it. The eyes get attracted to the most receptive. Sanandana did not bother about his personal safety, he just responded to my call immediately. Jealousy is the most deterrent obstacle to spirituality. Shun it forthwith. Padmapāda, spread the deer-skin, I have something to share with you all!"

That was how the first disciple from the inner circle came to be known as Padmapāda.

The work of preserving the heritage of written *Word* to the posterity was over; to spread its fragrance to the contemporary society had to begin. *Ācārya* Śaṅkara descended the slopes of Himalaya to the plains where many were waiting for light, a few were ready to test the light, and a few more were preparing to fight the light! But everyone was eager to behold the light called Śaṅkarācārya!

❐

5
Spreading Fragrance

Activity is life and life is activity. Every single moment all the beings are involved in some kind of activity or the other. Each activity begets a result or fruit, and has an effect on the performer as well as the surroundings. Keen observers of life and nature that our ancestors were, they understood that all of us, without exception act, for either getting the fruit of action, or do not act for avoiding it, depending on whether the action gives us happiness or discomfort. They also discovered that fleeting is the happiness derived through any activity. This discovery brought a *notion* that since the body is subject to birth, growth, wearing out, old age, disease and death, eternal happiness is not possible in *this life* and so, the concept of heaven and hell was created!

They realised that Nature governed their life externally and showered upon them with its blessings as well as fury. They worshipped the nature to extol and evoke the blessings. For each element or quality of Mother Nature, they had a presiding deity. *Indra* symbolised rain, *Vāyu*, all activity or movement, and *Agni*, fire and energy in all forms. Since fire always moves *upwards* they called him the carrier of oblations to the gods and deities. They purified every activity through the performance of *Yajña*, consisting of rituals. Thus, even the simple act of eating food was called as the *Vaiśvānara Yajña*—the sacrifice to the gastric fire! With the downfall of Vedic values, the society became wary of rituals which had become mechanical, without any substance as there was none to explain the mechanism of rituals. The advent of Buddha with his compassion and meditation took the society into the fold of Buddhism. One of the main objections the Buddha raised was against the *mechanical* and *empty rituals*. A millennium later, even Buddhism became too scholastic and decadent as the common mass of people became monks and nuns, who were not eligible for monastic life, and the high values and discipline, were compromised. Consequently, the society was directionless like a rudderless ship.

The Providence chose Kumarila Bhaṭṭa as its champion for *Sanātana Dharma* who dedicated his life for reviving *Karma Kāṇḍa*—the ritualistic portion of the Vedas. But he realised that without learning the *Nyāya*—dialectics of the Buddhist philosophy it was not possible for him to convince the society to return to the *Vedas*. He joined the *Saṅgha* as a monk on probation. He mastered their logic and was ready to leave the folds of the *Saṅgha*, when one day his teacher started criticising *Sanātana Dharma* and its blind rituals harshly. Being a sincere worshipper of our culture, especially the *Vedas,* Kumarila had a few tears in his eyes. Noting this, the teacher and the inmates questioned him about the cause for the tears. Kumarila frankly told them his real purpose of joining! The head monk ruled that the punishment for such unpardonable *crime of betrayal was death*! When they took him to a precipice, not wanting to allow others to push him of the cliff, he jumped uttering "*If* the Vedas are true, nothing will happen to me!" Nothing happened to him, except the loss of his left eye.

Kumarila went on to take many under his fold and succeeded in re-introducing *Yajña* in the straying society. Thus, it was that the society started performing the rituals and pleasing their chosen gods by offering oblations at sacrificial alters to *Agni*—the carrier of oblations to the gods, the destroyer of sins, and the giver of wisdom. Kṛṣṇa Dvaipāyana Vyāsa, knowing that Kumarila Bhaṭṭa was a formidable alley in spreading *Advaita*, had advised *Ācārya* Śaṅkara to meet him and initiate a discussion, which could give a new direction to the society.

Śaṅkarācārya proceeded to Prayāg—the confluence of Gaṅgā and Yamunā to effect a merger of *Karma* and *Jñāna* through rendezvous with Kumarila and his disciples. On his arrival, *Ācārya* Śaṅkara came to learn that to absolve him of the sins; Kumarila Bhaṭṭa had decided to enter the fire made of paddy husk. Having completed his mission, Kumarila, a master of the Vedas, a deep scholar in all branches of learning and an accomplished dialectician was about to depart from this world. Śaṅkara hastened to the place where Kumarila had already started offering his body to the *Agni* at the neck deep alters of paddy husk for a slow and painful death. Surrounding the pyre were Kumarila's disciples like Prabhākar, shedding tears for the impending loss of their master.

Śaṅkara reached the place to behold the wonderful sight. In spite of the excruciating physical pain, there was that glow of satisfaction of fulfilling the life mission on the noble countenance of Kumarila Bhaṭṭa. It was as if he had become *Agni* spreading the light and white heat of experience and wisdom. When he felt the presence of *Ācārya* Śaṅkara, he opened his eyes, a sweet smile adorned his face and he addressed the *Ācārya* as if reading the question playing in the consciousness.

"You may be wondering as to why I am immolating myself. In fulfilling my mission, I had committed two sins: I joined a Buddhist *Saṅgha* to learn their system of dialectics, so that I could use their own logic to win them over in the arguments. Once, when I had almost completed my learning, the *Ācārya* was too critical of the *Vedas* that brought tears to my eyes. They noted this and when asked for the cause of tears, I told them honestly my real purpose which was *Guru Drōha*—cheating my own teacher. The head pontiff ruled that I should be put to death by throwing me off the precipice. Not allowing them touch me, I jumped on my own shouting "*IF* the *Veda* is truly *revealed wisdom*, then I shall not be hurt", that was my second sin, for I had used the *Conditional 'if'*, expressive of doubt, and because I had learnt the Buddhist Scriptures by deception, I lost one of my eyes in that fall as a punishment. No matter how noble the purpose, righteousness does not allow me to digress from its path, and so I am immolating myself for the sins."

With a lot of affectionate respect for young *Ācārya* standing in front of him, he said,

"Time governs this life, bringing fulfillment or disappointment. But I have been very fortunate to serve our culture, and trust that I have done all I could in this life. I have had the privilege to hear about you and all your accomplishments. Life wants me to have a parting gift—an audience with a person of your caliber and dedication. Could you please recite the commentary you have written on the *Brahma Sūtras*?"

Śaṅkara was too happy to place his work in front of an accomplished champion of *Vedas*. As he started reciting, he started seeing a glow on the face of Kumarila Bhaṭṭa—the glow of experiential understanding, an aura of wisdom. Kumarila would interrupt to seek clarifications. He liked the introduction which gives the cause for the ignorance of Reality to be *Adhyāsa*—superimposition. When it was finally over, Kumarila observed with tears of joy in his eyes:

"Your work is truly phenomenal and I am convinced that my effort to introduce *Karma Kāṇḍa* through *Pūrva Mīmaṅsa* is fulfilled through this *Bhāśya* on the *Brahma Sūtras*. How I wish that I had met you earlier, and tried to write a *Vārtikam*—an explanatory treatise, on it! *Ācārya* Śaṅkara, I have a final favour to ask of you." When Śaṅkara assured him, he continued:

"Maṇḍana Miśra is one of my most capable disciples. He will be able to write an apt *Vārtikam* for this noble work. But you will have to win him over first, for next to me he is a very staunch champion of *Karma Kāṇḍa*. This meeting will benefit both of you, and ultimately our culture." His eyes were looking into eternity, as he said,

"In Maṇḍana you will have an able general for the campaign against negativity. Please allow me to take leave of you."

Kumarila Bhaṭṭa, who had fought fiercely against the forces that resisted the spiritual growth of our society, who had championed the cause of winning the ultimate trust of the society in our scriptures, and who had dedicated his every breath for our great culture, breathed his last with a smile of enlightenment on his glowing face. An era had ended, but not before preparing the ground for the next one of total fulfillment of spirituality which is inclusive of head, heart, action, which does not have any distinction between *this*—the world and *that*—the spirit, which has room for *everything* and *every being*, in its bosom. Śaṅkara, who had been given the role of the unifier by the Providence, would play it well, so well that he would stand out as the shining star on this stage of existence.

After the completion of the last rites of the great warrior Kumarila Bhaṭṭa, Śaṅkara took leave of his disciples. His next destination was Mahiṣmati, the place where Maṇḍana Miśra resided. Śaṅkarācārya reached Mahiṣmati instantly with his disciples as they had mastered tele-transportation. When he enquired about the residence of the great scholar, he was told that he could easily locate the house by the recluses chanting *Vedas* at the gate of his residence, some of whom were discussing deep philosophical questions. On reaching the spot, his disciples were awestruck by the clarity of the cadence and intonation of the Vedic *Mantras*, and the ongoing philosophical discussions on complex problems. Reading their mind, the *Ācārya* smilingly observed that even parrots can recite and *talk* philosophy! This comment paved way for the legend that Maṇḍana Miśra had trained even parrots in chanting the *Vedas* and discussing philosophical problems!

Śaṅkara was amused when he was stopped from entering even the courtyard, since the master of the house was busy engaged in the *Śrāddha*—the yearly ritual performed for the liberation of one's ancestors. But the engaging innocent smile along with his regal bearing influenced the disciples, who allowed him to pass with his retinue! In the huge hall, he saw Maṇḍana Miśra about to sit by the specially built altar. When his eyes beheld a young monk bearing the brilliance of a sun, he was surprised and felt a pang of jealousy. Replacing the emotion with the pride and arrogance of an accomplished scholar, he shouted insultingly at Śaṅkara, who continued to approach the altar with a compassionate smile.

Without losing his composure, Śaṅkara said he had come for the alms at the house of the well-known scholar, reminding him that it was the sacred duty of every householder to give it. The *Ācārya* pointed out that he had not come for ordinary alms but for getting the *Vāda-Bhikṣā*—alms of discussion from a householder who was also an established scholar! These words disturbed the champion of *Pūrva Mīmāṅsa*—the school advocating *only* rituals as the whole and sole aim of *Vedas*, which were from a youthful *Sanyāsin* who had renounced the mundane for the sake of self-realisation. He understood the truth behind the statement of Śaṅkara and knew that the monk who was making the request was an advocate of the wisdom of Brahman. Maṇḍana accepted the challenge and agreed to have a debate. He was certain that a mere child in monk's garb was in no way any threat to him!

The assembly suggested the name of Ubhaya Bhārati, wife of Maṇḍana Miśra, for being the judge for this debate. This illustrious lady was also an accomplished scholar, but pride being not one of her virtues she preferred to don the garb of an ordinary housewife! Noting the hesitation on the brow of Maṇḍana, Śaṅkara immediately responded by saying that he did not have any objection, as she would be just a judge. As per the rules of the debate, the defeated person would accept the victor's way of life. If defeated, Śaṅkara would wear the white clothes of a householder while Maṇḍana, the ochre clothes of a *Sanyāsin* if he was unable to win. Just before the debate, Ubhaya Bhārati put garlands on the necks of both the participants and declared the debate open.

The news of a young *Sanyāsin's* challenge to the one and only Maṇḍana Miśra had spread like wild fire and literally the whole city had thronged his residence. Not all of them had come there for appeasing their intellectual curiosity! Many wanted to behold the youth who had so much courage and confidence to challenge the stalwart. While the scholars came there to see their adversary—as they had been defeated by Maṇḍana—taste the defeat, or at least welcome one more co-sufferer to their lot!

His face illumined by austere life and the experiential wisdom, Śaṅkara occupied the seat allotted to him. There was neither the arrogance of his being a monk, nor was there any diffidence or concern for the outcome of the great debate. His countenance bore a quiet confidence in his experience, the unshakable trust in his *Guru's* grace, and the blessings of the great lineage of enlightened Masters behind him. Moreover, the real reason being not *his own personal victory, but to gain a comrade at arms for the revival of our culture, he just knew that he had the support of the whole Existence!*

On the contrary, Maṇḍana Miśra was aware of his larger than life image of being a destroyer in debates—any kind of debate, the age and inexperience of his opponent, and an impatience to finish this whole episode. Paradoxically, when he beheld that compassionate, ever-smiling youthful face, there was a mixed feeling of pity and regret for disappointing the youth! Though these feelings could be felt by him and to an extent seen by the onlookers in his posture and gestures, unfelt by him unseen by others there was an element of *fear* like a very soft thorn having the capacity to give an unrecognized pain! The question "*What if this*?" was only an infant in his mind which he ignored in the crowd of his past achievements.

Remembering the benign face of his *Guru* and mentally offering his salutations to the enlightened lineage, Śaṅkara made the opening statement, declaring his stand:

"Brahman—The Existence, Wisdom and Bliss Absolute (*Sat-Cit-Ānaṅda*) is the Ultimate Truth, without which *nothing is possible*, be it life or action. It is This Ultimate Truth that *appears* as the entire world due to *Māyā*—illusion, like the silver in shell. When this illusion is dispelled due to *Jñāna*—experiential wisdom, the world dissolves to the Brahman—the substratum that is No-Other than the individual self. All action (hand), feeling (heart) as well as reason (head) are only means to achieve this end of experiential understanding.

"This supreme wisdom based on understanding is *Mōkṣa*—liberation from the cycle of births and deaths. *Upaniṣads* scattered in the *Vedas*, are the authority for this proposition. Since they give out the *essence* of this wisdom which alone gives meaning to life and activity".

Maṇḍana Miśra remembered *his* preceptor Kumarila Bhaṭṭa, and cleared his throat. But Śaṅkara noticed a change in his countenance—his eyes became luminously soft; the arrogance which he used as an ornament was replaced by a childlike curiosity and receptivity to learn and absorb anything new and useful; and to the onlookers he appeared less threatening! He declared his stand:

"Life without action is not only meaningless but is not possible. Action is of two categories, the recommended action and prohibited action. The *Vedas* exhort action that prepares and makes the man eligible to enter heaven. It gives all the details of such actions—the *Maṅtras*—the chants, materials required, the methods, *mudrā*s—the gestures to be followed, the functions of different officiating priests, the duties of the beneficiary (*Yajamāna*). Thus, *Vedas* are of nature of commandments for the performance of rituals, if this is not accepted, *Vedas* become purposeless literature."

Two powerful minds clashed with arguments and counter arguments, each outdoing the other. When the onlookers heard one of them, they felt that he *has* to be right, but when the other logically destroyed his opponent's arguments, they were more than convinced that he *had to be right*! It was not just a debate for the sake of proving the intellectual supremacy.[30]

For *Ācārya* Śaṅkara, it was for winning a friend and a comrade for the greater work of revival of our culture and the renaissance of Indian society. He gave a small twist to this debate by asking a question:

"Do you recognise the contribution of Kṛṣṇa Dvaipāyana Vyāsa to our culture?"

His chest filled with great pride and great reverence in his heart Maṇḍana Miśra replied:

---

30. This debate being too academic, the author has availed his freedom to give an interpretation for the understanding of a non-philosophic reader and its usefulness in day-to-day life.

"Without any doubt whatsoever! But for him, we could not possibly have the Vedic treasure. It was Vyāsa who organised the knowledge into the four streams; it was he who gave us the method of preserving the correct intonation and cadence of the *Mantras*; it was again he, who gave the posterity the most practical rituals to our society."

"Then you may be aware for the common mass of people, who do not and who *cannot* follow all the dictums of the rituals, he gave the *Mahābhārata* which gives the story of human beings—their weaknesses and strengths, their trials and tribulations, the various types of persons both lowly and petty as well as lofty and great." As Śaṅkara said this, Maṇḍana interrupted:

"But that is just mythology without any relevance to this debate!"

Śaṅkara retaining his poise countered:

"I personally feel that a person of Vyāsa's stature would not have and could not have done anything just to fulfill the fancy of scholarship! Everything he did had the great purpose of, as you rightly pointed out, the regeneration of the society. So *Mahābhārata* was not just a story, but had a deeper aim of transferring the wisdom to the society."

"But *Mahābhārata* is irrelevant to this debate, we are discussing the superiority of *Karma*—action!?" Maṇḍana was getting impatient.

"Revered Sir that is the point I am coming to! *Śrīmadbhagavadgītā* forms the heart of *Mahābhārata*. It extols Arjuna towards action, who is giving all the arguments to desist from action. It gives action in all its aspects. *Karma* is only a *means* to achieve the end of *Mōkṣa*, the liberation and not an end in itself."

For the first time Maṇḍana felt that this youth had something very important to convey to him. A committed learner that he was, he showed genuine interest to know what it was and not just to win the debate! He said softly:

"I am aware of this part of the book, which convinces Arjuna not to shun action however ghastly, and to perform his duty. But I am at a loss to know how it is related to the topic of debate." Śaṅkarācārya appreciatively answered with a smile:

"The *Śrīmadbhagavadgītā* gives various dimensions of action—from gross to subtle. All beings are governed by their instinct of survival—hunger, sleep, fear and procreation, the action which is goaded by the instinct is common to all including the human beings. But we do not stop with that, we have something else, we are not just satisfied with our needs but we have *wants*! This *want* or *desire* makes us perform action which is governed by loss and gain, happiness and gratification, which has been put in the category of *Kāmya Karma—action* goaded by desire. Most in the society are at this level—involved with their petty selves consisting of '*I* and *mine*'. But man is only a process, *a work in progress*, and so he cannot stagnate in one stage for long, he starts looking at others who share the world with him, and develops a feeling of oneness with them. The practice of rituals or *Yajña* is to make the man aware of his duties and responsibilities towards them. In short, they give him the value of *Kartavya*.[31] The *Gītā* makes these obligatory.[32] But then, this action is mostly governed by loss and gain, and the eyes of the performer are *mostly* on the fruit of action. The scripture gives the secret of efficient and stress-free action. The beauty of *Śrīmadbhagavadgītā* is that it does not stop with this it proceeds to give the methodology of eliminating the *Kartṛtva*—of *I-doness*, from action. I have a very great regard for your respected *Guru*, who braved the adversaries almost single handedly in bringing the Vedic culture to its deserved glory. Under the *Ṛṣi Yajña*, you can take it to further glory by asking the questions, "*Is action an end in itself? Is heaven the ultimate goal of life?* and *If even after achieving heaven, we have to return to human*

31. *Pañca Mahā Yajña*—five great rituals extol the householder to be obliged towards *Ṛṣis*—Sages by gaining their wisdom and transferring it to the next generation, *Deva*—Gods, *Pitṛ*—ancestors, *Manuṣya*—fellow men, and *Bhūta*—all beings and elements.

32. यज्ञदानतपःकर्म न त्याज्यं कार्यमेव तत् ।यज्ञो दानं तपश्चैव पावनानि मनीषिणाम् ॥ श्रीमद्भगवद्गीता 18:5 ॥

life which is temporary, is it worth all the trouble?" We have to include the common man with his routine life of survival, in our endeavour to regenerate our grand heritage."

Śaṅkara had more than succeeded in changing the heart of Maṇḍana Miśra, who realised that though the achievement of his school of thought was great, it had included only a section of the society, and not society as a whole. He had the genuine humility when he asked the *Ācārya*:

"How can we include the common man? It will require a lot of effort as well as men with endless courage and grit! But I fully realise that it must be done!"

"Already I have a few persons with me, but I am certain, that with you by my side, we will attract more eligible persons and resources."

When the *Ācārya* said this, his eyes were seeing far into future and a smile had a conviction that it was not at all an empty wish. It had the long illustrious generations of the lineage of *Advaita*, and now another river of dedicated persons from *Pūrva Mīmāṅsa* had joined them.

But Maṇḍana Miśra had a few more clarifications to seek before giving in completely! He asked:

"How to proceed from the realm of activity to the realm of supreme truth or *Brahman—Sat-Cit-Ānaṅda,* as you stated?"

Śaṅkarācārya was in no hurry to reply the query. Instead, he looked at the assembly with love oozing out of his eyes, then looking at the scholar compassionately said:

"Action is to be performed for purifying the mind and sharpening the intellect. The pure mind has the capacity to see the Truth *as It is*, without any distortion. The burdened and a noisy mind can only create distortions, as one sees a snake instead of the rope in twilight! We will include the rituals to purify the mind, to sublimate the emotions and to sharpen the mind by adopting the rituals from *Karma Kāṇḍa*."[33]

---

33. The *Sandhyāvandanam*—with *Gāyatri Maṅtra*, the *Ṣōḍaśōpacāra Pūjā*—the worship of the Chosen Deity with sixteen offerings and other common rituals are the outcome of this confluence of the two schools.

When Śaṅkarācārya looked at Ubhaya Bhārati the judge, she got up and declared that the *Ācārya* had excelled her husband in the debate, and as per the convention Maṇḍana Miśra would embrace *Sanyāsa*. She invited both of them for *Bhikṣā*—the alms of food. With their meal over, she smilingly addressed the victor:

"*Ācārya*, you have had only half victory by winning over my husband. There is another half, because I am his other half!! Only when you win over me, you can be called as the victor of the great debate."

"I am more than willing, oh Mother. I belong to the class of *Advaita* which accepts all dimensions of Existence."

Said Śaṅkara in all innocence, little aware of one of the greatest tests for any monk. But he had to face it not unlike the gold entering the crucible to rid of all impurities, and to shine for all posterity.

❑

6
Ordeal by Fire

The air was filled with the fragrance of earth as *Godhūḷi*—the dust scattered by the cows' hooves as they returned home after grazing. The eastern horizon was turning dark from deep violet, while the West had turned deep red as the sun had set to awaken the other side for goading it towards activity. Śaṅkarācārya sat on the river bank in deep meditation. The silent and expansive mind of Śaṅkara was like a wave-less pond, unconcerned and alert, overflowing with the bliss from within. It had been a long day and the disciples sat at a little distance whispering the proceedings of the day, in all appreciation of scholarly Maṇḍana and his openness to receive what their master had to give. But the call of Ubhaya Bhārati for another discussion had puzzled them. They could not possibly imagine a lady—no matter how scholarly, getting into a discussion with a monk who had won over her husband! One thing was certain: the following day would be very interesting!

The residence of Maṇḍana Miśra was filled with crowds of eager learners, curious scholars and the common people who just wanted to have a glimpse of the young *Sanyāsin* who had won over the greatest champion of *Pūrva Mīmāṅsa.* As *Ācārya* Śaṅkara entered the venue there was silence, when they looked at him in awe. He smiled, through which he conveyed his unalloyed love for all of them. Spontaneously, they all cheered him, and prayed for his victory, for though they had not seen Ubhaya Bhārati get into any philosophical discussion, they all had heard of her deep learning, similar to our great women like Gārgi, Maitreyī who had debated with sage Yājñavalkya, of Sulabhā who had debated with King Janaka, as well as Lopamudrā and Arundhati who were partners in spirituality of their husbands.

Arguments and counter arguments were given for and against principles from different points of view. Just when the audience felt that it was very difficult if not impossible to come to any result, Ubhaya Bhārati suddenly asked:

"Discuss with me the science and the art of love between the sexes."

When she saw a puzzled expression on the bright countenance of Śaṅkara, who had been a celibate from his birth, and the only attitude he had for all women was that towards Mother, a smile adorned her face, she continued as if to explain:

"Let us now discuss *Kusumāstra Śāstram*.[34] You can describe the different forms and expressions; its nature and the centres; how it varies in the sexes during bright and dark fortnights; what are its manifestations in man and woman?"

The topic was definitely a bolt from the blue for Śaṅkara. In his devotion and his chosen mission, there had never been any occasion for giving any thought to this topic, which was and continues to be for those who are in deep sense indulgence. This definitely was for him an ordeal by fire! If he refused to enter into a debate, his claim that *Advaita* is *all inclusive* without any reservation would turn out to be only a shallow claim; while to discuss the subject without any real experience would be hollow! He sat in deep silence, so deep that it appeared to envelop the whole assembly. His disciples, including Maṇḍana Miśra, were shocked that this subject was raised. Noting hesitation on Śaṅkara's part and embarrassment on the faces of the disciples she said calmly:

"I request the indulgence of this august assembly. It is just a matter of time when the great *Ācārya* Śaṅkara will be honoured as *Sarvajña*—the Master of *all* learning including the art and

34. A work in aphorism form by sage Vātsyāyana, also known as *Kāma Sūtras*.

science of physical love. Moreover, the instinct of procreation is basic to all beings, especially human beings as it not only serves the purpose of progeny but is a source of joy. You have heard the *Ācārya* claim that *Ānanda*—bliss which is resultant of *any* action is *not qualitatively different* from Brahman, because bliss is Brahman."

Though some of the scholars were in agreement with Ubhaya Bhārati, most of them were apprehensive, that such misadventure could permanently harm the mission of revival of our culture, experiencing this branch of knowledge, was the fall of Śaṅkara. They felt that the debate was over! But when they looked at Śaṅkara with sympathy and concern, he opened his eyes and said with a smile:

"Mother, I agree with your statement! All types of bliss have only one source: *Brahman*! But throughout my life, I had neither time nor opportunity to even think on this topic. I will require some time to learn and experience this facet of life, before I venture into any further discussion."

Ubhaya Bhārati readily granted him time. The people disbursed with various conclusions. Some felt that the youthful *Sanyāsin* was needlessly taking a great risk; others felt that he was more interested in the title of *Sarvajña* than his mission (!); yet others felt that the woman had tricked him into this, to see him fall (!). But Śaṅkara was unperturbed, determined to make use of this opportunity to enhance his learning and perhaps gain more self-control. After *Bhikṣa,* Śaṅkarācārya left the town and started moving out of the town. Being aware of the conflict in the disciples' minds, he spoke reassuringly:

"You would be wondering as to whether it is necessary to gain this experience for winning a debate. Having dedicated to the cause of the revival of our great culture, we should always remember that our culture is *all inclusive*. It never *negates anything*! It has place for everything and everyone. What mother Ubhaya Bhārati said has a very great message for us, who are the servants, our culture. It is an opportunity to learn the art of dissociation from body and mind. I have learnt to dissociate with the feeling of *Kartṛtva*—doer ship or the notion "I am doing".

Deep inside, I have started experiencing the Changeless Reality which remains totally unaffected by space, time, and also internal as well as external conditions. A continual awareness persists during all my actions. It is as though, the Reality is always at rest, with only a single function of witnessing. Do you recall the two great verses from the *Śrīmadbhagavadgītā*?

"Knower of the Self and a yogi in spite of being in the process of seeing, listening, touching, smelling, eating, going, sleeping, breathing, speaking, renouncing, accepting, closing and opening the eyes, is convinced that the senses are interacting with the sense objects, while He remains unaffected *without any action.*[35]

"However, I cannot and will not utilise this body for the purpose. It has to be kept pure under all circumstances. For a *Sanyāsin* there can be no greater fall than breaking his celibacy. God will create an opportunity for the purpose. Let us now travel through the air and look for that opportunity!"

They started *Ākāśagamanam*. After covering a distance they saw a funeral procession. From the regal insignia, it appeared to be that of a king. The carriage was followed by the mourning ladies. The *Ācārya* gestured his disciples to follow him. Having entered a cave in a nearby mountain, Śaṅkarācārya spoke to his disciples:

"With help of a technique called *Parakāya Praveśa*,[36] I shall enter the body of the dead king. In time, after learning about the physical love through his body, I will return and re-enter this body. But you must guard this body against any harm, for if anything happens to it, I shall never be able to re-enter."

During his *Yoga Sādhanā* on the banks of Narmadā, Śaṅkara had learnt this technique. *Parakāya Praveśa* involves withdrawing the *attention* from the gross body (*Bhautika Śarīra*) as well as the subtle body—which consists of mind (*Sūkṣma*

---

35. नैवकिन्चित्करोमीति युक्तो मन्येत तत्ववित् । पश्यञ्शृण्वन्स्पृशञ्जिघ्रन्नश्नन्गच्छन्स्वपञ्श्वसन् ॥ श्रीमद्भगवद्गीता 5:8 ॥ प्रलपन्विसृजन्गृह्णन्नुन्मिशन्निमिशन्नपि । इन्द्रियाणीन्द्रियार्थेषु वर्तन्त इति धारयन् ॥ श्रीमद्भगवद्गीता 5:9 ॥
36. बन्धकारणशैथिल्यात् प्रचारसंवेदनाच्च चित्तस्य परशरीरावेशः ॥ पातञ्जल योगदर्शनम् 3:39 ॥ "The mind can enter another body on relaxation of the *cause of bondage*, and from the knowledge of passages."

Śarīra), and identifying with the causal body (*Kāraṇa Śarīra*). *Kāraṇa Śarīra* has the power of being anywhere. A master *Yogi* that he was, Śaṅkarācārya had mastered this technique to make it his own. Since he had become an efficient instrument of the divine, he knew that this wisdom would be vital for his mission.

Sitting in the cave in a meditative posture, he totally withdrew his attention from the body and left the cave with his *Kāraṇa Śarīra* through *Brahmarandhra*—the passage in the crown of his head, the disciples noticed that though the physical body had become lifeless, it appeared to be in the state of deep sleep. Śaṅkara reached the spot where preparations were being made for the cremation of the dead king. Having noticed that the king's eyes were slightly open, the *Ācārya* entered the body through them. The officials and subjects were pleasantly surprised to notice a movement in their king's body. All of them shouted in joy, on seeing their king returning from the jaws of death! He was brought back to the palace and there was festivity in the kingdom to celebrate a new lease of life for the king.

There was an order, arrangement and beauty wherever the eyes fell. The gardens around the palace, the architecture of the building, the paintings and sculptures were very well laid. The first thing that Śaṅkara noticed was that the king, who went by the name Amaruka, was a lover and worshipper of beauty and nature. The behaviour of the queen made it obvious that they shared a cordial and intimate relationship. From the conversations, it appeared as though neither the queen and nor the king needed any reason for celebrations. And that night music and dance, they had a genuine reason to organise celebrate the recovery of the king!

The queen observed an obvious change in the king. He was receptive and observant to learn. She had known him to be a person who flowed naturally towards enjoyment. Once in a while she would look at him in all affection, glad that she had woken up from the nightmare of his death. She was pleasantly surprised to find him extremely peaceful and there was little or no excitement which had been earlier part of his nature. He appeared to be totally living the moment and yet, also to be at a distance, as though, he was only a mute observer, a witness. However, she thought that may be that his recent encounter with death, which could never be taken lightly by anyone, had an impact on his mind and behaviour.

On his part, Śaṅkara involved himself in the affairs of state, welfare of the subjects. The ministers and officials were surprised at his alertness and the ability to take quick decisions; at his sense of commitment towards the subjects; and at his foresight of training others to take over the reins of the kingdom from him. They thanked the Almighty for not only bringing back their beloved king from the jaws of death, but also in changing his outlook towards life!

During other times, he would fulfill the purpose for which he had entered the king's body. He learnt that though the act of procreation is for the perpetuation of the species, human beings had discovered the element of happiness in the act. Like the variety of food discovered and developed by human beings, even the physical act of love was highly developed. During course of his learning, Śaṅkara not only studied the *Kusumāstra Śāstra* of Sage Vātsyāyana but wrote a commentary on it adding a spiritual dimension to the work.[37]

The act he noted was at four distinct levels of body, mind, emotions and being. On the grossest level the other was merely considered as an object through which one could satisfy the senses. At the level of mind there is sharing as the partners share common interests and the act is only a consequence. On the emotional level, the partners are in love with each other. Love characterised by respect and concern, as they live and act for the happiness of the other. The subtlest is the level of being, when both have merged into one without any feeling of otherness. Śaṅkara remembered the dialogue of Sage Yājñavalkya and his consort Maitreyī in *Bṛhadāraṇyaka Upaniṣad*:

"A man fully embraced by his beloved wife, is not aware of anything at all, either the external or the internal, so does this

---

37. This work in the name of Amaruka is lost.

infinite being, fully embraced by the Supreme Self, not know anything at all, either external or internal."[38]

Thus, the joy resulting in the act of procreation though qualitatively same, it has a drawback. During his interaction with the queen, he observed that the male and the female search each other for fulfillment. The dependence for the *other* is given beautifully in the Vedāntic statement:

"In contact with the sense objects and the sense experience, the happiness derived (as such) is unsurpassable (supreme). The *attraction* for objects is *the bondage*; freedom from this attraction is *the freedom*."[39]

While fulfillment is possible only, when one discovers that both male as well as the female principles co-exist *within*. Each one of us, man or woman is complete but the *obstinate habit* of seeking *outside* forces us to nurture dependence on external. If one increases the *Prajñā*—awareness and alertness during all the contacts of the senses with their objects, it is not very difficult to realise the truth *during* the experience. For Śaṅkara who was extremely alert and aware, it was quite easy. Thus, his bliss went on increasing even with small interactions. At the same time, Śaṅkara fully understood the bond existing between husband and wife. The queen would share all her emotions with King Amaruka; he noted her dedication and love for him; her preparedness to sacrifice anything even for his smallest wish; and her respect and concern were rather touching. Śaṅkara who was already very sensitive was moved.

The heart of *Ācārya*, who had become pupil Śaṅkara, opened to the world of emotions. To his pleasant surprise, he became aware of the treasure of emotions existing in the so-called mundane relationships. The bond between a chaste wife and her husband (*Madhura*)—for which he had never given any thought, taught him to become receptive to the other possible *Bhāvas* or the moods of relationships like between friends

38. यथा प्रियया स्त्रिया संपरिष्वक्तो न बाह्यं किञ्चन वेद नान्तरम्,
एवमेवायं पुरुषः प्राज्ञेनात्मना संपरिष्वक्तो न बाह्यं किञ्चन वेद नान्तरम् ॥ बृहदारण्यकोपनिषद् 4:3:21 ॥

39. दृश्यदर्शन संबन्धे सुखसंविदनुत्तमा । दृश्यसंवलिता बन्धस्तन्मुक्ता मुक्तिरुच्यते ॥ लघुयोवासिष्ठः 5:9:43 ॥

(*Sakhya*), between mother and child (*Vātsalya*), between servant and master (*Dāsya*), and between the disciple and Master (*Śānta*) and that all these *Bhāvas* are parts of the grand *Madhura Bhāva*. It struck him that the predominant emotion that pervades the whole existence is Love! Amidst these new experiential learning, Śaṅkara did not realise the passage of time as the intended time he had given the disciples was over.

Meanwhile in the cave, the disciples were concerned as their master had not yet returned. Padmapāda suggested that they visit the kingdom to find the welfare of their master, and that they should go into the palace disguised as musicians, so as to keep the identity of their master a secret. For he knew that the qualities of the *Ācārya* could not be hidden for long, anymore than the shine of a diamond! Somehow he felt that his master was in danger.

Deputing a few disciples to protect the body they reached the kingdom. When they reached the palace gates, they were told that the king had repaired to the inner courts and that he could not be disturbed. Padmapāda, who was in the guise of a chief musician, told that they were a group of musicians and they had heard of the king being a patron of music and arts and that they should be allowed to exhibit their talent. The security officer obliged and took them to the inner chambers.

The king recognised Padmapāda and ushered him. Prostrating in front of the king, they started the performance. It was on an incident from our history. Yogi Matsyendra entered the body of a diseased king to gain entry into the palace, after entrusting his body to his disciple Gorakṣa. While the Yogi thus reigned as king, the kingdom became extremely prosperous and peaceful. Having observed the change in the behaviour of the king, a wise old minister concluded that a great soul had entered into the body of the diseased king. And so he employed the services of court dancers and women to keep the king engaged in amorous activities. The king got so immersed in the affairs that he totally lost track of time! His concerned disciple came to the kingdom and reminded the king of his spiritual attainments and asked him to return. Matsyendra Nāth *remembered* and returned after leaving the body of the king.

Śaṅkara applauded the performance and smilingly said:

"It was excellent! You have succeeded in conveying a grand message to all of us in this palace. You will be duly rewarded. You shall find what you are seeking within this week. In the mean while, you can avail of the hospitality of the palace."

Understanding the intention of the master, Padmapāda said humbly:

"We are very grateful for this opportunity O Lord! But we cannot stay as we have to leave as quickly as possible."

Padmapāda left the kingdom with others to return to the cave and eagerly waited for the arrival of their beloved Guru.

Queen Niśiprajñā had observed the conversation between the king and the chief musician quite curiously, for she had noticed an element of recognition in her husband's eyes when the troupe had entered the inner court. She had also strongly felt that both had conveyed something important, the musician through their performance, and her lord in his brief sentences. As soon as the troupe left King Amaruka said gravely:

"O queen, I have something very important to tell you." Śaṅkara then told her the train of events that happened at Mahiṣmati and the debate and his consequent *Parakāya Praveśa*. The queen instead of getting shocked or angry smiled sadly and sighed to say:

"Lord! I knew from the day my husband's body got enlivened, that it could not have been possibly him. And in his space there had to be a very advanced soul. Your arrival in this kingdom has ushered peace, prosperity and joy. My husband was only interested in art, architecture and gardens which used to enhance his sense indulgence. On the contrary, you not only showed interest in the affairs of the state, but also the people. In the middle of all luxury and sense indulgence, there was something very sacred and pure, untouched by any contamination. Last night when I was in your arms, I gratefully beheld a flame in your chest where someone luminous was sitting in meditation. At that moment I was certain that you are not the one who appears to be."

Śaṅkara was apologetic when he said:

"We have so much to do and so little time, which forced me to take this step. But you have made this inevitable parting smooth. I always wanted to express my gratitude for this unforgettable contribution of yours in my life and to our culture."

Niśiprajñā said with watery eyes:

"I do not know anything about my being helpful in your great mission, but yes, you have brought joy into my life. I used to be treated only as an object of enjoyment, a thing to be used and thrown. Your company gave me a glimpse into the spiritual dimension of life. Your insistence on my being with you when you ran the state taught me to properly utilise the services of our able ministers and officers, and to motivate others to develop a sense of belonging to the nation. My prayers will always follow you."

"Before I leave this body to enter my own, I would like to gift you with a meditative technique, which will help you to be in the meditative state *during* all your activity. You beheld a flame and a luminous being in meditation. The same being dwells within you who *recognised* that very being in me! Try to get in touch with that being. It is not that difficult. We are able to perceive the world outside through senses. The eye sees the form, is recognised by the mind. Go within and then you will be able to behold the modifications." So saying, he recited a verse in his sonorous voice:

"The form is the scene and the eye the seer, eye is the scene and mind the seer; all the mental modifications are scene, the Witness is ever the seer and never the scene."[40]

Then he went on to explain the method of meditative contemplation—known as *Vicāra* thus helping Niśiprajñā to take the initial steps in the practice. Śaṅkara reassured that he

---

40. रूपं दृश्यं लोचनं दृक् तद् दृश्यं दृक् तु मानसम् ।दृश्या धीवृत्तयः साक्षी दृगेव न तु दृश्यते ॥ दृग्-दृश्य विवेकः 1 ॥
This is the opening verse of a great work of Śaṅkarācārya called *Dṛg Draśya Viveka*.

had shared his wisdom with her, assumed a Yogic posture and dropped Amaruka's body. After looking in all gratefulness at the temple that had given him shelter for learning something very important, he left the kingdom and reached the cave to be with his beloved disciples.

Śaṅkarācārya reached Mahiṣmati with his disciples ready for another debate. But as soon as Ubhaya Bhārati beheld the luminous being in the *Ācārya*, she greeted him most respectfully and said with folded hands:

"I see that you have become *Pūrṇa*—complete. When I had seen you last, you were an extraordinary being with sharp intellect, alertness and full of *Prajñā*—awareness. But now your heart has opened and you have totally succeeded in invoking the female principle[41] in you. Now you *are* a *Sarvajña*! The debate at this point of time is superfluous."

These words of eulogy made Śaṅkara realise that Ubhaya Bhārati too was in the same state of completeness and that her purpose of challenging him to a debate was mainly to help him achieve the state of completeness. She then served *Bhikṣā*—the food for the *Sanyāsins*. All the monks realised that it was not just the food for the body prepared by the enlightened mother, but spiritual nourishment needed for their beings which were embarking on a great mission of renaissance of our country.

"*Bhagawan*, we are all aware of the greater phase of activity awaits us. Will you please guide us how to act, and what is the essence of enlightened action?" Padmapāda asked.

"Never dwell on the fruit, *during*—when you are engaged in the action. This will make it efficient. Take the action as your duty. Remember that we are mostly aware of the world outside, the events, the beings and objects. But seldom are we aware of the *One who is aware; one who is acting*. This is where the meditation comes to our rescue! You become aware of the *Self*, who is just witnessing without involving or indulging. With the strong and sustained awareness of this *Self*, we succeed

41. This state is symbolised by *Ardhanarīśvara*—half man and half woman form of Mahādeva—the Great God, or the inseparable Rādhā-Kṛṣṇa.

in eliminating the *Kartṛtva*—the doer-ship, the sense of '*I* am doing'. The action then becomes spontaneous, effortless and most important, blissful."

Padmapāda had also observed the changes in his *Guru* after the *Parakāya Praveśa*. Changes like the divine softness, the spontaneous flow of sublime emotions like compassion and love. It was as if the lotus of Śaṅkara Bhagavadpāda had fully blossomed and the fragrance was surely spreading all around.

❐

Emotion
(Heart)

Footsteps of the Heart (Map)

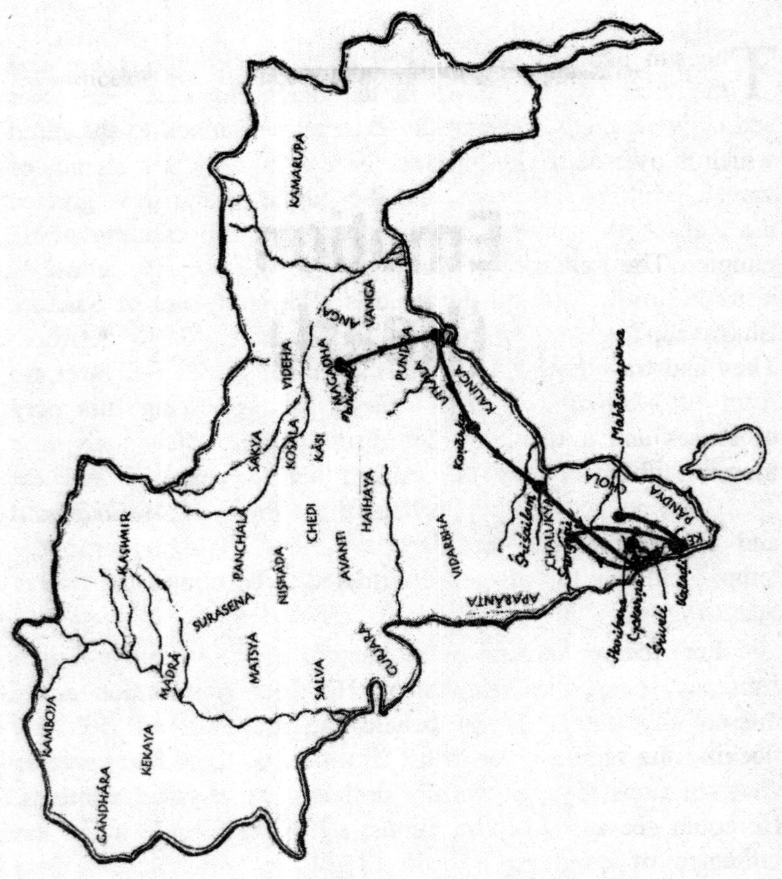

7
The World of Emotions

The sun had not yet knocked at the doors of horizon and the eyes could not see in the dark. However, the other senses were eager to bring the external sensations to the mind which is over-dependent on the sense of vision! Soft sounds of wavelets hitting the banks and the gurgle of the flow greeted the ears. A mild breeze brushed past the skin creating goose pimples. The fragrance of damp earth mixed with the aroma of jasmine flowers greeted the nostrils. The entourage of Śaṅkara Bhagavadpāda was resting on the bank of River Krishnā. They had travelled to Śrīśailam the sacred place of Śiva in the form of *Mallikārjuna*. The *Ācārya* sat witnessing this play of senses and mind, while his disciples were busy with their morning ablutions. As the eastern horizon blushed and the eyes became active, they beheld the temple of *Mallikārjuna* and *Bhramarāṁbikā*—his Divine concert. They entered the temple and saw the image—considered to be one of the twelve *Jyotirlingas*.

For *Ācārya* Śaṅkara every person, being and event was a source of blissful enlightenment. His keen observation never missed any details as he beheld the multitude of devotees flocking the sacred place. Most if not all of them had come to seek solutions to their worldly problems or physical ailments. He could see and feel that almost all of them were under the influence of emotions. Sensitive that he was, Śaṅkarācārya himself was overpowered by love and compassion.

The recent *Amaruka* experience had given wings to his imagination and he had started seeing beauty in all forms and shapes. He saw life bubbling and moving in wavelets of water; depth and grandeur in every puddle; riot of colours in flowers; trust in the eyes of infants; fun and frolic in bees and children; hope and aspiration in the dreams of adolescents; and wisdom in the eyes of the old. Most of all, he saw love, hidden deep inside every heart, but so deep that it was hidden under the blanket of desire, anger, greed, fear and jealousy, which had been the necessary aids for self-preservation in the long journey of involuntary evolution. This horizontal evolution was natural and as a matter of course.

For humans, however, being almost at the acme of biological evolution, another dimension opens: not biological but vertical dimension. We can *choose* to grow from *Paṣutva*—animal-hood to *Manuṣyatva*—human-hood, to *Divyatva*—God-hood. *Ācārya* had already noticed that the common mass of people was more emotional and everyone could feel love! With little introspection they all could return to the single source of all emotions—Love! They could be inspired to take to the willful or voluntary evolution. This choice to grow could be effected by helping them to transform the negative emotions to love. He felt that the best way was by spreading this grandest of emotions through his being!

Padmapāda, who was like the shadow of *Ācārya*, had keenly observed this change in his master. *Ācārya's* eyes which used to be alert and aware earlier, had acquired a very pleasant softness. Wherever they looked, they appeared to spread waves of concern, of care and of affection. Padmapāda explained to himself, that it may have been only *his* perspective. But he discovered that it was also felt by other disciples, especially Sureśwara, who experienced all encompassing love of his *Guru*. Whenever they were in his presence, they had a distinct feeling of being with their mother. Just like a mother, Śaṅkara had started thinking of the welfare of people. He felt certain that unless the ordinary people got involved in the process of cultural renaissance, there could be no appreciable change in the quality of life.

Ācārya was awestruck as he realised the genius of our sages who had not only understood the behaviour of human mind, but also the mechanism of emotions! He remembered the verse from the *Śrīmadbhagavadgītā* that gives the cycle of anger:

"A man dwelling on the objects of senses develops attachment to them; from attachment springs up desire, and from desire (if unfulfilled) results in anger. From anger arises infatuation; from infatuation confusion of memory; from confusion of memory, loss of reason and from loss of reason one goes to complete ruin."[42]

We think of such objects, the contact with which gives us happiness and avoid those objects or thoughts which are otherwise. Since most of us are not aware of the subtle we are convinced that happiness and misery are *dependent* on the objects or thoughts. Moreover, almost all the time we are obsessed by *Aham—'I'* and *Mama—'Mine'*. Consequently, *my problems* appear mountainous and we refuse to even acknowledge that others too are beset with equally if not more *daunting* problems! This over-indulgence in *Aham-Mama* creates and enlarges the negative emotions. Śaṅkara whose second nature was compassion saw that unless the common mass of people was given something to divert their mind from the puny *'I'*—the gross to something larger and subtler they will continue to be victims to the storms of emotions!

Ācārya was convinced that the experience through the body of *Amaruka* pointed towards an effective method for expanding one's consciousness! It is evident that we all have an attraction for beauty and without exception seek happiness and *avoid* unhappiness. It struck him that sense and awareness of beauty could be introduced to them through the worship of *Iṣṭa*—the chosen deity. If they could be introduced to the methods of channelizing and directing the emotions to something bigger or higher, each one of them could not only sublimate the emotions, but transform the very emotions into love characterised by sharing, respect and concern for the

---

42. ध्यायतो विषयान् पुंसः संगस्तेषूपजायते । संगात्संजायते कामः कमात्क्रोधोऽभिजायते ॥ श्रीमद्भगवद्गीता 2:62 ॥
क्रोधाद्भवति संमोहः संमोहात्स्मृतिविभ्रमः । स्मृतिविभ्रंशाद् बुद्धिनाशो बुद्धिनाशात्प्रणश्यति ॥ श्रीमद्भगवद्गीता 2:63 ॥

beloved. He was also aware of the effectiveness of the concept of *Iṣṭa* which could be made use of.

The sun lighted the *Gopuram* of the temple which was filled with the morning worshippers. It was as though the children were approaching their Divine Father to seek His attention and in turn dissolve their so-called problems. As the *Ācārya* poured his compassionate glance on them, it appeared—at least to his disciples—as though the devotees forgot about *their* problems to behold *Mallikārjuna* and experience His ever flowing blessings! The *Ācārya's* heart that could accommodate the whole universe felt oneness with it. This love, overflowed in the form of his recitation. Śaṅkarācārya recited an inspired and spontaneous praise on Śiva, the presiding deity of Śrīśailam. It filled the precincts and surroundings with his resonant and clear bell-like voice.

"I remember this morn, the remover of fear of involvement, the Chief of Gods, who carries the sacred *Gaṅgā* in his matted locks, who rides the Bull, the Lord of *Ambikā*—the Mother of the Universe; whose hands carry the sword and trident, as well as the gestures of fearlessness and blessings, and who dissolves the ailment of *Saṁsāra*—involvement and indulgence.

"I bow at this dawn, before the Lord of mountains and whose half being is *Girijā*—feminine, who is the primal cause of birth, life and dissolution of the universe; the Lord of the Universe, the personification of victory over the universe, whose very thought is pleasing to the mind, and who is the supreme medicine for the ailment of *Saṁsāra*.

"I adore at dawn, Śiva alone, who is the beginning and yet without any end, without any limitation and great, who can be known through *Vedānta*; who has no *differentiation* of name and form, and no six moods (lust, anger, greed, infatuation, pride and jealousy), and who eliminates the ailment of *Saṁsāra* by bestowing *No-other*."[43]

---

43. प्रातः स्मरामि भवभीतिहरं सुरेशं गङ्गाधरं वृषभवाहनमम्बिकेशम् । खट्वाङ्गशूलवरदाभयहस्तमीशं संसाररोगहरमौषधमद्वितीयम् ॥1॥
प्रातर्नमामि गिरिशं गिरिजार्धदेहं सर्गस्थितिप्रलयकारणमादिदेवम् ।विश्वेश्वरं विजितविश्वमनोऽभिरामं संसाररोगहरमौषधमद्वितीयम् ॥2॥
प्रातर्भजामि शिवमेकमनन्तमाद्यं वेदान्तवेद्यमनघं पूरुषं महान्तम् ।नामादिभेदरहितं षट्भवशून्यं संसाररोगहरमौषधमद्वितीयम् ॥3॥

The melody and mood of the recitation reverberated in the corridors of the temple initiating the disciples into the merger with their master as they totally lost their individual identities, which penetrated the hearts of the devotees and priests alike who had taken shelter under *Mallikārjuna*, to spread the fragrance of joy amidst them. It was unlike anything they had ever experienced before. The devotees turned their heads in the direction of the sound and beheld a young and brilliant *Sanyāsin*. They were in this sacred place in hope of finding some small measure of peace they sought. They felt as though their prayers were answered through this youth. They moved towards him in excitement and joy of finding someone who could give them relief from the vicissitudes of life.

When Padmapāda saw the simple folk rush towards the *Ācārya*, he tried to stop them for he was concerned about the disturbance they would cause. But with a smile Śaṅkara gestured him to allow them to come near him. He saw that most pairs of eyes carried the stories of woe, their simple demands and only a few of them had gratefulness. Looking into the eyes of a grateful devotee he asked:

"What brings you to this sacred spot?"

"I feel extremely blessed to be here! May be I can feel a divine presence."

Looking into the eyes of a distressed he asked the same question for which he got a reply:

"My life is full of problems which apparently have no solutions. Lord *Mallikārjuna* may have compassion on me!"

"What was that which you recited? It was so soothing, that we lost ourselves."

A devotee asked, and the same quarry was there in the eyes of other devotees. Śaṅkara replied in all compassion, love oozing out of his being.

"That was *Prātahsmaraṇam*—a morning prayer praising Śiva—the great God."

"It said something about the medicine for *Saṁsāra-Rōga*—ailment of *Saṁsāra*. What did you mean by that? As most of us are the slaves of *Saṁsāra*."

"What do you understand by *Saṁsāra*?"

"It is that which binds us to this world." When *Ācārya* looked at another devotee."

"It is entanglement with body, senses, mind and relationships and that which takes us away from God!"

Smilingly, Śaṅkara asked to no one particular:

"Is it the *Saṁsāra* which binds you or entangles you? More importantly, is the *Saṁsāra* identical for *all of us*?"

None understood the depth of the question. In all compassion that he was capable of, the *Ācārya* asked more deliberately.

"Taking *Saṁsāra* to be that which binds us, is it different or the same for *all of us*? Each one of you has come to Śrīśailam with prayers for the solutions of different problems or for fulfilling different needs. Now do you understand my question?"

The youth who had said that he felt a divine presence at this sacred place said with joy:

"It is different for each one of us because, our problems or the *Saṁsāra* depends on individual perception! A problem for one need not be a problem at all for the other!"

Śaṅkarācārya was very happy to hear the response. He continued:

"*Sādhu*! It means that each one of us has an individual *Saṁsāra*." Looking at the man who had mentioned that his life was full of problems he asked, "Do you think that your problems are more difficult than that of *others*?"

The man kept quiet for some time, and then replied,

"I am only aware of *my* problems because they are really intense!"

"My dear brother, have you ever bothered to look at those who are near you, your neighbours or others in your locality, or the town?" Śaṅkara asked him in all affection.

"I am so *involved with my own* problems, that I do not find time nor do I have any interest in the problems of others!" The listeners laughed.

"Exactly! You are so *involved*—as you rightly say, with *your own* problems that you have never bothered to look at others. That is the very reason why you *feel* that your problems are more intense than those of others. If you but stop giving *more* attention to yourself and just look around, you will find that almost everyone without exception has to face challenges—I refuse to call them problems—in life."

One old priest of the temple with a calm and pleasant face observed:

"Most of those who visit the temple are suffering and in pain or are facing some kind of paucity in life. I see them standing, sometimes even shedding tears! Compared to them I feel I do not have *any* problem!" Looking at the old priest affectionately *Ācārya* said:

"It is not that you do not have any challenges, but they have become insignificant compared to those whom you continue to see day after day." There was a pause and silence. He continued when he saw that everyone was listening to him:

"Oh mind, indulging in vain ideas like *I* and *Mine,* you are not treading the path towards true peace and happiness, but that of danger. You have no discrimination of the right and wrong. On the other hand, I am always content and blissful, as I do not depend on anything in the outside world. The proper thing for you then, is to remain quiet.

"As I am not different from the Supreme Reality, I am always content and without any desires. Being always content, I desire no welfare for myself. Since I wish your welfare, please take my advice and have *Śama*—be quiet."[44]

As the voice of *Ācārya* resonated it created the mood of peace and benevolence in the temple once again, filling the hearts of the listeners with joy.

---

44. अहं ममेति त्वमनर्थमिच्छसि परार्थमिच्छन्ति तवान्यईहितम् । न तेऽर्थबोधो न हि मेऽस्तिचार्थिता ततश्च युक्तः शमएवते मनः ॥

यतो न चान्यः परमात्सनातनात्सदैव तृप्तोऽहमतो न मेऽर्थिता । सदैव तृप्तश्च न कामये हितं यतस्वचेतः प्रशमाय ते हितम् ॥

॥ उपदेशसाहस्री 19: 2, 3 ॥

"*Saṁsāra* is nothing but the world each one of us has created for himself or herself with the help of '*I*' and '*mine*'. Why do you derive peace and feel blessed when you visit this temple dedicated to Lord *Mallikārjuna*? Why did you feel elevated when you listen to these recitations of the *Stotras* and the *Maṅtras*? It is because, when you come to this sacred spot you come very close to Mother Nature—the forest, the river, the flora and the fauna. And when you listen to these recitations the vibrations created make you *withdraw the attention* from '*I*' and '*mine*' at least when you are involved in the act of listening!"

The disciples were lifted onto an altogether different plane, while the devotees were in agreement with the words of the Master as they matched with their experience. Śaṅkara Bhagavadpāda concluded:

"Try to expand your attention from the narrowness of '*I—mine*' not only when you visit places of pilgrimage, but also when you are actively involved with your day-to-day life. Keep remembering the pleasant experiences you have had, even when you are with your family and friends or even foes—if you have any!"

The crowd started dispersing sharing their views and experiences in murmurs. Many remembered that they were yet to behold the sacred image of the Lord as they hurried to the sanctum! The disciples came near their *Guru* and sat surrounding him in a mood of total receptivity and respect. It was Sureśwara who asked with his palms joined:

"Master, I realise fully the futility of the rituals. They cannot possibly transform the heart and mind of the performer. But I also have a feeling that *Vedāṅta* cannot be either understood or practised by most in the society. What can we do?"

Śaṅkara looked at all the disciples. There was a strange satisfaction in that smile, as though the disciples were able to behold their role in the revival of our great culture, for they too had started thinking of the country and not just their personal salvation! He said looking at Sureśwara:

"First of all be reassured that *nothing is futile in our culture*. Everything has a place and a role to play. Rituals *if done mechanically* are not so useful, but when performed with understanding and awareness they purify the mind and sublimate emotions."

There was a distant look in the eyes of the *Ācārya*, which was as though he was seeing into the future. He continued:

"A householder involved with the responsibility of caring for his family does not find time and opportunity to take to spiritual practices. Nevertheless, he has the equal or more eligibility for salvation. We should start thinking for these people, because not only are they looking after the needs of their families but they are looking after us, for are we not dependent on them for our bodily subsistence?"

"How can we do that?" Padmapāda joined the discussion. Śaṅkara replied.

"This morning a few thoughts crossed my mind. Human life is a play of emotions—either the emotions play with us or *we play with them*! The main pivot of all emotions is '*I* and *mine*'. If we can introduce the concept of *Iṣṭa*—the chosen deity then we get an avenue to channelise our emotions towards it. Padmapāda, your *Iṣṭa* is Nṛsiṁha—the half-lion and half-human form of Viṣṇu. Can you tell me how you came to choose your *Iṣṭa*?"

"When I was a child," Padmapāda said, "I was fascinated by the story of Prahlāda the greatest child devotee of Viṣṇu. The Lord had appeared in the form of Nṛsiṁha in response to the total trust of the child that Viṣṇu is omnipresent, from a pillar in the palace of his father. I too wanted to have the vision of Lord Nṛsiṁha, and so performed penance in a forest. On many days a hunter, who was amused to see me doing penance, had the habit of asking me the purpose of my penance. One day I told him that I wanted to have the vision of the wonderful being, having a human body up to the neck and a lion's face above. After a few days, the hunter brought Nṛsiṁha tied with creepers! I asked the Lord in great wonder 'How is it that in spite of the fact that you are so difficult to attain even by the *Ṛṣis*, the hunter could get you so quickly?' The divine being responded that even the *Ṛṣis* are not able to concentrate so whole-heartedly like this hunter and that even my concentration was wanting. He disappeared after blessing me."

"That is what is needed! Most men in the society have this trust due to simplicity. We should help them use this trust. We have temples of various gods and goddesses, and people do visit them. We shall develop such spiritual practices, which can be easily performed by them. If we are able to give them some simple rituals so that they can do *Upāsanā* of their *Iṣṭa,* then just by following a daily routine they can derive the benefit of *Cittaśuddhih*—purification of head and heart. We shall take the help of Sureśwara." Master had not only spoken his intention but also planned the next course of action. The wonderful practice of *Ṣōḍaśōpacāra Pūjā*—the worship of the deity with sixteen articles was born with Sureśwarācārya as the mid-wife!

❐

8
Harnessing Emotions

The sun was at its zenith and so was the rush of pilgrims into the temple. The noon rituals for Lord *Mallikārjuna* were in progress. Many of the pilgrims beholding the sacred image for the first time, were besides with emotion swelling deep within were shedding tears of joy. Some of them who were visiting *Śrīśailam* for the first time had been preparing for this pilgrimage for years. The precincts of the temple became a haven of retreat for others from their day-to-day life. Amidst the cacophony of voices, the sound of the priests chanting *Rudram*—the sacred chant for Lord Śiva[45] was prominent. *Ācārya* was sitting on the parapet by the side, observing meditatively and enjoying the psychedelic emotions crossing the minds of people.

Bhagavadpāda noticed a disturbed youthful priest. Though he too was in the chant, he was absentminded and preoccupied with something that weighed upon his mind. But soon as he beheld the calm graceful and smiling countenance of *Ācārya*, he came near and prostrated. He felt at ease in the company, for he felt that this noble person had solution to his problem. After the formal greetings the youth said humbly:

"*Bhagawan*, my name is Hari and I am a priest in this temple and have been in the service of the Lord for the past few years. I have no cause for complaints, but have some personal problems, which require immediate attention. I feel I am just following what my ancestors have been doing for generations

45. *Taittirīya Samhita: 4:5*

without break conducting rituals, of course, with sincerity. My grandfather is the head-priest and is a picture of veneration. My father too is a very good man. When I placed my problems before them, they just smiled and said that the doubts will dissolve after years of practice!"

"Hari, you may ask without any hesitation." Relieved at the response, Hari asked:

"I learnt the Vedic chants and have committed them to my heart. But when I chant, my mouth and voice do the chanting but my mind keeps roaming! As long as I am *not aware of this*, there is no problem, but soon as I do, I start feeling guilty! In recent times I have even started feeling that perhaps priesthood is not suitable for me."

Śaṅkara smiled benignly, his words were full of understanding:

"First of all this phenomenon of restless mind is not peculiar to you alone. Every one of us experiences it. Because that is the basic nature of the mind! So stop feeling guilty for something for which you are not responsible. Another thing is blessed you are to be born in this sacred place and into a family which is in service of the Lord for generations." So saying the *Ācārya* continued:

"Among all living creatures, human birth is rare indeed; much more difficult it is to attain full manhood; rarer it is to have *Sāttwic* attitude towards life. In spite of having these rare attainments, to have steadfastness in the righteous way of life is yet rarer.[46] The only thing I want to know is, are you interested in doing something else than the *Paurōhitya*—the priesthood?" To which Hari responded spontaneously:

"No *Bhagawan*, the fact is I cannot imagine of leaving this place. As I told you earlier, I do not have anything against my condition or occupation. The gravest concern is my mind which refuses to be at where I am and what I do!"

"Like I said, most *are not aware of the condition of their minds* but you are, and that is something to be satisfied about.

---

46. जन्तूनां नरजन्म दुर्लभमतः पुंस्त्वं ततो विप्रता तस्माद्वैदिकधर्ममार्गपरता विद्वत्त्वमस्मात्परम् ।
आत्मानात्मविवेचनं स्वनुभवो ब्रह्मात्मना संस्थितिमुक्तिर्नो शतजन्मकोटिसुकृतैः पुण्यैर्विना लभ्यते ॥ विवेकचूडामणि 2॥

Can I meet your grandfather or father? Let me talk to them first and then we will find a happy solution to your *so-called problem*!"

* * * * *

Sun had set and the surroundings had been covered by a dark blanket. Hills were filled with the soft sounds of crickets and night birds. Most of the devotees had left the precincts of the temple after the evening worship; the last gong of the bell had rung. *Ācārya* Śaṅkara was sitting, absorbed in the expansiveness of Self. The disciples sat near savouring the peaceful, benign and satiating silence radiating from their master. Three persons representing three generations were approaching the group which had taken the responsibility of dedicating themselves for the transformation of the future of this great country.

The aged person with a very calm and pleasant countenance was the grandfather of Hari, turned out to be the priest who had observed that afternoon, that compared to others, he did not have any problems! The second person was his father, while the third was Hari himself. All of them offered their salutations and sat in front of *Ācārya*. The three of them felt very familiar and at ease, as if they had known him all along! Without any formalities the *Ācārya* started the conversation:

"Hari appears to be facing a problem! Has he mentioned it to you?"

The grandfather said with a smile:

"Yes, and we told him that we all face this and it is nothing new!"

The father joined in:

"I keep telling him that instead of dwelling too much on the condition of the mind, he should concentrate on the recitation and rituals." Śaṅkara looked at Hari questioningly.

"*Bhagawan*, I told you that unless my mind becomes steady I cannot concentrate and that is the point of conflict." *Ācārya* was silent, apparently without any reaction! But nobody was uncomfortable, for the silence was full and had a lot of understanding behind it. Then they heard his sweet bell-like voice ringing melodiously in their ears.

"The first steps for a child are full of anxiety and perhaps even fear. When someone enters the river for the first time, his concern for safety is very real for him! So for Hari his wandering mind is of great concern. I told him that many if not most are not even aware of this very common problem. So Hari, the first thing is that you do not be too worried about it. Let me ask you something: did you have this problem when you *learnt the Maṅtras*?"

Hari became contemplative, as if going back into time. He answered after a pause:

"I was always curious and alert as they were new to me and I wanted to learn as fast and as best as I could. But as and when I committed the *Maṅtras* to the memory I noticed that *while my mouth recited, the mind started wandering*."

Śaṅkara looked meaningfully at the disciples and said with pride in his eyes:

"This boy is an *Adhikāri*—eligible person, very few are aware of the vagaries of mind. Such persons alone can plunge into spirituality." Looking at Hari, he observed:

"*Caṅcalatā—randomness* is the nature of mind. With effort it can be brought under control. Now I would like to have a consultation with your elders about the method of worship. How do you perform the worship?"

"I am Madhusūdana." The elder of the two began, "We were taught to first of all prepare for the worship, like cleaning the sanctum, collecting flowers, water for the worship. Prepare the food offering to the Lord." He looked at his son to continue.

"We start reciting the *Rudram* and commence the worship by bathing the Lord, decorating his Idol with ashes, flowers, etc. Then make the food offering and then perform the *Maṅgalārati*—by showing the lamp."

Ācārya enquired:

"You both narrated the preparations for the worship. *Do you* prepare yourselves in any way before the worship?" For which the father responded:

"We purify our body by taking bath and wearing clean clothes."

Looking at Sureśwarācārya, the master asked:

"We have the practice of *Nyāsa* in the Vedic rituals. Please explain this practice in detail." Sureśwara closed his eyes and said after a while:

"*Bhagawan*, when the preparations for *Yajña* are completed and the *Yajamāna*—one for whom the *Yajña* is being performed, invokes various deities in himself. The idea behind this practice is for identification with the deities. There are usually two types of *Nyāsa*: *Aṅga*—body parts, and *Kara*—hands. When the *Yajamāna* thus identifies with the deities by associating parts of his body—like heart, head, shoulders, etc., or the five fingers of hands, he is totally absorbed in the ritual." Śaṅkarācārya was silent for some time and then said:

"Can we not include *Nyāsa* in the daily worship? We can adapt the *Maṅtras* to suit the particular *Iṣṭa*—chosen deity. You may ask as to how this part of the ritual helps in the daily worship in temples. If the worshipper is not aware, generally the ritual becomes an empty gesture! The *Nyāsa* will keep the mind on the activity he or she is involved with. I want to know from you revered sir," Śaṅkara asked looking at the eldest of the *Purōhits*:

"You have had the privilege of being in the great tradition of *Paurōhitya*. How many gods are being worshipped in our land?" Madhusūdana smiled and said:

"Generally six, that is, Śiva, Viṣṇu, Śakti, Kumāra or Kārtikeya, Gaṇapati and Sūrya—the sun are accepted. But the method of worship differs from deity to deity and place to place." Hari wanted to say something the *Ācārya* looked at him with a smile.

"Why are there so many deities, instead of having a single deity? It has created so much of avoidable conflict among people." Śaṅkara looked at Padmapāda meaningfully.

"The human nature differs from one individual to another. For instance, if a person is meditative or an introvert, Śiva suits his disposition. If someone is action oriented or an extrovert, Viṣṇu is for him. Nature of mind is such that it has a conviction that whatever is acceptable to an individual *should necessarily* be the *only* deity! This has caused a lot of conflicts—avoidable as you rightly say—among people. As for the difference in the methods of worship, there is no standard method and is adopted according to the nature and place! But as *Bhagawan* pointed out we can develop a standard method of *Pūjā*—worship, to suit all the six traditions." The *Ācārya* agreed and said:

"In *Nyāsa* we cannot only include the *Kara* and *Aṅga* but more importantly, the faculties which have the presiding deities, like speech *Agni*—fire, *Prāṇa* (the vital force behind all activity)—*Vāyu*—air, vision—sun, mind—moon, hearing—directions, body—earth and others, which are experienced by the *Hṛdayam*—the consciousness.[47] This will help in the development of *Prajñā*—awareness." *Ācārya* continued looking at the priests:

"We can start with the *Pūjā* of Mahādeva—the great Lord, from tomorrow."

All of them had retired for the night of rest. Śaṅkara was awake; he felt that he had to wait for a sign before really proceeding with what they had discussed. In the second quarter of the night, he felt a presence, and when he looked in the direction he was overjoyed to behold sage *Vyāsa*. Getting up he offered his salutations as the sage sat down and Śaṅkara stood with his palms joined.

"I could not but come to see you at this very important stage of your work. It was Mahādeva himself who put the thought of *Nyāsa* in your mind! You were very right in concluding that it can be adapted to suit individual *Iṣṭa*. This will definitely help the worshipper in improving his *Ekāgrata*—concentration of the mind. You can take the services of Sureśwara and Padmapāda. Sureśwara will develop the ritualistic part, and Padmapāda the emotional content of the *Pūjā*." Kṛṣṇa Dvaipāyana Vyāsa continued:

"I have one correction to make: even before including the faculties like speech, vision and others it would be more

---

47. This is known as *Laghu Nyāsa*, when the worshipper invokes these faculties from the heart region.

beneficial to invoke the gods in the different parts of the body." So saying he started reciting the *Mantras*:

"Let Brahmā be at the organ of creation; Viṣṇu in the feet; Hara in the hands; Iṅdra in the shoulders; Agni in the intestines; Śiva in the heart—consciousness, Vasavaḥ—wind gods in the throat; Saraswatī be on the tongue; Vāyu in the nostrils; the sun and the moon in the eyes; Aświni Kumāras in the ears....[48]

"This suggestion for feeling the gods in one's own body will come a long way in getting rid of the dependency on rituals at some point of time. We have to remember that the ultimate reason for all activities is *God Realisation—we all are one with God*! Otherwise in spite of all the care you are taking to make the worshipper more and more aware will end up in one more empty ritual!"

Śaṅkara saw the flaw immediately and smilingly rejoined:

"*Bhagawan*, now I totally realise that in the task you all have entrusted me, I am just an instrument, and you all are behind me. I will do the necessary correction. I have one more quary: How did you manage to edit the *Vedas* and all the other *Śāstras*, at the same time, travel around the country on foot?"

Looking admiringly at Śaṅkara, Veda Vyāsa said:

"Like you just said, it is by being a perfect instrument of the mission. *By never keeping any weight of activity—be it discoursing, remembering and transferring the scriptures, counseling or travelling. This you can very easily do by being in total Mauna—silent mind. That was why they gave me the title of Muni—which means one who is silent within*!"

Veda Vyāsa said with a distant look in his eyes:

"I would like you to also look into another section of the society. Are you aware of *Śrīmadbhāgavatam*, one of the last of my works?" When he saw Śaṅkara nodding his head

48. अग्निर्मे वाचि श्रितः । वाग्हृदये । हृदयं मयि । अहममृते। अमृतं ब्रह्मणि । वायुर्मे प्राणे श्रितः। प्राणो हृदये । हृदयं मयि । अहममृते । अमृतं ब्रह्मणि ।सूर्यो मे चक्षूषि श्रितः । चक्षुर्हृदये । हृदयं मयि । अहममृते । अमृतं ब्रह्मणि । etcetera.

प्रजनने ब्रह्मा तिष्ठतु । पादयोर्विष्णुस्तिष्ठतु । हस्तयोर्हरस्तिष्ठतु । बाह्वोरिन्द्रस्तिष्ठंतु । हृदये शिवस्तिष्ठतु । कण्ठे वसवस्तिष्ठतु ।वक्त्रे सरस्वती तिष्ठतु । नासिकयोर्वायुस्तिष्ठतु । नयनयोश्चन्द्रादित्यौ तिष्ठेताम् । कर्णयोरश्विनौतिष्ठेताम् ।..... ॥

affirmatively, he continued, "In spite of my efforts to edit the *Vedas*, to write *Mahābhārata* or write the *Vedānta Sūtras* I felt a sense of incompleteness and that was when I remembered to write the play of Lord in different forms and the lives of his devotees. After finishing this work, it struck me that spirituality is not for only those who take to the life of *Brahmins* and *Brahmacārins*, it is the birthright of every single individual. So *Bhakti* can be a way of life, and not just a method of worship. You can think in this direction. This will help you to include commonest of the common people."

This led to an insight in Śaṅkara as he merged with the silence of Vyāsa Muni and the world around. When he came to, he was alone as Vyāsa the Master had left. He heard the cock crow announcing the arrival of a new day for learning and teaching.

It was a very special occasion in the temple of *Śrīśailam* that day. The devotees were seeing a youthful *Sanyāsin* conducting the *Pūjā* and the monks and the priests chanting in the loud and clear voices some unfamiliar *Mantras*. It was as though *Śiva* himself was performing the ritual to his own image! There was sanctity, holiness and tranquility in the atmosphere. Not only the persons involved with the ritual, but also those who had come to pray and seek favours forgot the very purpose of their being there! They did not feel like asking for *anything* for they felt fulfilled. All they could feel was a sense of gratefulness for their being in the temple at this sacred moment. Their beings were in the present moment, in presence of something which was beyond description! Some of them were shedding tears of joy unable to contain their joy. Of all persons, priest Madhusūdana felt completely blessed as he realised that only today he had become a part in the grand role of temples in the society.

Earlier in the morning Śaṅkarācārya had discussed with his disciples and the priests about including the initial part of the *Nyāsa*. When Madhusūdana, the senior most of the priests was asked to perform the ritual, he had humbly responded:

"*Bhagawan*, this is the first time we are in the process of introducing something new, would it not be more appropriate that you do the *Pūjā* along with your disciples and we do the recitation of the *Mantras*? I am certain that Śiva—my *Iṣṭa*, happily agrees with me!" Padmapāda had added on behalf of the disciples:

"*Bhagawan*, Sureśwara will be assisting you while we all will chant the *Mantras*."

Responding with a sweet smile of his, the *Ācārya* had said meaningfully:

"I must say that I shall perform the ritual only today. I would very much like to see the custodians of the temple culture take on the responsibility!" Looking at the priests, he added, "You have the responsibility of creating the vibrations of holiness for the society—the common mass of people, who visit the temples for solace. If they start directing their emotions towards the deities of the temples you would have fulfilled the very purpose of these grand temples."

* * * * *

Entourage of Śaṅkara Bhagavadpāda winding its way through the jungle trail had reached a small hamlet consisting of a few huts. It appeared to belong to a community of hunters. Just by seeing them, the headman came rushing to offer his salutations. Looking at him with all compassion, the *Ācārya* said:

"You seem to be troubled. Can I do anything to alleviate it?"

"*Swāmi*, I do not know what and how to say it!" When Śaṅkara Bhagavadpāda encouraged him, the headman said with difficulty.

"*Swāmi*, Bhairava and his group of *Kāpālikas*—who practise human sacrifice as a part of their religion, are enticing away our children with a promise of bright after life. Gradually, our tribe is being depleted from over two hundred to just a couple of scores.[49] All of us are in pain and are worried about our survival."

Śaṅkara could actually experience the agony of the tribe *physically*! His being took him to his own mother who had been

---

49. A group or set of twenty.

bearing the pain of separation from her only son. His eyes were filled and he consoled the man with his throat choked in emotion:

"I can understand your pain and concern. Can you or anyone of you take me to the head of *Kāpālikas*?"

"But *Swāmi*, going there is extremely dangerous." But when insisted he added, "Since it is for the very survival of our tribe, I shall take you there even if it may cost me my life."

The clouds rumbled and the wind blew fiercely and the thick trees on the forest slopes swayed violently. The tribal headman moved looking back once in a while at his compassionate companion. He was awestruck at the fearlessness of this monk who was risking his life for his tribe, though they were complete strangers. Śaṅkara on the other hand was blissful enjoying the dance of fury of nature. It was as if he was witnessing the *Tāṇḍava*—the dance of Śiva! In that calm benign and smiling face, lay the confidence that since he was chosen by our culture for *its* work, *it* would look after him.

The foliage was so thick that light hardly entered the forest to see the small trail. But the man leading him was an expert. Observing that *Ācārya* was as fresh as he was when they had started, the headman asked in all appreciation:

"*Swāmi* how is it that you are not tired?" Śaṅkara smiled and said:

"I am involved in doing my Mother's work and that gives me strength."

"But your mother is not with you, then how can you do *her* work?" asked the headman innocently.

"I am not referring to my physical mother but our Mother Culture. You may not see her but she is very much with all of us!"

The headman did not understand, and nor did he ask for further clarification! As they reached the destination, four fierce looking characters approached them, the headman fell on his knees and begged the men to allow them to see their chieftain. Śaṅkara entered a cave lit by torches alone. A standing image of Kāli with garland of skulls of the victims beheaded during the sacrifices. There was this obnoxious smell of blood and putrefying flesh. On a stone throne sat a man, with his disheveled hair and blood-red eyes who seemed to be in a state of perpetual anger! With a resounding voice, he asked in arrogance:

"Who dares to disturb the peace of this cave?" The *Ācārya* answered in all calmness and poise.

"Oh Chief of Kāpālikas I have come to give you peace which you have never known." His compassionate smile seemed to disturb the man, who asked him with all irritation:

"You are only a boy, and dare to offer *me* peace? Who do you think you are? Don't you know that I am always in search of men whom I offer at mother Kāli's altar?"

"I am Śaṅkara the disciple of Goviṅda Bhagavadpāda, and I am very much aware of your predisposition to sacrifice human heads at Mother's altar. What have you gained by sacrificing so many human beings, who are like you? Don't you know that the practice of offering human sacrifice is against the fundamental human nature?"

The chieftain was amused at this smiling youth who was teaching *him—who was considered as the most fearsome of the Kāpālikas*! Keeping his amusement aside he said in all impatience:

"And you think you are right, and that I am totally wrong! I have a great objective."

Looking into the eyes of Śaṅkara, he continued:

"By such sacrifice I will take my followers to *Kailāsa*—the abode of Śiva, and those who have been sacrificed would have already reached their destination and are in the company of Lord Śiva!" Smiling compassionately at Bhairava for his dangerous ignorance, Śaṅkara said:

"How can murder of the victims and the consequent pain to their parents and relatives take you to *Kailāsa*? Please tell me, are you *really* at peace? The real peace is when you are one with nature, in tune with other beings who too have equal right to live as they wish. Who are you to force your view of life on others by terrorizing and enticing your victims? It has only made you irritable, angry and violent."

"NO!!" Bhairava thundered. "I am assuming the nature of my *Iṣṭa—Kapāli* or Śiva sporting a skull in his hand!" Śaṅkara was undisturbed by the outburst, he asked calmly:

"How do you worship *Kapāli*? Do you consider Him as a Master?"

"No, He is my father! And who are you to ask me about my *Iṣṭa*?"

"Do you consider yourselves to be his *only* children?" Śaṅkara continued.

"He is the Father of the whole universe."

"If he is the Father of the universe, how can he be cruel to his own children?"

Bhairava noted the grit and fearlessness of this youth with appreciation and replied:

"*Kapāli* is the form of Śiva as the Destroyer and that is why we do *his* work."

"That is what I am asking you, in all these years of such brutal actions, have you become a better human being? Or is it that you have fallen below *Paṣutva*—the animalistic nature? From what I have seen, even the tiger or lion does not kill for fun; it is for appeasing its hunger, whereas, you are literally murdering people in the name of your *Sādhanā*. Have you had the experience of *Kapāli*, have you seen Him?"

"I am doing these very things to have His experience. I will stop the day I succeed." Bhairava replied.

"Is there no other way?" There was an appeal in Śankara's voice. After giving it a thought, Bhairava said:

"There *is* a way. If I sacrifice an enlightened soul who has identified with the whole of creation, who has mastered his senses, mind and intellect, and who is ever ready to give up his body."

"I can, and am ready to give up my life, if you can but stop this carnage in the name of *Sādhanā*" Bhairava was flabbergasted, it was unbelievable. But he was pleased!

❐

9
Towards Devotion

Śaṅkara Bhagavadpāda sat under a shady tree surrounded by his beloved disciples. A small stream meandered on their left, the gurgle reminding of its journey in the mountains. A mild breeze carrying the pleasant fragrance of herbs and flowers blew hesitantly as if afraid of disturbing the deep discussion among the group. However, Padmapāda had not been comfortable after the return of his master. He could not ask the *Ācārya* directly as he knew that if the master wanted him to know, he would have been told of the meeting with Bhairava at his den. Unable to contain his curiosity, he had tried to talk to the tribal headman, who had just told him that *Swāmi* had convinced the Bhairava in stopping the carnage. He heard his master say:

"We will have to introduce the method of *Pūjā* so that the ritual will be standardized throughout. But we cannot do it ourselves. The priests who learn from us will have to spread in their region. Sureśwara, it seems you want to say something."

"*Bhagawan*, I motivated Hari to go around the area and help to spread the method. He would have started his work already!" *Ācārya* noted this quality of organizing people in Sureśwara and said looking at all others.

"All of us will have this great work of bringing not only those who are already involved in our mission, but also to inspire others in joining us. Let me tell you something very important, for all of us who are in this inner circle, we have been chosen by *Śruti Bhagavati* for her work. And our salvation lies in it.

The very nature of our work is such, that unless and until *we live what we are trying to teach*, it will not succeed."[50]

Ācārya's eyes fell on Padmapāda and noted his absentmindedness. But he continued to give instructions to others. When all of them had dispersed he called Padmapāda to his side affectionately and asked:

"You were not present during the discussion!" Falling at his feet, Padmapāda said with tears in his eyes:

"*Bhagawan*, I am disturbed after your return from Bhairava's cave. I do not know exactly what it is, but somehow I have a feeling that your life is in danger!"

Śaṅkara laughed like a child and said looking with all affection:

"Padmapāda, all of us are connected intimately. I will suggest that you start the *Upāsana* of Nṛsiṁha—your *Iṣṭa*, may be you could do *Japa*. That will alleviate your fear and also, who knows, offer protection!"

Upāsana, which actually means *sitting near*. From that moment onwards Padmapāda started the *Japa*—constant repetition of the *Mantra* of his chosen deity Lakshmi Nṛsiṁha. And to his pleasant surprise, he found that his fears ceased and instead, he found his mind calm and alert, ever prepared to face any challenge. His master noted this with satisfaction.

The dark intimidating sky of new-moon night was overcast with clouds. Hoots of owls could be distinctly heard amidst the chattering of frogs and crickets. The villagers rested in the laps of slumber. The disciples too had retired for the night after a busy discussion on the course of action each one of them should take. All of them had wondered why their beloved master had already started planning for the future, when their master had years ahead of him! Everyone was convinced that there was a reason for every action of their beloved teacher. Theirs was not to doubt but to follow his instruction to the letter and spirit. But not Padmapāda, instead of directing his energy on worries he

---

50. Swami Vivekananda used a small prompt "Be and make!" First be what you teach, and then alone can you teach.

had invested it on his *Iṣṭa*. He had started feeling the *presence*, which was becoming palpable, so intense that it seemed capable of being touched! Consequently, he felt his strength waxing.

Departure of Śaṅkara Bhagavadpāda was felt neither by the disciples nor by the villagers. He had told the headman while returning from Bhairava's den, that he had convinced him in desisting from any more carnage, and so none knew of the arrangement the *Ācārya* had made with Bhairava. As he walked slowly but confidently towards his certain death, his mind started reciting:

"There is neither teacher nor scripture, nor pupil nor teaching, nor you nor I, nor this perceived universe; for, the awareness of one's true nature has no differentiation. Therefore I am That One, Auspicious and Pure That alone remains"[51]

He was filled with a feeling of gratefulness to Śri Goviṅda Bhagavadpāda, his *Guru*, as he remembered that this was one of the ten verses he was inspired to sing due to His presence. He did not know whether he would ever clear the debt of enlightenment he owed to his Master, but was glad that he was trying to save many lives by surrendering his head to Bhairava at Kapāli's altar.

On reaching the place, the waiting sentinels of the persecutor took Śaṅkara Bhagavadpāda to a stream for giving him a ceremonial bath. Thunder and lightning struck and it rained as if the nature was really sad to part from this young brave and talented son of hers. Śaṅkara started distancing from his body as he identified himself with the pure infinite and eternal spirit. He saw himself walking towards the cave… In the village farther away, sitting in *Padmāsana*—the Lotus posture, Padmapāda totally identified with *Nṛsiṁha*—his *Iṣṭa*.

When *Ācārya* Śaṅkara came to, he saw a person lying prostrate on the floor paying him obeisance, his soft, mild eyes shedding tears of repentance. He said amidst sniffles:

"Forgive me *Bhagawan*, you did come to me—an unfortunate wretch, to give me peace that I had never known.

---

51. न शास्ता न शास्त्रं न शिष्यो न शिक्षा न च त्वं न चाहं न चायं प्रपञ्चः ।
स्वरूपावबोधो विकल्पासहिष्णुः तदेकोऽविशिष्टः शिवः केवलोऽहम् ॥ दशश्लोकि 7 ॥

The Bhairava has been liberated from me and now I am just your slave, transformed and reborn through your divine powers." *Ācārya* made him rise and said:

"It is the Divine in *your own self* that transformed you and not me!" Then his eyes fell on Padmapāda standing nearby with his palms joined in salutation. Padmapāda had an ethereal aura, in which could be clearly seen Nṛsiṁha—the *Iṣṭa* of his beloved disciple.

Everything was clear to Śaṅkarācārya who stood up, inspired by the vision started reciting spontaneously, a garland of verses to Lakṣmi Nṛsiṁha.

"O abode of those who are entangled in the web of *Saṁsāra*, you are the sharp hook to catch the crocodile of attraction for sense objects; my throat and head is choked with worldliness; please take me into your cool shelter O Lakṣmi Nṛsiṁha. Having fallen into the depths of the well of *Saṁsāra*, I experienced the misery of its serpents; this humble servant of yours begs you to take him in your benign fold O Lakṣmi Nṛsiṁha."[52]

"*Bhagawan* how is it that I am here? And who is this man shedding tears?" The disciple, who was awestruck with wonder asked. *Ācārya* said:

"Padmapāda, you were brought here by your *Iṣṭa*. Your identification with your *Iṣṭa* and also *Guru* is so much that when you felt that his life was at risk, Lord Lakṣmi Nṛsiṁha came for your *Guru's* rescue. But now I realise that it was actually to rescue a troubled soul from straying! This *was* Bhairava, the head of *Kāpālikas*, who is now a different person due to the compassion of your *Iṣṭa*." Looking at Bhairava the *Ācārya* said:

"You have a very great potential to serve the same society you had tried to harm."

"But *Bhagawan* I would like to be with you and serve. Your sacred company will help me to overcome the sense of guilt in me." There was appeal in Bhairava's eyes.

---

52. संसारदावदहनाभीकरोरु–ज्वालावलीभिरतिदग्धतनूरुहस्य ।
त्वत्पादपद्मसरसीं शरणागतस्य लक्ष्मीनृसिंह मम देहि करावलम्बम् ॥ 3 ॥
संसारकूपमतिघोरमगाधमूलं सम्प्राप्यदुःखशतसर्पसमाकुलस्य ।
दीनस्य देव कृपया पदमागतस्य लक्ष्मीनृसिंह मम देहि करावलम्बम् ॥ 5 ॥

"Don't waste your energy on guilt or repentance, go to the villagers and try to fill the emptiness in the hearts of the parents you had hurt by sacrificing their offspring. You will go there, may be face their irritation and anger, and by bearing the wrath, assure them that you are their friend and not enemy. Fear is a stubborn emotion, which can be dissolved only in the elixir of compassion and love. Now go and take your followers with you."

When the persecutor who had transformed into a seeker went away, happy that he had been given an opportunity to change his life and perhaps mend what he had done, Padmapāda looked at his master with a question in his eyes.

"I know what you are thinking Padmapāda. This is the only way to test the sincerity in Bhairava and the grit in the victims. There will be some reactions but the Lord's work was complete." *Ācārya* responded, and continued.

"My dear, this event was an eye opener to all of us. When Bhairava asked for my head in turn to totally stop all human sacrifice, I had thought that if even a single life can stop all carnage, it was worth it, and I readily agreed. I had this distinct feeling that if *Śruti Bhagawati* has more activities for me, she will take care, if not, she will retrieve me! But now I feel more than I have ever felt that this whole episode had lessons for all of us!

"It was a test for my trust in the mission, *which has chosen us*. I felt that this whole mission, from the very beginning has been and will ever be, for our grand culture that has truth, compassion, love, dedication, renunciation and service at its foundation. It was an opportunity for you to be with your *Iṣṭa* and to test your dedication for the chosen work, because it was not for protecting your *Guru* but the work which has brought us together. It was a chance for us to get convinced in the divinity in everyone including a *Kāpālika*!"

"*Bhagawan* please explain what really transpired in this whole episode?" The disciple asked. *Ācārya's* eyes were distant when he responded with a glow on his face:

"This event has fear as the main emotion. Bhairava was really afraid of death and wanted eternal life with Lord Śiva in Kailāsa; the victims too got entrapped in his promise of life hereafter; the villagers—for obvious reasons, were afraid; I too was in the dark as to what I was expected to do. The easiest option would have been to leave the village and the villagers to their fate. But *Śruti* came to my rescue and my *Guru's* grace made me stay back and try to solve the problem. When asked whether there was any way to stop all this violence, Bhairava said that if he could sacrifice an enlightened person at the altar he would stop it. Since compassion for the villagers was more important than the work, I agreed. You have been connected to me due to your infinite trust in me and had the genuine feeling of my life being in danger. You were concerned about my safety. To eliminate this concern—which is nothing but a little *fear*, *Upāsana* is the best way in which you try to be with your *Iṣṭa* constantly."

"But how did I reach the cave that I had never seen before, and how did Bhairava transform?" Śaṅkara smiled and said:

"That is another lesson I learnt! By its very nature, the divine cannot harm, it can only *transform*. Lord Nṛsiṁha had not only stopped the Bhairava from severing my head, but it had *proceeded to sever the violent strain in Bhairava's heart*! This brings a new understanding: a devotee's *Upāsana is not only for his personal growth, but it can also contribute in the removal of negativity in the surroundings*."

Just then, there was a lot of noise outside the cave. Somehow discovering the absence of the *Ācārya* and his beloved disciple from the village the disciples and villagers, and surmising that perhaps Bhairava had found new victims, had proceeded to the den with the help of the village headman. Padmapāda rushed outside the cave to find the villagers angrily shouting at the now transformed Bhairava and his followers! Seeing Padmapāda alive they became silent and eagerly looked at him, who said in all calmness:

"Both *Bhagawan* and I are safe and healthy! Bhairava is a changed man and so are his followers." Just then they beheld the divine personage of *Ācārya*.

"I have instructed Bhairava to help you rebuild your broken lives. He will stay with you and will serve you in all possible ways."

"Can he possibly bring back our children? Can he fill our irreparable loss? Don't you think he will keep reminding us of his heinous crime if he stays with us? Will his crime go unpunished?" A villager who had lost his two sons, asked without even stopping for breath! Śaṅkarācārya smiled and looking at the person who had asked the doubt on behalf of all the victims and Bhairava compassionately said:

"I understand your pain and do know that your loss is irreparable. Please tell me how do you propose to punish him for his unpardonable crime?" A youth who had only one eye, because of this defect, he was rejected and had been replaced by his very close friend, said with all fury:

"With his and his followers' lives! They deserve death!" his face red with anger. The *Ācārya* was silent allowing the crowd to absorb *his* silence. Then he asked compassionately:

"Will that bring back the departed to life?" They did not answer as they knew it was not possible. He asked another question:

"Don't you see that by executing them you are only imitating them? They were sacrificing the people for *their* mistaken goal of eternal life, while you are executing them in response to your vengeance." The headman saw reason behind these words. He said:

"*Bhagawan* you are right, but how can we forgive them for what they have done?"

"You had seen this man in the past do you see any change in him now?"

Ācārya asked, pointing at Bhairava. Every one of them noted repentance, a sense of guilt and a silent appeal to give him an opportunity to mend his ways. While his followers had the same fear in their eyes, which each one of them had during the reign of terror and violence. They continued to be silent, but this silence had acceptance of truth in it. Śaṅkara Bhagavadpāda continued in a voice filled with compassion for victims as well as the former persecutors:

"We should realise that any wrong act has ignorance at its root. It is like you are walking in the forest on the night of new moon, you hurt yourself and others in the process. He was misguided by his wrong understanding that by the sacrifice of heads at the altar of *Kapāli* he will get eternal life at *Kailāsa*. All of you, including the disciples, should remember that whatever *is not seen or experienced has more influence on the mind than what is in front*! The mind too has a basic nature: it easily dwells on *what is not, rather than what is*!"

The clouds had cleared, and the sun spread it warm light on the land. The foliage had been washed fresh and was scattering different hues of green. It appeared as if the nature was announcing the end of storm—outside as well as inside the minds of listeners. *Ācārya* continued, looking at Bhairava:

"Hereafter you shall be known as *Bhadra*—the auspicious." Then looking at the villagers he said, "I have seen that your village is barren without any resources. This place has plenty of fruit bearing trees and ample fertile land for agriculture. All of you should migrate to this place. Bhadra will build you houses and provide you protection along with his *companions*. Their martial skills will help you during any untoward danger in your lives." Bhadra responded with his voice choked in emotion:

"*Bhagawan* I would like to commit myself to the welfare of this new village. I know that I can never fill the emptiness in the hearts of the parents and relatives of our victims, but we shall all try to convert this place into an ideal community that is free of fear."

"The main aim of religion is this capacity to live amicably with others. Try to spread this love and compassion around so that every village may emulate you!" Everyone was satisfied with the judgment of Bhagavadpāda. A new leaf had been turned in the region with co-operation and love amidst people.

Sureśwara was wonderstruck at this lofty understanding of religion. He gratefully remembered his mentor Kumarila Bhaṭṭa who in all compassion had directed his *Guru* to him, for eliminating the *holier than thou* attitude—his Himalayan ego! He felt that within such a short period he had learnt and experienced much under the feet of Bhagavadpāda, whose compassion knew no end, to even take *his* help in standardizing the *Pūjā* in the temples. The recent episode with *Kāpālikas* had further taught him to convert his emotions to devotion. He had been of the conviction earlier, that head and reason were the only requirements for leading a healthy human life. How wrong the view was! This realisation brought a smile to his lips. The *Ācārya*, ever observant and aware that he was, noticed it and asked:

"What is it Sureśwara, that brings smile to your lips?" The disciple looking at his master said:

"I was smiling at my own foolishness! I used to be so proud of my knowledge that I failed to even note the existence emotions and their role in our life. I used to think that action and understanding are the only tools for a purposeful life! *Bhagawan*, how can persons like me begin to *feel*?"

Śaṅkara Bhagavadpāda looked at a stream meandering hundreds of feet below. They both were sitting on a rock waiting for others to join them. The retinue was on its way to the place where Ṣṛṅga *Ṛṣi* had performed arduous penance. The master spoke after a long silence.

"Sureśwara, you have been interacting with the *so-called* ordinary people. You would have realised that *Vedānta* is beyond their understanding. They have ordinary wishes and ordinary means to fulfill them. But we, who have been entrusted with the revival of our culture, cannot ever hope to do our work without their help. Their greatest quality is *their capacity to feel*, which many of us have lost in the mire of arguments, logic and reason! They are rather spontaneous, to not only the pain that is their own, but of others. They can *relate themselves with the whole universe*! The very question you have asked has an answer! *By feeling*! Try to remember and if possible *relive the time when you decided to dedicate your life to* Kumarila Bhaṭṭa, *the person who inspired you*."

Sureśwara's mind travelled back to the time when he was in the *Āśrama* pursuing education. The great Kumarila Bhaṭṭa had addressed them and appealed to their conscience to meet the challenge given by Buddhism. He had approached his *Guru* to allow him to be with Kumarila and serve our culture. When the *Guru* had hesitated, Sureśwara had shed tears and expressed that this alone would bring fulfillment to his life. He *had felt intensely* at that time. His master's words brought him out of his reverie:

"Whenever you learn something new how do you *feel*?"

"I *feel* an effervescence of joy inside me." replied Sureśwara.

"By *not allowing the mind to comment—good, bad, beautiful, ugly,* start observing your surroundings. Do not analyse any perception or experience, just *feel*!" Since the instruction had come from the master, Sureśwara complied readily. He *felt* the same affinity and trust he had when he was at the feet of Kumarila Bhaṭṭa. Another journey had begun.

❐

10
Hues of Devotion

Amidst the roar of advancing and retrieving waves, the cry of sea gulls could be heard. The foam joined the orchestra by adding its soft sound of effervescence. The small crabs and shell creatures played tug of war with the waves joyfully moving on the wet sand. The sun was behind the onlooker whose shadow was in front, creating patterns of on the waves and the wet sand. The onlooker was Śaṅkara Bhagavadpāda who had reached *Gokarṇa* on the west coast with his entourage. Gokarṇa is a sacred place of pilgrimage having an ancient temple of Śiva. The sacred *Liṅga*—symbol of Śiva, is supposedly part of the Liṅga brought by Rāvaṇa the demon king of Śri Laṅka from Kailāsa. The disciples could see that their *Guru* had identified with the ocean. They knew that anything and everything triggered him to plunge into the cosmic consciousness. Padmapāda as well as Sureśwara could feel the expansiveness experienced by him.

As they entered the temple Śaṅkara beheld the image of *Mahādeva* in the form of *Ardhanārīśvara*—the right half being that of Śiva, and the left half being that of Pārvati. In a spontaneous emotional state, he sang in praise of the Lord in this wonderful form:

"I meditate on the form of Śiva, the destroyer of cupid, who is illumined by His own white radiance and the left side by the lightning like brilliance of His consort Pārvati. In this form of union, the hand of Śiva shivers due to tne movement of deer as it leans to nibble at the grass-like beams that spread forth from

Devi Pārvati, while the parrot in her hand struggles to peck the corn-like quanta of brilliance from Śiva's effulgence! This mutual Divine Radiance dispels the foreboding darkness of the poison-mark[53] on Śiva's throat and envelops me with *Advaita*—No-Otherness."

As they came out of the temple to behold the expansive sea, the disciples who could only see the *Liṅga*, wanted to know how their master had been able to see the non-existent form of *Ardhanārīśvara*! Padmapāda asked:

"We know that there is an adorable form of Śiva as *Ardhanārīśvara*. How can we understand this form?"

Sitting on the soft sand, *Ācārya* beckoned them to join him. Identifying his breath with the waves, he responded after a full pause of silence:

"The whole existence is governed by two principles—*Prakṛti*—the female and *Puruṣa*—the male. One of the basic tendencies of the mind is that it *divides* or *differentiates*, which has been called as *Bheda Vāsana*.[54] Though the Reality transcends name and form, mind tries to understand it through name and form!"

"Why is it that the mind tries to do so?" It was Sureśwara who asked this question.

Ācārya was silent for a while, with his eyes on the ocean in front and a blissful smile on his face, he responded to the question with a question:

"Can you contain the *whole ocean* which is in front of us through your eyes? The eyes can see only that *portion* of the ocean which is in the purview of their vision, because the power of vision is small compared to the ocean. Similarly, Reality is

53. Mythology mentions that during the *Amṛitamanthana* many objects came forth which were kept by gods, while the poison was consumed by Śiva which left a blue mark on his throat, giving him the name *Nīlakaṅṭha*.
54. *Laghu Yoga Vāsiṣtha* mentions two basic tendencies of the mind—*Bheda Vāsanā*, tendency to differentiate and *Bhoga Vāsanā*, tendency to experience.
भोगैकवासनां त्यक्त्वा त्यज त्वं भेदवासनाम् ।भावाभावौ ततस्त्यक्त्वा निर्विकल्पः सुखी भव ॥
॥ लघु योगवासिष्ठः 3:9:37 ॥

beyond the purview of senses, mind, intellect, and ego. But still we try to understand it though the *instruments* available to us. These instruments have been called as the *windows—Khāni*. A window limits our vision because of its frame! As I was saying, Śiva and Pārvati are not two but are joined very intimately with each other. Like the fire and its *power* to burn, water and its *power* to wet! Pārvati is *Śakti*—the *power* of Śiva! That is the symbolic significance of *Ardhanārīśvara*. When you see the image of Śiva, do not keep Pārvati away from her Lord!"

Both the disciples had an insight into what the *Ācārya* hinted. They all sat in blissful silence amidst the sounds of waves, the birds and the fishermen returning to the shore after their successful catch. It was symbolic, for the disciples too had returned to themselves after catching the hints from their beloved master! After spending a few days there *Ācārya* proceeded in the north eastern direction to a place called *Hariśaṅkara* which has a temple dedicated to the two of the principal deities of the Hindu Godhead—Hari or Viṣṇu and Śaṅkara. The right half of the image is that of Hara or Śaṅkara and the left half is that of Hari. According to the legend, one demon by name *Guhāsura* became invincible and started persecuting the sages, who approached Hari to rescue them. But due to the boon received from Brahma the creator, he could be vanquished only by the combined powers of Hari and Hara.

At the temple, the *Ācārya* in his meditative state had a clear insight into the symbolism of the image. He said to his disciples:

"*Guha* really means the seat of consciousness or heart. Whenever it gets corrupted due to ignorance, it becomes invincible and dangerous to the person as well as his fellow beings. Hari represents the sustainer principle that maintains the balance of the creation, while Hara, the eliminating principle that removes the hindrance. Hari strengthens the trust and other positive qualities like compassion, understanding and love, and Hara eliminates the six enemies of the mind—lust, anger, greed, infatuation, pride and jealousy. Hari symbolises activity while established in Yoga,[55] while Hara represents meditation that calms the mind."

Śaṅkarācārya then chanted the verses in praise of the dual deity. The beauty of this *Stotra* is that each verse describes both the deities simultaneously as it has duel meaning! The verses describe the incarnations of Viṣṇu and also manifestations of Hara.

"May Rāma, who with prowess attained by the wisdom of divine missiles, defeated Rāvaṇa, and who had Sītā as his consort, bestow happiness upon us." The same when addressed to Śiva meant:

"May the Great God Śiva who dispels ignorance by his radiance, and who destroyed *Kamadeva* (cupid) having ten pronged manifestations and who has the daughter of mountains as his consort bestow happiness upon us.

"May we receive the protection of Mahāviṣṇu with Garuḍa by his side, who incites terror in the serpents and who in his incarnation as Kṛṣṇa with a peacock feather in his crown charmed even the mind of Pūtanā?" And to Śaṅkara it meant:

"May we be protected by Lord Śiva, in whose lap Vināyaka is seated embracing Him with his trunk, who has Gaṅgā on His crown and moon decorating Him, whose name is sanctifying, who appears in the minds of those meditating on Him?"[56]

Having spent some time at Hariśaṅkara[57] the *Ācārya* proceeded south with his retinue to the shrine dedicated to Śiva located at Kollur. The temple with its sylvan surroundings

55. योगस्थ कुरु कर्माणि सङ्गं त्यक्त्वा धनंजय । सिद्ध्यसिद्ध्योः समोभूत्वा समत्वं योग उच्यते ॥ "Arjuna, perform your actions dwelling in Yoga, by relinquishing attachment and indifferent to success and failures; equanimity is called Yoga" — *Bhagavadgītā* II:48

56. विलासिनाऽलीकभवेन धाम्ना काम द्विषन्तं स दशास्यमस्यन् ।देवो धरापत्यकुचोष्म साक्षी देयादमन्दात्मसुखानुभूतिम् ॥ हरिशंकर स्तोत्रम् 7 ॥

विनायकेनाऽऽकनिताहितापं निषेदुषोत्सङ्गभुवि प्रहृष्यन् ।यः पूतनामोहकचित्तवृत्तिरव्यादसौ कोऽपि कलापभूषः ॥ हरिशंकर स्तोत्रम् 9 ॥

57. This place came to be known as *Harihar* due to a massive temple in the name of *Harihareśwara* built by the Hoysala Dynasty in the thirteen century which was nearly four hundred years later.

of dense trees like mango, jack trees, coconut palms and pomegranates was soothing to the body and soul. They—especially the *Ācārya*, entered the temple in an inspired mood. With his eyes brimming with tears of bliss the great sage sat in front of the *Liṅga*. What he saw in his mind was not the image of Śaṅkara, but was that of Mother. After a while he called the priest of the temple to let him have a closer look at the *Liṅga*. He saw that there was a golden line on its crown and it was not in the centre but more towards right, indicating that the deity was that of Mūkāṁbika.[58] He directed the trustees of the temple to install a Mother's idol. He described the benign beauty of the Mother of the Universe in a spontaneous garland of one hundred verses which came to be known as *Soundaryalaharī—Waves of Beauty*. This *Stotra* has been acclaimed as one of the literary masterpieces of *Ācārya* Śaṅkara, and is religiously chanted by *Śāktās*—the devotees of Mother.

Śaṅkara was in such a mood, when he saw beauty in *whatever he saw*, he identified himself with not only all beings but even the inanimate things, as everything was nothing but a manifestation of the Divine. He had become one with the heart of the universe, beating for all of its creatures, breathing with them and vibrating with the five elements. The ongoing transformation was noticed by the two disciples and identified as they were with their beloved master, they too had a glimpse. Sureśwara felt blessed for the defeat he had from his master, as though he had become water that naturally flows under the feet of a mountain! Padmapāda accepted the experience as though it was *Prasādam*—the consecrated food from the temple.

They reached *Śrīveli*, a small hamlet of persons involved in the study of scriptures and practising righteousness. The news spread and the joyous inhabitants rushed to offer their respects and hospitality to the *Ācārya* and his disciples. One person, Prabhākara by name approached with concern and sadness in

58. It is believed that based on the spontaneous inspired description of Śaṅkarācārya the trustees of the temple installed the idol of the Mother of the universe there. This work is also claimed to be the practical guide for *Tantra Sādhanā*.

his eyes. His wife on the other hand was unable to hold back her tears leading a boy, seven years of age, with bright face but with his eyes dilated with their inability to focus—as if he was below normal and idiotic. They all prostrated offering their respect. When *Ācārya* looked at Prabhākara questioningly, this is what he had to say:

"My only son is seven years old, his mind appears to be undeveloped as he is unable to even speak, how can we expect him to study our scriptures? Have mercy on us!"

The *Ācārya* saw that the boy continued to be in the prostrate posture. Śaṅkara affectionately lifted him and made him sit near him. When he encouraged Prabhākara to continue he said:

"He has not spoken a word till now. When the boys of his age call him to play, he never joins them. Seeing him sitting silent the boys beat him, but he never protests nor does he show any annoyance. Sometimes he comes for food, while other times he abstains from it. He does not heed to any instruction and yet I have never tried to correct him by way of punishment. Should I resign him and leave him to his fate?" Instead of saying anything to Prabhākara, compassionate *Ācārya* looked at the boy and asked:

"O my child, gladden me with your reply; you in whom delight wells up: Who are you? Of whom are you? What is your name? Where do you come from and where do you go?"

To this the boy replied:

"I am neither man nor God nor celestial, nor am I *Brahmin* or *Kṣatriya* or *Vaiśya* or *Śūdra*, nor a *Brahmacārī* or a *Gṛhasta* (householder) or *Vānapṛstha* forest dweller nor a *Sanyāsi*. I am of the nature of wisdom. I am the *Ātman*, which reveals itself incessantly, which is the cause for all activities of the mind, senses, but which is devoid of all limiting descriptions (*Upādhis*), and am pure as sky and which is the substratum of our entire life and activity, as the sun, the foundation of all activities of the world. Just as the face (reflection) produced by the mirror has no existence separate from the real face; there is no real existence of the *Jīvas* (embodied souls) that are no more than reflections of the *Cit* (consciousness) in *Buddhih*.

That self-revealing *Ātman* is alone the source of all reflections."[59]

The *Ācārya* was overjoyed to listen to the wonderful exposition of the Self from the boy, while the parents were flabbergasted at the clear and vibrant recitation in chaste Sanskrit! Placing his hands on the head of the boy the master said to the parents:

"How will the boy who refuses to talk be of any use to you? You cannot persuade him to enter *Gṛhastāśrama*, for he has the experiential knowledge of the Self, like the person who can see the *Āmalaka* (gooseberry) on the palm of his hand. Let this boy be with me and join me in the work of rejuvenation of our culture." The parents of the child were unwilling to give the boy away to the *Ācārya*. Śaṅkara then told them the story of the boy:

"Perhaps you may recall having gone to a pilgrimage with your wife when this boy was just two years old. When you both were going along the bank of a river you saw a monk sitting in meditation. Leaving the boy near *Mahātma* both of you went to bathe in the river. As you returned you noticed that the child had slipped into water and was floating. You jumped into the water and retrieved the child but it was too late, for the child had died. Grieved at the loss of your child you approached the saint and wept before him. Compassionate that he was, he looked at the child and it came back to life. Actually, it had so happened that the *Mahātma* had given up his body to enter into your child's. The boy standing near you is that saint." On hearing this, Prabhākara and his wife offered their son to Śaṅkara

---

59. श्री शंकराचार्य
कस्त्वं शिशो कस्य कुतोऽसि गन्ता किं नाम ते त्वं कुत आगतोऽसि ।एतत् मयोक्तं चार्भक त्वं मत्प्रीतये प्रीतिविवर्धनोऽसि ॥ 1 ॥
हस्तामलक
नाहं मनुष्यो नच देवयक्षो न ब्राह्मण क्षत्रिय वैश्य शूद्राः ।न ब्रह्मचारी न गृही वनस्थो भिक्षु र्नचाहं निजबोधरूपः ॥ 2 ॥
निमित्तं मनश्चक्षुरादिप्रवृत्तौ निरस्ताखिलापाधिराकाशकल्पः ।रविर्लाकचेष्टानिमित्तं यथा यः स नित्योपलब्धिस्वरूपोऽहतात्मा ॥ 3 ॥
मुखाभासको दर्पणे दृश्यमाने मुखत्वात्पृथक्त्वेन नैवाथ्स्त वस्तु ।चिदाभासको धीषु जीवोऽपि तद्वत् स नित्योपलब्धिस्वरूपोऽहमात्मा ॥ 5 ॥
॥ हस्तामलकीयम् ॥ This happens to be the only work of *Hastāmalakācārya*.

Bhagavadpāda though rather reluctantly! The *Ācārya* looking at the boy affectionately addressed his disciples and devotees gathered around him:

"The verses sung by the boy will hereafter be known throughout the world. By reflecting on the meaning of these verses, seekers will come to realise the Truth as clearly as an *Āmalaka* (gooseberry) placed in *Hastam* (palm). Henceforth, I name this boy *Hastāmalaka* and the verses he sang as *Hastāmalakīyam*. On account of their greatness I will compose a commentary on them." Thus, it was that the third apostle joined the band of missionaries of our culture.

The entourage reached Ṣṛṅga-Giri on the banks of the river *Tungabhadrā*. It was here that Śaṅkara had seen the peculiar sight of a cobra offering shade to a toad when he was on his way to Narmada. The flora and the fauna appeared to be welcoming them!

He told the disciples of his experience, and his decision to have a centre to propagate *Advaita*. A beautiful temple was built for *Śāradā*—the Goddess of learning. About this time, a disciple named Giri joined the group. Noted for his service, Giri[60] attended to the personal needs and was like a shadow of his master. Giri never talked in front of his master and always walked behind the master. He would stand behind the *Ācārya*, whenever there was any discourse, and listened carefully whatever was being uttered by the master. The other disciples took his presence for granted as they knew that he could not understand any Sanskrit.

Once when the *Ācārya* reached the spot—a shady tree, and sat on his seat, the disciples chanted the invocatory *Śānti Mantra* before the discourse. But the master did not start his discourse; instead, he kept looking at the empty spot, where Giri was in the habit of standing! When the disciples realised that he was waiting for Giri, some of them thought, why we should wait for a wall—for Giri was as receptive as a wall! Nevertheless, they

60. In the life of Paramahaṅsa Sri Ramakrishna, Lātu Maharaj was very much like Giri, who by offering personal service to his Guru had achieved Ṣelf Realisation; Swami Vivekananda named him *Swami Adbhutānanda*.

had to await the arrival of Giri. The subject of all this waiting was washing clothes of his master, and after finishing his work at hand, rushed to the tree. When he arrived at the scene, all the disciples saw a transformed Giri—radiant and inspired. Falling at the feet of his master, Giri stood with his palms joined in salutation and recited a spontaneous garland of eight verses in praise of his *Guru*. The verses were in Sanskrit, that too in the *Toṭaka* metre—considered being difficult! The disciples were flabbergasted realising their folly.

"Oh, the best of all preceptors! You are the knower of all the *Śāstras,* which form the ocean of nectar; you are the abode of the essence of Truth, which is the theme of all the *Upaniṣads*. I ever bear your pure feet in my heart. May you become the sole refuge for me, Oh Śaṅkara? You are the possessor of the intellect that contemplates on and enquires into the wisdom of the Self. All of us are benefited by your radiance. I adore you, the knower of the Supreme Lord and the ego separated through discrimination. May you become my sole refuge for me, Oh Śaṅkara?"[61] Looking at all the disciples in compassion, the master said:

"We are the committed soldiers of our culture. She has been called as *Śruti Bhagavati*, our compassionate mother. When she does not see any difference among her children, how can we possibly differentiate amongst the lettered and unlettered persons? Remember *Śruti Bhagavati* has chosen us to do her work because we are too insignificant to *choose anything*. Anyone and everyone can become our comrade and unless we too develop a heart like hers, we cannot serve her!" He continued:

"Whenever we are involved in a noble activity we have to guard against a natural tendency from taking over us: *Holier than thou* attitude. Most of the people in the society are involved

61. विदिताखिलशास्त्रसुधाजलधे महितोपनिषत्कथितार्थनिधे ।हृदये कलये विमलं चरणं भव शंकर देशिक मे शरणम् ॥ 1 ॥ भवता जनता सुखिता भविता निजबोधविचारणचारुमते ।कलयेश्वरजीवविवेकविदं भव शंकर देशिक मे शरणम् ॥ तोटकाष्टकम् 3 ॥
This is called as Gurvāṣṭakam or Toṭakāṣṭakam consisting of eight verses in praise of Guru.

in self-preservation, *which is only natural*! By looking at them, we may gloat about being special or non-ordinary. If at all there is anything different in us, it is that *SHE* has chosen us, may not be due to our talent *but she wants us to learn something very important*. I personally feel that She wants us to be in her likeness—develop a heart that can accommodate the whole universe. Shirk from all pettiness, but at the same time do not entertain any guilt over your behaviour. When there is darkness there are bound to be some accidents! It happened to me while at Kāśi, a hunter and his wife had to remind me what *Advaita* is! I shall remain ever grateful to them."

"*Bhagawan*, after the Kāpālika episode, I am experiencing certain emotions which I had never done before. Though I am older, I feel like a child in your presence; though you are a man, I feel as though you are my mother; though I am grown-up man, I feel like crying without any shame; and though they are tears, there is so much of relief and joy when they wet my cheeks! What is happening to me, *Bhagawan*?" It was Sureśwara pouring out in front of his master.

Both of them were taking a stroll on the bank of Tungabhadrā. The flow was quite turbulent. Looking at it the *Ācārya* observed:

"Just like this river, mind too is an incessant flow of thoughts. In your case, earlier it used to be unidirectional, logical and most importantly, purposeful. While championing the cause of Vedas, you had forgotten how to be childlike. But after the Kāpālika episode, you have started feeling or to put it in your words, you have started moving towards the heart. The suffering of the villagers, the persecution of Bhairava, helped in making you think of *others and their problems*. *Sāttwic* and unselfish by nature that you are, the emotions helped you to move towards devotion. Thought has a potential emotion in it, and *Bhakti* is all about transforming that emotion into devotion." Looking into the being of Sureśwara, *Ācārya* continued affectionately:

"Sureśwara, you have come to realise that heart is very important to us. If we want to be of some use to the society that has more number of emotional than intellectual people, we should have both head and heart. If all our actions are governed by this principal factor of being useful, our task becomes easier."

A plan of action to continue the work for ages to come was taking shape in the mind of Śaṅkara Bhagavadpāda. They moved towards the temple of Śāradāmbā—the mother of wisdom. Śaṅkara smiled in response at the image of the mother who was showering radiance on them. Sureśwara felt at peace with himself and with the world around him.

❐

11
All in One, One in All

Ancient trees stood on the slopes of the hills washed by the rains; their foliage was reflecting the morning sun, spreading the message of plenty. They all had been silent witnesses to the events of at least five to six centuries. The earth was dressed in various hues of green; the small boulders had grown velvety green moss; a rivulet moved noisily, eager to join the mainstream of Tungabhadrā. A fox was nursing its litter of four pups. As Śaṅkara stood absorbing nature's plenty, his eyes met with those of mother fox, who casually looked at him and noting no danger, laid her head to rest. Having finished his ablutions early, Śaṅkara decided to take a walk in the forest. Nature had always had a very benign effect on him as he felt connected not only with it, but also with those great sages who had spent their lives in contemplation and meditation amidst abounding nature. It was not just an idle thought, but a live experience to him as he identified himself with the sylvan surroundings, as though all the sages of the past, who had performed austerities and had experienced the divine, were by his side blessing his work!

Padmapāda, not finding the master in his usual place, which was a shady tree on the bank of Tungabhadrā, went in search. Soon Sureśwara, Hastāmalaka, and Toṭaka joined him. They all were concerned about his safety. They all were relieved to find him near a stream gurgling down the slopes deeper inside the forest. He was sitting, his eyes half open, and a radiant smile adorned his face. Sensitive that they were they did not disturb him, but sat at a distance. As soon as they sat, they effortlessly entered the state of meditation. After a while, when they opened their eyes, they heard his soft and loving voice, it had not only affection but also a very powerful suggestion in it:

"The *Śrīmadbhagavadgītā* observes 'He, who sees Me dwelling in all beings, and sees all beings dwelling in Me, I am never out of sight of him, nor is he ever out of sight of Me. He who established in Unity, worships me as residing in all beings as their very Self, that *Yogi,* though engaged in all forms of activities, dwells in Me.'[62] Coincidentally, these verses appear after *Bhagawan* Kṛṣṇa introduces Arjuna to mind control and meditation. What could be the reason for that?" He looked at all his beloved disciples, who were more than ready to absorb what he was going to say. He continued after a small pause:

"This is the beauty of *Mahābhārata* and the genius of *Bhagawān* Kṛṣṇa Dvaipāyana Vyāsa. Whatever he has written has very deep meaning and relevance! We have heard from our ancestors that meditation is mandatory for *Ātma Jñāna*—Self-Realisation. Unfortunately, our understanding of *Ātman* or the Self was limited and restricted to one single person. The Self has no limitations. It includes all; it contains all; it encompasses all! But yes, we start our journey through the limited self, perceived by everyone as 'I' and 'mine'. The journey starts there but we get stuck to the limitation." Seeing a wrinkle on the brow of Padmapāda, the *Ācārya* looked at him:

"*Bhagawan*, you have rightly pointed out that my meditation is restricted to my own self. But tell us, when we saw you here and sat near you, something happened to us, which resulted in silence culminating in joy." Bhagavadpāda smiled and continued:

"We have misunderstood *Ātman*—the Self as, that which can be experienced only with our eyes closed! We *have* to change that. How? We have been endowed with the senses—of sight, sound, smell, taste, touch and a matching mind and heart to *use* them. We have also been told—and it *is* our experience—

62. यो मां पश्यति सर्वत्र सर्वं च मयि पश्यति ।तस्याहं न प्रणश्यामि स च मे न प्रणश्यति ॥ 6:30 ॥
सर्वभूतस्थितं यो मां भजत्येकत्वमस्थितः ।सर्वथा वर्तमानोऽपि स योगी मयि वतति ॥ श्रीमद्भगवद्गीता 6:31 ॥

that these senses distract us from experiencing the *Ātman*! This is a paradox and how can we reconcile? Our faculties and instruments are for the purpose of experiencing the world around us. Our perception however, is limited by the limitations of the senses. They have been called as *Khāni*—windows[63] which can open only outside. We are warned that if we are *involved* with our senses, we cannot see *Pratyagātman*—the inner Self." Śaṅkara smiled when he saw a puzzled expression on their faces.

"Our ancestors were the children of nature and they loved their mother. All the contemplations, dialogues, and conclusions in the *Upaniṣads* took place either in the forests or places abounding in natural beauty. So when they enjoyed nature it was not just to quench the thirst of their senses, *but to experience the Divine through the balance and beauty that pervades the nature.* Because beauty gave them bliss, peace and a kind of oneness with the objects they perceived. The dawn, the infant Sun, the mist or fog, the clouds and the thunder, everything fascinated and filled them with wonder! But many if not most of us are bound to and by the limited senses, like we restrict the sky to the frame of the window, which is limited! We have to *make use* of the limited senses to imagine the unlimited nature.[64] Spirituality is the search for the divinity in the mundane; for the eternal in the evanescent or temporal!" Eyes of Bhagavadpāda were in eternity as he uttered these words. The disciples could feel *his* expansiveness embracing them. They could almost touch it!

Sureśwara was the first to stir from the state as a question raised its hood in his alert mind:

"*Bhagawan*," he asked trying his best not to disturb others, "How to transcend our *limited vision*?" Śaṅkara smiled sweetly appreciating his concern for others and said:

"Whatever you see or perceive is not what it appears. You see a man three cubits tall, dark or fair, fat or thin. He has

63. पराञ्चि खानि व्यतृणत्स्वयम्भूस्तस्मात्पराङ्पश्यति नान्तरात्मन् ।कश्चिद्धीरः प्रत्यगात्मानमैक्षदावृत्तचक्षुरमृतत्वमिच्छन् ॥ कठोपनिषद् 2:1:1 ॥

64. Blaise Pascal (1623-62) the French scientist and philosopher said, "in space, the universe engulfs us and reduces us to a pin point; but through thought, we embrace that universe."

thoughts, perceptions, impressions, reactions, habits, dreams and so on and so forth. He is an unlimited being supporting his own world of relations, friends, foes… Your senses only try to give you a glimpse of that being. But we try to fit this unlimited being into a small limited glimpse given by the senses and mind. Be fresh like a child, receptive and open. You will then discover a vibrant, fresh, ever-new and beautiful world around you!" Padmapāda appealed to the master.

"*Bhagawan*, can you please teach us the proper way to do *Dhyāna*?"

"First of all, we should realise that there are as many ways to lead the mind into meditation as there are people! Each one of us is unique. You must have observed that in spite of the fact that a nose, two eyes, two ears and a mouth which are common to all of us, each one is totally different to the others. It is more so in the case of our mind and intellect. Our impressions, nature, habits and behaviour depend on so many factors that it is difficult to suggest a common method of taking the mind to *Dhyāna*!" He continued after a pause.

"In any action there has to be an element of joy without which, it becomes an empty gesture! The joy of spirituality lies in *discovering the method peculiar to an individual for taking the mind into the state of Dhyāna*. All our scriptures only give very broad suggestions. We have to individually strive to discover our particular method." Seeing a wrinkle on the brow of Toṭaka, *Ācārya* looked at him questioningly.

"*Bhagawan*, you were careful to say, *to help the mind to go into Dhyāna*; or *taking the mind to Dhyāna*. Is not *Dhyāna* an act?" Appreciating the alertness in the disciple, the *Ācārya* replied:

"*Dhyāna* is not an act, but a state of mind. We can do something to slip into the state of *Dhyāna*. All one can *do* is to prepare the mind, by purifying it. This preparation can be done in as many ways as there are men. Sometimes one can use many methods, depending on the state of mind!"

Suddenly, there was this joyous pandemonium of birds. It was as though they were making their own commentaries on living! The sun had risen warming the slopes, trees percolating its warm light through their leaves; a lone peacock was calling out for his companions. All of them were greeting a fresh new day, as if celebrating life. Never far off from nature, Śaṅkara too joined the celebration through his benign smile! Everything was quiet once again. He continued:

"You must have noticed the sound of birds, some excited, some joyful, some appealing. Each sound had its own mood. But collectively, there was joy in it! And presently there is silence. If you observe anything in nature—and in nature I also include our mind—there is this alternate activity and silence. This phenomenon can be made use of in helping the mind to go into meditation."

Ācārya Śaṅkara then proceeded to initiate them into methods of mind control. They received benediction from the master, poise and joy, in proportion to their eligibility. The methods taught by the master were then recorded by the disciples. This record of verses of the master came to be known as *Yogatārāvali*—a collection of twenty-seven verses, after the twenty-seven stars in the Hindu almanac. However, the disciples had to cover a lot of ground before getting into the Universal consciousness as the future events would reveal!

Events happen around an enlightened master by themselves and they have something great to offer to not only the people involved at that time but leave impressions for the posterity. One afternoon, Sureśwara approached the master with a request to permit him to write *Vārtikam*—explanation giving a critical exposition on the commentary of revered *Ācārya* on the *Brahmasūtras*. The master noted the sincerity and eligibility of the disciple and asked him to start the work. When Sureśwara retreated to contemplate on the scripture, a few disciples approached the master. There was concern and apprehension on their faces. *Ācārya* looked at them with curiosity, and though he knew the cause of their feelings he asked them to freely express their fears! One of them made bold to say:

"*Bhagawan*, we feel that your permission to Sureśwara will not really help in the propagation of *Advaita*." Śaṅkara smiled and asked innocently:

"Why do you feel that way?" One of them responded:

"Sureśwara was Viśwarūpa or Maṇḍana Miśra, the champion of *Pūrva Mīmāṅsa*—the ritualistic portion of the Veda. Kumarila Bhaṭṭa, his *Guru* is known to be a traitor of his Buddhist teacher; Maṇḍana had reluctantly accepted defeat in that memorable argument with you; and most importantly, he was a *Gṛhasta* who became a *Sanyāsi* as a part of the agreement that the loser accepts the *Āśrama* of the victor and so even *Sanyāsa* was forced on him. Moreover, how can a person who held a completely opposite view write on the pristine philosophy of *Advaita*? How can he be trusted?" Gathering courage, another disciple added:

"We have Sanandana who has implicit trust on you, to the extent that he even did not bother to find whether he could walk on water. Responding to his trust over his *Guru*, mother Gangā supported his feet by providing lotuses under his feet due to which you named him *Padmapāda*. He is known to be your shadow, and is well versed in the texts, and other scriptures. Since *Brahmasūtras* are the epitome of *Advaita*, we feel Padmapāda should be entrusted with this responsible task." Though he smiled, there was a touch of sadness in that smile, *Ācārya* said:

"Sanandana is certainly eligible to write the *Vārtikam* on the *Vedānta Sūtras*. But let Sureśwara, who has started this work also continue." The disciples left, though not fully satisfied! Like a mother who is fond of all her children, Śaṅkara called Sureśwara and said:

"I feel that you should not begin your *Vārtikam*. The other disciples do not seem to have enough confidence in your competence because of your earlier view! Instead, I want you to write an independent work on *Advaita*. This will more than clear their suspicion."

Sureśwara understood the situation and went away to execute the bidding of his master. When he saw the retreating figure of Sureśwara, Śaṅkara had a premonition that the *Vārtikam* may not be written at all! Again he smiled as he saw that even this disturbing incidence had a great purpose. This time his smile was real! After a few days, Sureśwara brought the work and kept it at the feet of his master. This work was called *Naiṣkarmya-Siddhi*. In this work of great beauty and depth, Sureśwara establishes that action does in no way affect the *Ātman*. Pleased with the work, *Ācārya* showed the work to the disciples. They felt convinced that Sureśwara was more than eligible to carry on the work of their master. Some of them were visibly ashamed of their doubt. Sureśwara however, was in no way disturbed, for he had not only contemplated on the truths revealed in the work, but had *lived* them.

A few days later, *Ācārya* Śaṅkara was with the other disciples, when he addressed them in all compassion:

"That was a test of your understanding and conviction in *Advaita*. I feel you all fell short, by not only entertaining the doubt about the sincerity and eligibility of Sureśwara but more importantly, your own conviction on *Advaita*! We all are a dedicated band of soldiers of our culture, who have dedicated our lives for the cause. We must be clear in our mind as to what is it that we are supporting? Can you tell what the most important characteristic feature of our culture is?" He observed that they were looking down and when no one answered, he said with affection:

"It has the greatest capacity to accept and absorb the whole universe in it. We are trying to meditate on *Brahman*, *not because it is an ideal or a goal to be reached, but because we are one with it*. Through your suspicion about the intension of Sureśwara, you were not really exhibiting your concern for *Advaita*, but there was jealousy which shows that you still have not accepted your own brother disciple, how can you possibly identify with *Brahman*? It only shows that you have a lot more to learn. But do not be ashamed, you have not done anything wrong." He added after a pause:

"*Śruti Bhagawati* keeps testing our sincerity and eligibility repeatedly! I too was tested and had failed miserably!" He then went on to narrate the incident of the hunter on a *Ghāt* of Kāśi. Guilt eliminated, the disciples got encouraged, they all proceeded to meet Sureśwara for sincerely apologizing for their behaviour. Sureśwara was very graceful to say that his earlier life had been for a different ideal, and he had lived *that* ideal when he championed it. And so, it was natural for his brother disciples to entertain a doubt about his capacity. But now, his whole life and energy was for *Advaita*.

Next day the *Ācārya* called Sureśwara and said:

"This life will be totally dedicated to the mission that has chosen all of us. You will be working, but in a spirit of *Advaita*. Your conviction and devotion to our culture will inspire all of us to re-dedicate our lives for the cause. I entrust you with the responsibility of guiding the first centre of our mission, it will be called the *Śṛṅgeri Śārada Pīṭham*." With a faraway look in his eyes, *Ācārya* added:

"In near future, you will be reborn for writing a *Vārtikam* on the *Brahmasūtra Bhāśya*. It will be very widely accepted and used text for understanding and the practise *Advaita*.[65]" Sureśwara said humbly:

"*Bhagawan*, I am your disciple, and this is my second birth. I will try my level best to do your bidding. I am blessed to be a part of your team and twice blessed for being of some service to our culture." When their eyes met Sureśwara could feel an ethereal love oozing out of Śaṅkara Bhagavadpāda's eyes and more importantly his being. Indeed he was blessed to bathe in the loving compassion of the *Ācārya*!

"One who works for me alone and has me for his or her goal is devoted to me, who is free from attachment and bears no enmity towards any being—he or she attains to me alone, O Pāṇḍava."[66]

The master commenced his discourse to his disciples that day with the recitation of this *Śloka*. Everything about the milieu was congenial. There was a gentle breeze blowing from the east; the sun was in the act of bidding au revoir for the day;

65. In the eleventh century, Vācaspati Miśra wrote *Bhāmati*.

66. मत्कर्मकृत्मत्परमो मद्भक्तः सङ्गवर्जितः । निर्वैरः सर्वभूतेषु यः स मामेति पाण्डव ॥ श्रीमद्भगवद्गीता 11:55 ॥

jasmine blossoms were being showered on them by the creeper on the tree; and gentle stream flowing on their right. It could be felt by all those present that Bhagavadpāda was in an inspired mood. The disciples felt that the whole nature was in a listening mood; nay *he had become the nature* which was talking to them addressing them almost individually.

"This is perhaps one of the most wonderful *Ślokas* in the *Śrīmadbhagavadgītā*. If one is able to practise the essence of this verse one is assured of Self-realisation. This is the last verse of the *Viśwarūpa Darśanam*—the chapter in which the Lord shows His Universal Form, the proof that *He is in all and all are in Him*. If all our activity is directed towards Him and offered to Him, there can be no other thought. The moment one starts thinking about the results, about appreciation, or about the name and fame, one becomes *petty* and naturally goes away from Him—the Cosmic Self. How can one do it? By being His devotee, which alone is pure love, as the contemplation on Him eliminates all attachment, *Rāga*—or attraction and *Dweśa*—aversion, which results in non-attachment. A *Bhakta* necessarily a *Nirvairaḥ*—he has no enemies." He paused to look and listen to a peacock.

"May quietness descend upon my limbs, speech, breath, eyes and ears; may all senses wax clear and strong. Everything is *Brahman*, reveal the *Upaniṣads*. Never may I deny *Brahman*, nor *Brahman* ever deny me. I with Him and He with me, may we abide always together. May the Truth of the *Upaniṣads* be revealed to me? AUM! Peace! Peace!! Peace!!!"[67]

"All of us know the meaning of this *Śānti Mantra* from the *Sāma Veda*. This perhaps is one the basic mistakes we commit! We *know*, because it is only a part of our memory and not our experience! We should always remember that memory or knowledge is only a residue of information we have gathered or experienced in the past. We all have covered a vast ground as far as the knowledge or even experience is concerned. Time

67. आप्यायन्तु ममाङ्गानिवाक्प्राणश्चक्षुः श्रोत्रतथो बलमिन्द्रियाणि च सर्वाणि । सर्वं ब्रह्मौपनिषदं माऽहं ब्रह्मनिराकुर्यां मा मा ब्रह्मनिराकरोदनिराकरणमस्तु अनिराकरणं मेऽस्तु ।तदात्मनि निरते य उपनिषत्सु धर्मास्ते मयि सन्तु ते मयि सन्तु ॥ ॐ शान्तिः शान्तिः शान्तिः ॥ साम वेदः ॥

has come for us to take that great leap into our being. One small detail remains to be implemented in our life. The *Maṅtra* observes *Everything is Brahman*. If everything and every being is *Brahman*, then why should we differentiate? What is there to differentiate? What can we deny or negate?"

These were not just questions, but strong suggestions for them to follow. Coming as they were from Śaṅkara Bhagavadpāda, who was established in the unity of existence, the disciples literally felt as if they were leaping into the being. The Being Who is in all, and All in Him! It could not be called as experience, because for experiencing there has to be the *Tripuṭi*—the triplet of one who experiences, the experienced and the experience for the three had merged into One, One without the other. It could not be even called One, for there was *No-Other*.

❐

12
The Pilgrimage

The valley was full of flowers of various hues, in bloom, spreading ethereal fragrance all around; the peacocks, the blue jays and numerous other birds flaunting their plumes; the wag tails, cuckoos, and nightingales singing in tune with the breeze brushing past the leaves of trees. It was spring at Śṛṅga-Giri which was pretty as a picture. Amidst all this joyous celebration of nature the disciples of Śaṅkara Bhagavadpāda were absorbing the nature's beauty. But more intensely, they were partaking from the spiritual wealth of their master. They were slowly but steadily able to feel their oneness with existence with all its beings. They did not know why, they felt the physical pain of an animal—an ox, when it was whipped by its master; they could feel the load of firewood by seeing a woman carrying the bundle on her head; they experienced freedom in a bird's flight; joy of a mother with a babe in her arms;… It was as if the whole world had become their body!

Padmapāda was an exception to this, for he could not enjoy the banquet of bliss. After the episode of protest by the disciples on deputing Sureśwara for writing a *Vārtikam* for the *Brahmasūtra Bhāśya*, though the other disciples had apologized and he too had genuinely sought forgiveness, it had continued to trouble him. The only question that haunted his being was why had he been so suspicious? By questioning the eligibility of Sureśwara, he had questioned his master in his ability to allot responsibility to his disciples! Padmapāda came to a conclusion that it was due to his *Ahamkāra* that he was devoted to his *Guru*.

The *Ācārya* was aware of the turbulence of conflict going on in his mind. Waiting for an opportunity, he called Padmapāda to join him for a walk on the banks of *Tuṅga*. Looking into the sad eyes of his beloved disciple *Ācārya* asked in all compassion:

"What is the cause of anguish amidst joy of spring?" Padmapāḍa responded with tears in his eyes.

"*Bhagawan*, there is a lot to be done before I become eligible for your compassion and grace. I want to reduce my faults. After much deliberation, I have decided on the next course of action." The master showed curiosity in his eyes and said nothing. Padmapāda continued.

"*Bhagawan*, I would like to take a pilgrimage." Śaṅkara smiled and asked innocently.

"And how do you think pilgrimage will be of any help?"

"*Bhagawan*, I know that the greatest place of pilgrimage is at the feet of *Sadguru*, that the greatest *Maṅtra* lies in the words of the *Guru*, that the object of meditation is the form of *Sadguru*. But even having spent so much time with you and following you like a shadow, it appears as if my negativities have not been eliminated. Moreover, by doubting Sureśwara, I have doubted and questioned *your* judgment. I would like to repent for that great sin by staying away from you. I feel that the pilgrimage alone will absolve me of that wrongdoing. I will visit the holy places and perform penance. I will also have the good fortune of having the *Satsaṅga*—the holy company of saints and sages in those places." When Padmapāda finished speaking, *Ācārya* noted that he was very eager to get the permission of his *Guru*! It was pointless to convince him as he had already made the decision. Understanding the heart of the beloved disciple Śaṅkara said in all compassion.

"Dear Padmapāda, it appears you have already made up your mind to go on this pilgrimage. Even if I try to tell you something against this venture, you will not listen to it! Go safely, may the purpose of this pilgrimage be fulfilled!"

Padmapāda, as observed by his *Guru*, was in a self-righteous mood of atonement. He wanted to perform austere penance through this pilgrimage. When Padmapāda was about to take his leave, *Ācārya* gave a few suggestions.

"Remember Padmapāda, *Brahman* has five facets or expressions. *Asti*—existence, *Bhāti*—self-luminosity, *Priyam*—love, *Nāmam*—name, and *Rūpam*—form. The first three form Its *Swabhāva*—basic nature, as it has also been named as *Sat-Cit-Ānaṅda*. The other two—*Name* and *Rūpam* are its manifestations. We become the victims of forgetfulness due to fact that we get entangled with *Nāmam* and *Rūpam*. *Śāstras* declare that when man falls on the ground, he takes the help of the very same ground to get up.[68] You are a *Bhakta*, having a very great capacity to love. Intensify your love towards all. When I say *all*, *it includes you*! Do not be too harsh on yourself because it is Love which can forget and forgive. Forget what happened here and forgive yourself for the forgetfulness of *Advaita*. You can do this by trying to see your *Iṣṭa* in every being. This will help you to *transcend Form*, and keep chanting His name—which is pleasing as well as soothing to your heart. You will thus, be able to transcend even the Name!"

Having received the directive of his *Guru*, he prostrated in all gratefulness. It struck him that his beloved *Guru*, had given a practical method of *Sādhanā* very casually, but the hint was so powerful that it filled him with enthusiasm. As he walked away from *Śṛṅga-Giri* he started contemplating on the content of the advice. The *Maṅtra* that had filled his being from his very childhood surfaced on to his mind, and pervaded his breath; his feet followed the rhythm of his breath; whatever the eyes beheld, appeared to be the articles of worship of his *Iṣṭa*—Nṛsiṁha, the man lion. He was overwhelmed by an expansive feeling, a feeling that appeared to envelop the existence as if, the existence had him in its warm embrace, or was it him embracing the existence? All he experienced was the joy that filled his being that radiated all around. Then he walked…and continued walking.

On that day Śaṅkara was discussing the methodology of *Vedāṅta* with his disciples. Suddenly, his eyes closed and he

---

68. यस्यां भूमौ निपतितः तामालम्ब्य विमुच्यते ।

stopped talking. When he came to normal consciousness, there were tears in his eyes. The disciples, who had never witnessed such display of emotion, were surprised. *Ācārya* got up from his seat and walked away. Sureśwara rushed and enquired after his mastered, who responded gravely:

"It is my beloved mother. She is beckoning me to be with her. Look after the flock Sureśwara, till I return." Sureśwara stood and bowed his head with his palms joined in salutation. When he opened his eyes his master had disappeared!

Āryāmbā was sitting, leaning against the wooden pillar on the parapet outside the hut. She had finished her morning ablutions. She was looking at the flow of River Pūrṇa. The gurgling sound and the flow itself gave her peace. Her beloved son had asked her to observe the river whenever she missed him. This had been her daily practice since his departure years back.

She could not help remembering his serene smiling face, his sweet patient voice, his unconditional love and respect for her.... When suddenly she experienced a shot of pain in her chest, she had difficulty in breathing. Once again, that smiling face and mellow voice came to her urging her to get up and enter the hut. She reached the bed and lay down in exhaustion. Yes, she felt, that her time had come to depart, time to join her ancestors, her beloved husband. With all the energy she could gather, she whispered:

"Śaṅkara, where are you my child?"

In that very instant, she heard the footsteps, and she knew he had responded to her last call as promised! Her beloved Śaṅkara was at last with her, what more could she ask of her God? A radiant smile lit up her face, as though the time gap was filled and *her Śaṅkara was back never to leave her again*! Śaṅkara too was beside with emotion. With joy emanating from her being she looked into the eyes of her son to say:

"Śaṅkara, it appears that you have achieved what you always wanted." Her beloved son responded:

"*Ambā*, still there is so much to be done. But yes, I do have had glimpses of my *real being*!" Āryāmba smiled and said:

"What do I understand about what needs to be done or about your *real being* as you say! I have very little time left. Can you give me something before I depart from this world?"

Spontaneously, Śaṅkara recited a verse, whispering into her right ear:

"What empowers you to perceive, the Sun during the day, lamp during the night? With what do you experience the world when there is no light? And by whose power do you behold the mind and intellect, with your eyes closed? Everywhere and every when, it is the Supreme Light of 'I-Am' that lights up this Existence."[69]

The enlightened son's being was transferred into that of the old mother through the verse. It was as though her inner being responded to his affectionate call. Her face lit up in the joy of the glimpse. She smiled and said, and this time there was a strange power in her voice, as though it was her last command to her dear son:

"Your presence and your voice have given me enlightenment. Since my very birth, I have been a devotee of Kṛṣṇa. Let me remember Kṛṣṇa—our *Kuladevatā* in my last moments on this earth."

With his eyes closed, his right hand holding his mother's hand, left palm on her forehead, Śaṅkara saw the lord in all splendour, the child who had given joy to all the people of Vrindavan; the youth who had given direction and support to Pāṇḍu Princes; the charioteer who gave that sermon on enlightened action on the battlefield of *Kurukṣetra* to Arjuna who had lost interest in all action; the complete man who had attained Godhood. Spontaneously, the precious verses on Kṛṣṇa poured out through Śaṅkara's bell-like voice. With same devotion she had felt while in the family temple dedicated to Kṛṣṇa she heard her son:

"Without meditating on Whom, men fall into the species of perpetually afraid deer without knowing Whom, fall into the

69. किं ज्योतिस्तव भानुमानहनि मे रात्रौ प्रदीपादिकम् स्यादेवं रविदीपदर्शन विधौ किं ज्योतिराख्याहि मे ।
चक्षुस्तस्य निमीलनादि समये किं धीर्धियो दर्शने किं तत्राहमतो भवान्परमकं ज्योतिस्तदस्मि प्रभो ॥ एक श्लोकी ॥

mire of fear of birth and death; without remembering Whom men become mere insects, may such compassionate Kṛṣṇa, Who is the Protector of this Existence, may He be seen by my eyes. Who destroys the fear from beings surrendering to Him, taking shelter under Him, Who eliminates ignorance, who is dark and handsome, companion of cowherds, and the friend of Arjuna may such compassionate Kṛṣṇa, the Protector of this Existence, be the object of my eyes."[70]

Her eyes distant, looking into infinity, Āryāmba became totally peaceful, body-mind-soul and took that leap into her being, to behold God-Truth-Bliss. She experienced her *Iṣṭa*—Śri Kṛṣṇa. Śaṅkara, who was with her being, felt the peace that he could almost touch that brought tears of joy in his eyes. He was indebted to her, who had carried him in her womb, brought him into this world, nurtured him; fed him and most of all, given him the freedom to opt what the destiny had chosen him to accomplish.

News of the death of Āryāmba, that Śaṅkarācārya was with his mother, and that he would be performing the last rites of his mother, spread in the village of Kālaḍi! The orthodoxy rushed to the house and started giving arguments for the prohibition of a *Sanyāsi* performing any household rituals including the last rites. Scholars that they were, they quoted scriptures. Śaṅkara was unperturbed, and after hearing the last of them, responded calmly:

"Learned elders, I am very much aware of the scriptural dictums. I would like to remind you that all rules and dictums *are for the people, but the people are not for the scriptures*. They are only guidelines for the society. But under exceptional circumstances they can be overlooked." Immediately there was commotion when one of them commented angrily:

"How can you who are supposed to be the flag bearer of our *Dharma* say something so irresponsible? If people start finding

---

70. विना यस्य ध्यानं वृजति पशुतां सूकरमुखां विना यस्य ज्ञानं जनिमृतिभयं याति जनता ।
विना यस्य स्मृत्या कृमिशतजनिं याति स विभुः शरण्यो लोकेशो मम भवतु कृष्णोऽक्षिविषयः ॥ 6 ॥
नरातङ्कोट्टङ्कः शरणशरणो भ्रान्तिहरणो घनश्यामो वामो वृजशिशुवयस्योऽर्जुनसखः ।
स्वयम्भूर्भतानां जनक उचिताचारसुखदः शरण्यो लोकेशो मम भवतु कृष्णोऽक्षिविषयः ॥ 7 ॥ कृष्णाष्टकम् ॥

convenient explanations for their shortcomings there will be no *Dharma*."

"You may be aware that it was because of my mother, that I am a *Sanyāsi.* In spite of the fact that I am her only son, she gave me permission to renounce the world. The only request she had made was that I would be by her side in her last moments on this earth, and that I should perform the last rites. I had given my word to her that it would be so. I feel sticking to one's word or in other words to truth comes under *Dharma*." Then looking at all those people, Śaṅkara said with serious determination, and there was a kind of finality in his voice:

"I can never be free from my mother's debt. This is the only thing she had asked from me. No matter what the scriptures say, or the society's dictum, I will perform my mother's last rites."

"In that case we cannot give you permission to use the *Smaśānam*—the burning ground for the purpose." So saying all of them left, without bothering to even think how and where he would offer her body to the fire. There was no disturbance whatsoever, when Śaṅkara stood up and planned his next course of action. The same determination which he had when he had chosen to renounce the world was seen on his brows!

Wearing white clothes usually worn by a son while performing the rites, Śaṅkara cut the plantain stalks and arranged them in a pyre, for there was no mango or any other fire-wood in the vicinity. He lifted dear mother's still body affectionately and carried her to the pyre. While walking he remembered *her carrying him with all care and love.* The same poignant emotion overpowered him. She had not only carried him outside, but within her womb, bearing all the discomfort for his sake. As she lay on the pyre peaceful in her eternal sleep, he had one last look at her gentle affectionate face. Creating fire with his Yogic power, he lit the pyre, offering her mortal remains to *Agni*—God of fire. As the wet stalks burnt without any resistance, five verses on mother came spontaneously from his being:

"The sorrow caused by the unbearable pain at the time of my birth, the spell of weakness due to distaste caused by me while I was in your womb, the misery you had put up with for one year with wet and dirty bed because of me, and most of all for the agony you bore while carrying me for ten months, is itself something which even the most exalted son cannot repay through any form of action. Oh Mother! Unto you my salutations!! When you fondled me as a child, these affectionate words came out of your mouth: 'you are a jewel, you are my eyes, O my dear one, my son, may you live long!' To that mouth I am now offering dry grains! At the time of delivery you had cried aloud in pain 'O Mother, O Father, O Lord Śiva, O Kṛṣṇa, O Goviṅda, O Hari, O Mukuṅda' O *Amba* I offer this obeisance to you."[71]

Śaṅkara was overwhelmed by bliss as the tears flowed freely down his cheeks. At that very moment, he *knew* that his *Ambā* had merged with the infinite, transcending death in all its forms! He also realised that these few tear drops were the only means to express his gratefulness to the Existence that had brought them together in this life, and to his *Amba* who had brought *him* into existence!

Padmapāda started realising the truth behind his master's advice. The continuous *Japa* of the name of his *Iṣṭa* he started *seeing* the form of Nṛsiṁha initially in the mind, with his eyes closed, but gradually even with open eyes. For Padmapāda, every form was *His*, and every name was *His*. Every place including the pathway to the place started vibrating with *His* holiness. This was what his *Guru* had told them all along, that holiness and pilgrimage was *inside* but we can take the help of external places. What really happens is, that we give more prominence to the place, the temple, or the nature around and get so much *involved* with them that we forget the real purpose of pilgrimage.

After visiting many holy places, Padmapāda reached his own home town, on his way to Rāmeśwaram. All his friends and relatives were overjoyed to see him after many years. They recalled the time he had spent with them. Amidst all this

71. One of the rituals before lighting the funeral pyre is to offer grains into the mouth of the dead. This collection of five verses came to be known as *Mātṛpañcakam*.

excitement however, Sanandana as they had known him, was calm and detached. His friends observed that perhaps he was not really happy to be back or perhaps he had changed! Sanandana said:

"I am happy to be amidst you all. But there are a few things weighing upon my mind which may be the reason that I look disinterested. I have been trying to write a *Vārtikam* on my Master's commentary on the *Brahmasūtras*. I have written only five chapters dealing with the first four *Sūtras*." His uncle who too was a scholar of repute was interested:

"Sanandana, can I have a look at it?" The nephew gladly showed it. The uncle was extremely happy to note the scholarship of his nephew, but it was against the doctrines he had stood by so far. The way Sanandana had refuted the doctrines of other schools with powerful and unanswerable arguments that caused concern in his mind. He found that the teachings of Prabhākara, of which he was a follower, were especially refuted. Though overcome by sectarian jealousy at these criticisms, he professed great appreciation for the work. The nephew who was proceeding to Rāmeśwaram, gave the work to his uncle for safe keeping, and left his home town.

As he reached Rāmeśwaram, he was overwhelmed by the grand temple. Its lengthy corridors, the immense size of the *Gopurams*, and the spiritual vibrations enveloping all around, fascinated him. As he approached the sanctum, and beheld the symbolic image of *Rāmeśwara*—the Lord of Rāma, in that instant he realised his own puniness compared to the temple, the smallness of the temple itself in front of the ocean, and of the earth in comparison to the universe! It was then he felt himself free of this comparison and of the *otherness* which is the cause for all the comparative misery! He sat leaning against the grand sculpted pillar in sheer wonder. It was sometime till he felt a small pat on his shoulder, when he beheld a gentle face of an aged priest, who was saying something:

"Are you feeling well?" Padmapāda heard himself respond:

"I never felt so well in all my life!" so saying he touched the feet of the priest. The priest blessed him and asked him to accompany him *into* the sanctum, as they entered they heard an uninterrupted sound of *Praṇava*. It was a sign, that Padmapāda had completed his pilgrimage. Falling prostrate in front of the Idol in gratefulness, he slowly got up, only to see the smiling face of his Master Śaṅkara Bhagavadpāda in it! He said to himself:

"Yes! I had to go through all the effort to see you *Bhagawan*!"

On his way, back, Padmapāda returned to his home town, only to find that his uncle's house along with his work *Pañcapādika* was gutted in the fire. He was told by one of his friends that the house was set ablaze on purpose so that even the house where the book on *alien* thought was kept, was destroyed! But the spiritual experience at Rāmeśwaram was so grand that everything else appeared petty and inconsequential. His uncle was full of remorseful excuses, but Padmapāda asked him not to feel guilty, for he knew that he could reproduce it by the grace of his *Guru*. He was now eager to join his Master, who had appeared in his dream that morning instructing him to proceed to Mahāsurapura.[72]

In a way both master and his beloved disciple had completed their pilgrimage which had opened up their hearts. To Śaṅkara Bhagavadpāda, the pilgrimage to Kālaḍi—the place which had been chosen for his advent, and more importantly to the place which had given him an cpportunity to feel and be the mother's heart which could envelope the whole universe with love; to Padmapāda, the pilgrimage of holy places that had culminated in Rāmeśwaram which had graced him with the opportunity to have a glimpse into the heart of existence—the heart of his *Guru*!

❐

72. Most probably the present *Mysore*.

Intellect and Intuition (Head)

Campaign of No-Other (Map)

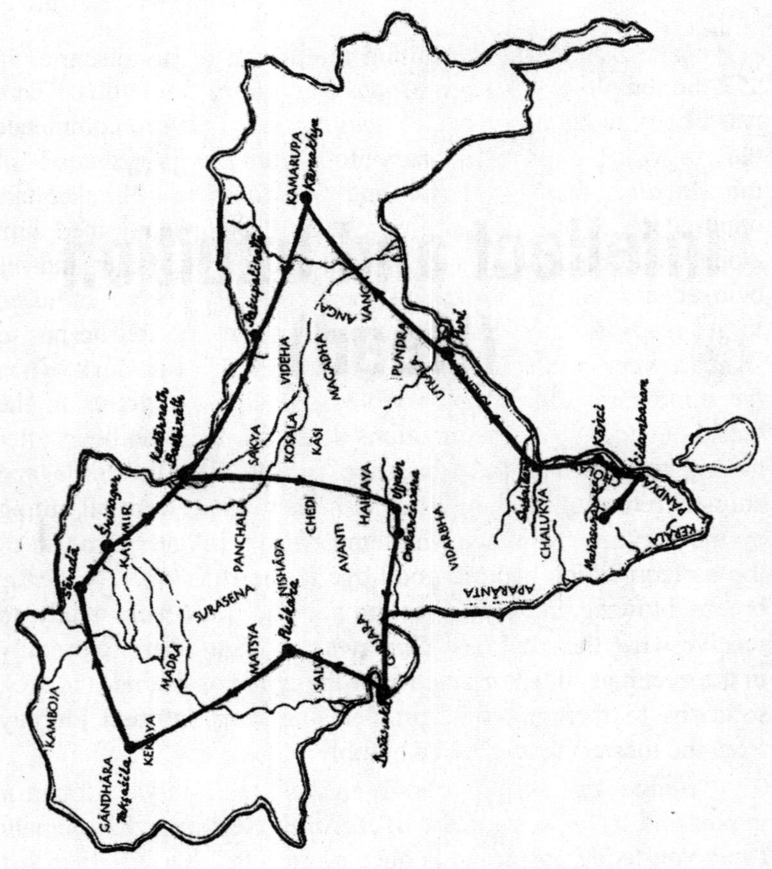

13
Viveka and Vairāgya

Ācārya Śaṅkara was awaiting the arrival of his disciples in the temple of Viṣṇu, at *Mahāsurapura,* in Karnataka. There was clarity in his mind, determination in his being to commence the *Digvijaya*—his missionary tour for the propagation of the *Advaita*, and to clarify and convince the philosophers opposed to it, in accepting it. When Padmapāda joined him along with others, there was blissful reunion of Master and his beloved disciples. Even by his mere look, they were enthused to get ready for the challenge ahead. And yet he felt he has to share a very valuable *Vidyā*, with them. It was dusk when the mind turns inwards, having completed its ventures in the world outside, when the emotions settle down in the heart after having terminating the exhaustive travels, like the birds and animals returning to the nests and homes. They were all sitting on the western corridor of the temple lit by the amber blush of the horizon which had bid good bye to the sun. With the gentle breeze blowing in their direction the disciples were ready to receive what their beloved *Guru* was about to share. Normally in the evenings, it was a practice of the group of disciples to seek solutions to their practical problems in their spiritual journey from the master. Toṭaka asked humbly:

"*Bhagawan*, during your absence all these days, I found it impossible to *be* in the state of *Advaita*. But from the moment I met you today, my being is once again tuned into *IT*! Is it that as your disciple I have the experience only in your presence?" *Ācārya* smiled and looked into the eyes of each disciple by turns.

Then he spoke, his voice gentle and sweet, enveloping their being.

"In these past few years that we have been together, we have learnt and almost mastered the art of non-attached action, the art of sublimating our emotions and directing that very energy towards the resurgence of our grand culture, and of course you have also learnt the technique of controlling the mind. During this journey, you have been having glimpses of Reality, mostly on your own, and sometimes when we are together. First of all, I would like you to remember, that these glimpses were not *solely because of the company*. If you try to recall, you will find that whenever you had any glimpse, you were in a highly sensitive and receptive mood that has nothing to do with the external factors. Toṭaka, each one of us, in fact every being, is eligible to *be* in *Advaita.* But somehow we have *forgotten* as we are *involved* in the mire of *Sthūla*—the gross, and are neglecting *Sūkṣma*—the subtle."

As he uttered these words, the disciples realised that all the other sounds had totally merged into silence, full and peaceful. Their eyes closed in reverence to something lofty, which they could feel but could not express. Again the voice of their master slowly appeared, not unlike a powerful light when one is groping one's way in darkness.

"Before we start our final phase of work—by final I do not in any way mean the last, but the task which we will venture into as a team, I would like to share a *Vidyā*. Let me start by asking you: What is the most daunting task for a seeker?" Everyone remained quiet as they knew it was not a question but a statement!

"It is the process of quietening the *Ahamkāra*. And *Ahamkāra* has three different facets. The first is 'I-act'; the second is 'I-experience' and the third, 'I-know'. All of us are endowed with three faculties: Hands or action, Heart or feelings and emotions and Head, reason and analysis. All of us are very much aware of these and use them when necessary."

What they were listening, was not new to them. But knowing their *Guru* to be deliberate in using words, they awaited the purpose of this repetition, Padmapāda was more eager than the rest. *Ācārya* continued looking at him:

"When we know that something is good or bad, there is this *Icchā*—desire to seek the good, and avoid the bad. The effort for seeking or avoiding depends on the *Icchā*. All of you know that all our effort and activity is towards the acquisition of what we understand to be good *from our point of view*. There is honesty and sincerity in our effort *only when there is desire*. But if we do not know the aim of our effort, then there can be not *Icchā*, without it we possibly cannot act! All of us as a team know the aim of all our effort to be the unification of all the diverse schools of thought *without damaging their diversity*. It is for this reason that we have to understand the *unity amidst the apparent diversity* among them. My dear ones, you have to be the unifying thread of diverse gems of our culture."

Ācārya realised as he looked into the eyes of his beloved disciples, that they were getting ready to receive what he had to share. Each one of them had been a sincere and committed soldier embarking on the campaign of uniting all the forces of our culture. However, as each one of them was unique, each had a unique perspective. Though all the disciples were united by *the purpose*, they had to understand what the *Ācārya* had to share at their level. That was the reason he was going to speak on *Śraddhā* and *Viveka*. There was that motherly affection when he continued speaking:

"Human life is governed by *Śraddhā* and *Viveka*. *Śraddhā* is faith, belief or trust, and *Viveka* is discrimination.[73] Those who have neither *Śraddhā* nor *Viveka* experience downfall in their life. But the majority is endowed with *Śraddhā*. Their life is dependent on it even for small little things. This faith is on the words of others—elders, teachers, scriptures and the enlightened persons. *Śraddhā* in other words, is dependent on others' *Viveka*. The common people live on this level, as they never feel the necessity of analysis or discrimination. Gradually,

73. श्रुत् इति सत्यनामम् आस्तिकतायाः अभिधानम् । "*Śrut is synonymous* with *Śraddhā*—faith, belief, and trust".

विचिर्पृथग्भावे विवेचनम् विवेकः। "Separation or analysis is *Viveka*."

as one progresses one starts observing life closely and learns to evaluate it through analysis. For example, we *know* something or someone to be good or bad. This evokes *Icchā*– a desire to get attracted to good and to avoid the bad. A person at this level has both *Śraddhā* in the words of teachers or the scriptures and also a little *Viveka*. And then there is pure *Viveka* when there need not be any *Śraddhā*."

Śaṅkara Bhagavadpāda allowed these words to sink in by remaining silent. The disciples became aware that *Ācārya* was preparing them for a great task that lay before them. Heart of heart they thanked the providence for choosing *them* to be His companions, to become instruments of change. Though they had heard these before, the truths this time appeared to give them new insights. Sureśwara felt that in a seeker's life this repetition of truths is mandatory for implementing them. He remembered his own life before accepting the *Sanyāsa*. He had become so vain that he had stopped learning! During this retrospection, he realised that Truth was seen from different perspectives, and solely depended upon the level one is in. As and when one broadens one's vision, one begins to accept and appreciate all views. So the task before each one of the disciples to accept other disciples *totally* as they are and then go into the society with love and understanding, to lift the society by showing it the broad perspective. He was brought out of his reverie by his master's compelling voice:

"Whenever we perform any action, there has to be the *Saṁkalpa*—intention behind it. If it is pure, the action is pure and pure action purifies the mind. When one is totally involved with the action and remembers neither the past nor the future, but has only the present action, then that action is pure. Naturally, *Vāsanās*—which are nothing but the past impressions and dreams of future—do not have any place during pure action. It is during such moments, when the mind is *Śuddha*—still and pure, one can get glimpses into Truth. Remember always, that 'action is only meant for the *purification of Cittam and not for the realisation of Truth*'."[74]

74. चित्तस्य शुद्धये कर्म न तु वस्तूपलब्धये ।

"*Bhagawan*, will you please explain it once again?" It was Toṭaka. *Ācārya* responded with a smile.

"*Cittam* is that knowledge—the store of information that becomes *Saṁskāra*—deep impression which influences any future action manifesting through body, senses, mind, intellect, emotions and ego. The word *Vastu* is actually *Swarūpajñānam*—awareness, which *knows* the *activity* of body, senses, mind, intellect, emotions and ego. *Swarūpajñānam is mandatory for any experience or knowledge. Swarūpajñānam* is never influenced by *Saṁskāra*, and is aware of the rising, being and settling of *Saṁskāra*. But *Swarūpajñānam* is not possible if one is under the influence of the external." He could see that it was still not clear to some.

"This knowledge is not at all new, but it is our heritage we have received through our scriptures. In future, the essence of this knowledge will travel everywhere to restore the sanity of humanity! '*I am a human being*' is becoming such a rare statement because we are being overpowered by our *individuality*. Remember the most important fact, *all the differences, arguments, confusion, wars and misery are based on individual differences that are based on sex, community, caste, religion, and nation.* Unless this *Paricchinnatā*—differentiation is rooted out, the society cannot be in harmony and of course, happy!"

A soft breeze carried the mild fragrance of night blooming flowers; a hoot of an owl could be heard, perhaps calling out for its companion. Bhagavadpāda continued, without disturbing mood that got created in the mind of disciples by the flower and birds:

"The fragrance of the flowers and the hoot of the owl we just heard, are unconnected and are apparently different. But *who* experienced them both?"

"It was the mind that received these impressions, which is one."

"And who *recognised* them?" Śaṅkara asked with a smile.

"It was *Buddhi*!" Padmapāda replied.

"How did the *Buddhi* recognise them?"

"It was through stored memory of the past." It was Sureśwara, this time.

"And who is the master of all these faculties?" Śaṅkara asked his disciples.

"It is *Ahamkāra*—ego!" Everyone responded.

The deliberate pause forced each one of them to contemplate and examine the fact heard by them. They realised that the master was slowly guiding them into a great insight which would help them the understand themselves which alone could help them understand the world around. Sensing this, the *Ācārya* smiled and said:

"Yes, understanding starts from self and then the *other,*" stressing the last word.

"The *Paricchinnatā*—differentiation can be rooted out only through *Viveka*—analysis. It is a common experience that most of us do listen to the truths from the enlightened or from the study of scriptures, but the conviction is so fragile that it is forgotten or may be it remains only at the level of discussion. We say that the *Ātman* is eternal, is deathless, it transcends time and so on. But they are all empty words, and are not our experiences. For most, *even Ātman is just another word*! Always remember that '*the web of words is a deep forest that causes aimless wandering for the mind*'.[75] So, it is very important that we learn the art of *Vicāra* to build a strong conviction. Now let me ask you a basic question: what is it that *distracts* us from the Truth?" Hastāmalaka replied quietly:

"It is our stubborn conviction that happiness or misery depends *solely* on the external gross world."

With a lot of appreciation in his eyes, *Ācārya* continued:

"This *stubborn* conviction—as Hastāmalaka pointed out, is the result of the process which you all explained earlier. The senses receive something; the mind *follows* them, and the intellect understands it as desirable or undesirable. This whole approach itself is the source of distraction. Don't you remember

75. शब्दजालं महारण्यं चित्तभ्रमणकारणम् ॥ विवेकचूडामणि 60 ॥

that verse from the *Śrīmadbhagavadgītā*?" He looked at Padmapāda, who responded:

"As the wind carries away a barge upon waters, even so the wandering senses, take away the mind which follows them."[76]

"The mind thus becomes a helpless slave of the senses. 'The deer is always fascinated by melodious sound and the hunter sings to charm the deer. The elephants, especially in the mating season, become extremely attached to the sense of touch, and walking without caution, they fall into the pits dug out specially for them. Moth is enchanted by the form and gets attracted to the brilliance of the flame, and it flutters towards its death. The fish perpetually hungry, in its gluttony swallows the bait. The poor honey bee, gets attracted by the fragrant smell of flowers, pursues its industrious vocation of collecting honey from the flowers for hoarding in its hive until at last, heartless man sets fire to the hive in order to loot the wealth of honey of the bee. What then is the condition of man who is attracted to all these senses?'[77] This principally is the cause for the stubborn conviction in the gross world, as we can *perceive* it through senses, and men of the world usually get swayed off their feet."

The disciples were awestruck at their Master's keen observation of nature! They were convinced that through his love and guidance he would transform them from seekers to his Self-realised companions. It made them think that though they had overcome the sway of senses to a great extent their mind still entertained the conviction that happiness and misery are dependent on the external circumstances at least to a small extent. As if reading their mind *Ācārya* continued:

"All of you have been involved in some spiritual practices according to your nature. You all feel—and to a very great extent you are right—that the practice will bear a fruit you covet, may be in the sublimation of senses or quietening of mind or pacification of emotions. But try to ask yourself as a third

---

76. इन्द्रियाणां हि चरतां यन्मनोऽनुविधीयते । तदस्य हरति प्रज्ञां वायुर्नावमिवाम्भसि ॥ श्रीमद्भगवद्गीता 2:67 ॥
77. शब्दादिभिः पञ्चभिरेव पञ्च पञ्चत्वतापुः स्वगुणेन बद्धाः ।कुरङ्गमातङ्गपतङ्गमीनभृङ्गा नरः पञ्चभिरञ्चितः किम् ॥ विवेकचूडामणि 76 ॥

person: '*what is the belief behind the practice*?' You will find that *by doing something, we achieve something.* We will go into this a little later.

"The ignorant thinks that he is the body. A man of bookish knowledge considers himself to be a combination of body and *Jīva*—soul. But a realised sage with his *Viveka* and *Vijñāna*—experiential wisdom, knows that he is *Brahman* and looks upon the eternal *Ātman* as his self.[78]

"It is *Dehātmabhāva*—the stubborn conviction that one is the body, that creates this basic illusion and dependency on the senses and the mind that are meant to help us perceive the gross world, *influence* us and take us under their sway and in a way *we become their instruments, nay even slaves*! As human beings we have been endowed with a unique gift: that is, the consciousness of the external world *as well as* the internal, through the *Sphandana*—the vibration of *Aham, Aham*—'I'. All other beings have only the awareness of the external and not the internal. As and when one tries to become more and more aware of *Aham* the grip over the external *loosens*. Remember, the world never binds you, *but your interest in the external does*; the sense organs or their objects never ensnare you, but *your indulgence does*."

Padmapāda wanted to say something, noticing this *Ācārya* looked at him encouragingly:

"*Bhagawan*, there are a few verses in the *Śrīmadbhagavadgītā* which describe this situation. Arjuna enquires from the Lord as to what impels man to commit sins as if under a compelling force. The Lords replies: 'It is desire, it is anger, begotten of the element of *Rajas*, insatiable and grossly wicked; know this to be the enemy in this case. As flame is enveloped by smoke, mirror by dust, and embryo by the amnion, knowledge is enveloped by desire. So Arjuna, knowledge is covered by this eternal enemy of the wise, the insatiable fire in the form of desire. The senses, mind and the intellect are said to be its origins; enveloping knowledge through these,

78. देहोऽहमित्येव जडस्य बुद्धिर्देहे च जीवे विदुषस्त्वहंधीः ।विवेकविज्ञानवतो महात्मनो ब्रह्माहमित्येव मतिः सदात्मनि ॥ विवेकचूडामणि 160 ॥

desire deludes the embodied soul. Therefore Arjuna, control the senses first and kill this wicked desire that obscures *Jñāna* and *Vijñāna*.'[79] *Bhagawan*, how do we control the senses, so as to overcome their sway over us? Normally, we find it very difficult to control either the senses or the mind which are by nature restless."

Bhagavadpāda was now seeing that the seeds he had sown in the fertile minds of his disciples were not only sprouting but they were showing the signs of growing into mighty trees that would shelter many a pilgrim of the soul. *Ācārya* responded with a smile:

"In my opinion *Śrīmadbhagavadgītā*, is one of the greatest *Śāstras*, which is complete in itself! The *Ślokas* are from the chapter on *Karma Yoga*—The Yoga of action. The very next *Śloka* gives a grand technique. 'The senses are subtler than the body; but subtler than senses is the mind. Subtler than the mind is the intellect; and what is greater than the intellect is He—the Self.'[80] Why does the Lord give the hierarchy of human faculties at this point? We are aware that it is difficult to control a faculty from its own level. But if we can shift to the subtler level, it becomes possible. Let us experiment. Close your eyes."

There was a long silent pause. Since their eyes were closed, the disciples were all ears only to their master's voice. He started instructing them:

"Let us now listen to the sounds. Before we do that, *remember not to judge any sound as pleasant or unpleasant; good or bad. Just listen to it, and pass on to the next sound.* Start from the farthest sound you can hear, and then gradually come nearer."

They heard distant sounds of birds, breeze rustling through the leaves of trees, the closing gong of the bell in the temple, a cricket vibrating its wings.... To their pleasant surprise, they

---

79. काम एष क्रोध एष रजोगुणसमुद्भवः । महाशनो महापाप्मा विद्ध्येनामिह वैरिणम् ॥ 3:37 ॥
धूमेनाव्रियते वह्निर्यथाऽऽदर्शो मलेन च । यथोल्बेनावृतो गर्भस्तथा तेनेदमावृतम् ॥ 3:38 ॥
आवृतं ज्ञानमेतेन ज्ञानिनो नित्यवैरिणा । कामरूपेण कौन्तेय दुष्पूरेणानलेन च ॥ 3:39 ॥
इन्द्रियाणि मनो बुद्धिरस्याधिष्ठानमुच्यते । एतैर्विमोहयत्येष ज्ञानमावृत्य देहिनम् ॥ 3:40 ॥
तस्मात्त्वमिन्द्रियाण्यादौ नियम्य भरतर्षभ । पाप्मानं प्रजहि ह्येनं ज्ञानविज्ञाननाशनम् ॥ श्रीमद्भगवद्गीता 3:41 ॥

80. इन्द्रियाणि पराण्याहुरिन्द्रियेभ्यः परं मनः । मनसस्तु परा बुद्धिर्यो बुद्धेः परतस्तु सः ॥ श्रीमद्भगवद्गीता 3:42 ॥

discovered that the sounds which could disturb them under normal circumstances were *just sounds, without any quality of good and bad, etc.* For a long time the master and the disciples remained absorbed, enjoying the silence and peace. The voice of *Ācārya* rose from silence without disturbing the mood; the disciples opened their eyes to behold their master whose blissful face was illuminated by the moon beams.

"What happened? All you did was to resolve *not to judge*. This resolution came from your *Buddhi*. As you all are aware, *Manas* just gathers the information gives by the sense objects—in this case it was ear, and passes on to *Buddhi*, which compares with the past information and *judges*. You took this decision *not to*, from *Buddhi*, which is subtler and it did not make any impression on you! You neither stopped hearing, nor indulged in the sound but were just *Sākṣi—witness*." Looking at each one of his disciples Śaṅkara Bhagavadpāda told them affectionately.

"You did not have to renounce the sense objects, nor did you put more effort, and just by this decision on a subtler level the *importance you used to give to some particular sounds as good or bad, dropped on its own*! This is called *Vairāgya*—dispassion or disinterest towards the objects of senses. For some of you it may be quite simple to control your senses, just by an auto suggestion. But when you are working for the masses, you will be required to teach them step by step methods."

"*Bhagawan*, what happens when we stop judging?" It was one of the disciples who joined the *Saṅgha* recently. *Ācārya* responded:

"Whenever the senses come in contact with their respective objects, the sensation is received by *Manas*. Most of the sensations are ignored by it, again based on *Saṁskāras*—the past choices made by the *Buddhi* which again are based on the *Rāga* and *Dweśa*, and some are passed on. The decision *not to judge* helps us to be a *Sākṣi*—non-involved witness, keeping both *Rāga* and *Dweśa* under control." There was a full pause before *Ācārya* continued.

"When a person observes the life to be repetitive as well as mechanical, he starts asking some basic questions like 'what is it that my heart seeks?; what is eternal amidst the temporal?; what is the root cause of misery?' He notices that though he achieves what he had desired, the happiness is only temporary, because the thing achieved itself is impermanent. Such a person embarks on this divine journey as he seeks answers to them, through either *Śāstras* or the enlightened persons. The *Satsaṅga* initiates a disinterest in the gross and he starts putting the first steps in the direction. After the purification of his mind either through actions that are free from indulgence or involvement[81] or spiritual practices like *Prāṇāyāma*, *Pratyāhāra* and *Dhāraṇā*, he starts getting the taste of *Vairāgya*. The real *Vairāgya* is when one *chooses a destination*, and all the other gross desires of body, senses and ambitions of mind dwindle into insignificance. The process of such *choosing* is *Viveka* and the resultant sense of direction is *Vairāgya*."

All of them without exception had learnt that *Vairāgya* was not strenuous as it is made out to be, but is an attitude or resolution taken by a seeker *not to give importance to things*; an awareness of the facets of mind, and to use them and *not to be influenced by them*, is *Viveka*!

"You can spend some time to practise what we tried today, before you retire for the night. Tomorrow we will take up other aspects." *Ācārya* concluded.

The night had set in, the world outside had gone into the lap of slumber. From the hill they could visualise the world they were called upon by *Śruti Bhagavati* to awaken. But for that they had to be awakened. Each one of them felt responsible to do the bidding of their master. Though they had limited time, they were certain that he would awaken them. A reassuring thought crossed their mind: why should they worry when He was with them and that too under the benign canopy of Mother's grace?

Padmapāda and Sureśwara chose secluded corners in the corridors of the temple to settle down for the night—not for retiring, but to contemplate on what they had heard from their beloved master, while the other two of the inner circle,

81. Indulgence is at the level of body and senses, while involvement is at the level of mind.

Hastāmalaka and Toṭaka remained with *Ācārya*, to serve him if need be. As they lay down nearby so that they could rush at his beck or call, they realised that never had he called them for any service, and it was always the *Ācārya* who would awaken them by his movements in the early mornings! And yet they knew that being near to their master had always helped them in their growth!

Padmapāda recollected the words of his master that we are under the *illusion* that *by doing something we achieve something*. He asked himself as to how could that be an illusion? At the same time *Ācārya* had told them that this will be taken up for discussion later. He tried to retrospect his own life. His coming to the master, and his guidance in achieving anything, be it the *Japa* or the *Upāsanā* on his *Iṣṭa* he had *done something*! How could any effort be *an illusion*? However, suddenly as the word *Śraddhā* surfaced, his mind became silent, and he was rid of all the questions as well as their answers. It dawned on him as a flash of lightning, that but for his implicit *Śraddhā*, he had not *done anything* and yet it was there all the time. And his silent the mind turned inward, away from the external, away from all movement, entering the still, deep subjectivity he became what he had always been, a witness; witness to the activity called *Buddhi*, *Manas*, *senses*, and *body*.

Sureśwara had taken an entirely different line of thought for his contemplation. He tried to recollect the experience when he wrote *Naiṣkarmya-Siddhi*, that whatever the action, it does not have any effect on the Self—eternal and all encompassing. Since he had been obsessed with actions before meeting the master, he had felt so relieved and had felt grateful. It had remained for some time but had gradually diluted into a vague memory in some corner of the mind! He contemplated that at the root of any action, be it gross activity, or feeling or even knowing is the *Aham—Aham Kartā* (I am a doer), *Aham Bhoktā* (I am an experiencer) or *Aham Jñātā* (I am a knower). And suddenly, the *Sphandana* of *Aham*...*Aham*...started as a monotone to the music of intellect, mind, senses and body. He felt expansive, blissful and totally unattached. Both of them had arrived at the same destination on their own.

Hastāmalaka had just *remembered* his *real* nature and without any effort whatsoever and was silent…still. But in that silent stillness he could feel the presence of his master. Toṭaka had not done anything but remained alert for the master's call, as he always did, keeping the *Ācārya* foremost in his being. He had the same alertness as the three of his brother disciples! Now what was it that made all the four of them, to be in such a state of alertness, only Śaṅkara Bhagavadpāda could tell!

❑

14
Antarmukhatā— The Inner Gaze

The resonant gong of the temple bell announced the *Brahma Muhūrta*—the hour of *Brahman*, considered as the most auspicious by the seekers. The disciples and their master were ready to start on an inner journey. Bhagavadpāda sat facing south and his beloved companions sat facing east. Everything was still, as if the world had stopped. With their eyes closed the disciples were listening intently to their master. Along with the voice of *Ācārya*, they were able to feel the inner voice, silently humming—*Aham*...*Aham*...*Aham*...I...I...I. He was guiding them, holding the hand of each individual with his voice full of concern and love, helping them through the mire of the gross, and leading them into the subjective world. After the passage of some time, they started becoming conscious of the gross. It was Sureśwara who initiated a discussion.

"*Bhagawan*, while writing *Naiṣkarmya-Siddhi*, I had these glimpses. But with passage of time as brother Toṭaka had observed, it just got dissolved. What remained was only an intellectual understanding. Just a while back, your voice guided us through and my brothers will agree that all of us had a glimpse. Somehow I feel your presence has a lot to contribute for our state. Can you please clarify this further?" *Ācārya* smiled and with all patience replied:

"That is what I am trying to convince you! Your conviction that the external factors have effect on your life is an illusion which most of us have created. You have to overcome this stubborn view, because you are not going to be seekers but teachers! For seekers it is enough to have glimpses and to get established in truth, but not for teachers."

As Śaṅkara Bhagavadpāda got up from his seat, all of them joined him. Some of them were a little apprehensive when their master gave them the responsibility of teaching the society. *Ācārya* smiled and reassured them:

"We all are the chosen ones, not by any individual but by our eternal culture, and thus the fortunate few. Mother *Śruti* will guide us at every step of the way. All that is required by us is to have *Śraddhā* and to gratefully accept it by becoming the willing instruments in her hands! After worshipping all pervading *Viṣṇu* the guardian deity of this place we shall meet here."

"We commenced our march towards self-development with a *Saṁkalpa*—a strong resolution either due to an understanding that the human life has a greater purpose than mere survival; or inspiration dawned on you when you met someone or came across some revealed truth from scriptures. Many take up this journey with all enthusiasm but after travelling a distance, give it up due to external difficulties, like objection of relations, etc., or more importantly, due to internal problems like unsteady mind, unclear intellect and doubt. It is due to the divine grace that we all are together and are slowly inching towards our destination. As we discussed earlier, our number is limited while the task before us is great and need more persons to fulfill the task. We have the responsibility of training such persons who will join us in our campaign."

The group had re-assembled on the western temple corridor. The granite floor, a gentle breeze carrying the fragrance of flowers from the temple garden created a receptive milieu in their minds. The worship performed by Śaṅkara Bhagavadpāda with his graceful gestures and resonant melodious voice chanting the appropriate *Mantras* had attracted the attention of the temple officials. At the behest of the Chief Priest, one of them had gone to the palace to inform the king of a young *Sanyāsin* with an entourage of disciples, some of whom were older than him. Pious and deeply spiritual that he was, he had rushed to the temple in ordinary clothes so that he could freely meet the monk and perhaps gain something for his own life's journey! He too sat in the last row, incognito and humble like any other man of the society!

"*Sanyāsins* are necessarily limited in any society, as they have to burn the bridges of relationships to renounce the world. As *Sanyāsins* we have to keep a respectable distance from society. The need of the hour is to inspire the enlightened citizens and to help them in contributing for the cause of rejuvenation of our great culture. They will remain *within the society* to lead by example. The common mass of people will see that even by leading simple day-to-day life they can achieve peace and harmony."

Ācārya looked around and saw a few new faces amidst the listeners. Many of them were the priests who had insisted that he should perform the worship of the Mother. There was one face, handsome with a determined chin and gentle eyes which met his and smiled at him. He too responded in kind.

"As you are aware, life as such is a combination by *Karma*—action or hands, *Bhāvanā*—emotion or heart, and *Buddhi* or head. Since we cannot do without action, and are influenced by emotions, we direct them for the purification of mind. That is what Lord Kṛṣṇa hints through the *Śrīmadbhagavadgītā*." Seeing wrinkles of restlessness on the new face, *Ācārya* said:

"Maharaja, you want to say something?" The person to whom he addressed appeared surprised, as he had taken all the care to hide his identity! Approaching he prostrated. After sitting, he said with obvious embarrassment:

"*Bhagawan*, I have not come here as a king, but as a seeker. I am Kṛṣṇarāya, and cannot say that I have understood *Śrīmadbhagavadgītā* nor do I claim to be any scholar. But does not a person find fulfillment through any one of the *Yogas*—*Karma*, *Dhyāna*, *Bhakti* or *Jñāna*?" *Ācārya* responded after a pause:

"Yes, one can use any of the methods or even their combination for self-realisation. Those men in the society, shouldering the responsibility of family and the society at large definitely get glimpses with perseverance, enough to lead them to enlightenment.

"Some of my companions had raised a doubt that though they had glimpses of truth, they remained as glimpses, which wear off with time, when mind goes after the gross as usual! Since they feel responsible for giving a direction to the society and for them, they are convinced that such glimpses are only small beginnings for a greater journey. They have to lead exemplary lives, not only to set high ideals and values, but never to lose the purpose of their chosen life or their real identity."

Everyone in the audience, especially the disciples became more alert to receive the gems the master had to share with them. Kṛṣṇarāya was full of awe and admiration for this group of *Sanyāsins* who had come to his small kingdom to stay. He indeed felt fortunate.

"What is *Adhyātma*—spirituality? It is a search for the eternal *behind* the temporal. Whatever we see or feel by our body, senses and *Manas* is temporary, subject to constant change. Then why is our *conviction* in the world is so stubborn? Because we can perceive it and when we come in its contact, there is pleasure or pain, happiness or misery depending on our *Saṁskāra*. So we are constantly trying to go after the pleasure and also try to avoid pain. But in our pursuit of happiness all we get is fleeting happiness. We seek permanent happiness *within* the temporary changing world; we seek permanent relationships in the changing society. This happens to be the helplessness of human beings. Since we are not aware of any other things but the gross world perceivable to senses and mind, we try to *change the objects rather than our* perspective! Consequently, we are in total despair. But this despair alone, helps us ask the question, 'amidst all this temporal, is there *anything that transcends the change; is there an Eternal Principle*?"

"Lord Kṛṣṇa gives a beautiful hint for *Dhyāna*. 'O son of Kunti, the contacts between senses and their objects, which give rise to the feelings of heat and cold, pleasure and pain, are transitory and fleeting; therefore, Arjuna, *Tāṁ titikṣaswa*—tolerate them. That man is wise, for whom pain and pleasure are alike—as they all pass of with time, and who is not tormented by these contacts becomes eligible for immortality.'[82] In these verses, the Lord is talking about an *entity that perceives the world*. The search for this entity is *Adhyātma*."

"Many of us know the fact of impermanence of objects as well as the experience, but only intellectually. If fact, the most surprising thing about human behaviour is that we even *see* the people dying in front of us, but we act *as if* we are eternal! Why is that so?" It was the head priest this time. *Ācārya* closed his eyes for a moment as if looking within for an answer.

"That is because of the nature of our senses and *Manas*—that function of the mind which gathers external information through senses. A wonderful *Maṅtra* in *Kaṭhopaniṣad*, and perhaps the only *Maṅtra*, describes this: 'The Reality has endowed the windows of senses to open only on the outside, due to which we can perceive only the outside and not the inner Self; whoever having aspired for immortality, that brave and patient man turned his senses *inward* to behold the Self within.[83]' In one stroke, it not only explains the human frailty of the inability to look within, and its total dependence on the outside; and also defines *Adhyātma* as the *Inner Gaze*." There was a lingering smile on the benevolent face of Śaṅkarācārya. He continued after a pause.

"What does the *Maṅtra* mean by *Āvṛtta-Cakṣu—the eyes turned inward*? Here we should take the eyes as all the senses. But it has also declared that they can only *open on the outside*! This is one most wonderful method adopted by our *Ṛṣis* for describing a difficult concept: the method of paradoxes. At the beginning of the *Maṅtra* it describes the nature of senses to be windows that open only on the outside, in the very next line it

---

82. मात्रास्पर्शास्तु कौन्तेय शीतोष्णसुखदुःखदा । आगमापायिनोऽनित्यास्तांस्तितिक्षस्व भारत ॥ श्रीमद्भगवद्गीता 2:14 ॥
यं हि न व्यथयन्त्येते पुरुषं पुरुषर्षभ । समदुःखसुखं धीरं सोऽमृतत्त्वाय कल्पते ॥ श्रीमद्भगवद्गीता 2:15 ॥

83. पराञ्चि खानि व्यतृणत्स्वयम्भूस्तस्मात्पराङ्पश्यतिनान्तरात्मन् । कश्चिद्धीरः प्रत्यगात्मानमैक्षदावृत्तचक्षुरमृतत्वमिच्छन् ॥ कठोपनिषद् 2:1:1 ॥

mentions about a brave and patient man *turning his eyes inward*. How can that be possible? Though the senses can and do gather only the information from outside, it hints that for looking *within* you do not require the help of the senses. It is only your stubborn habit to depend on the senses for *everything*!

"The word *Dhīra* not only means a brave man but also a man of patience. He patiently curtails the activity of the senses, with the help of *Manas*." Seeing wrinkles on some brows, he continued:

"Senses are necessarily outgoing as they have developed over our long journey of evolution. The first and the foremost activity of life in particular and existence in general, is survival. There is a *Subhāśita*: 'food, sleep, fear and procreation are common amongst *all beings;* man alone is endowed with *Buddhi*—discrimination, without it man is an animal.'[84] *Buddhi* not only means the faculty of analysis and decisiveness, but the *capacity to turn the attention to both the outside as well as the inside.* We are aware of the world outside—of nature around, of the people and beings *outside us*. You are seeing me, of the persons sitting in this temple, of the birds or the breeze. Then there is the *inside world* consisting of your thoughts, of emotions, of the aspirations and dreams, you are also aware of that world for which we do not need the help of any senses. Shall we all conduct an experiment? We shall sit and be aware of the world around us. Try to use one sense at a time."

In the silence that followed, almost everyone was able to feel the nature more intensely than ever. For a change, none of them got disturbed by the noisy parrots sitting on a nearby tree; or a dog barking at another; or the smell of smoke emanating from the temple kitchen;...it was as though they were just sense objects coming in contact with their respective objects. The voice of *Ācārya* too was part of the nature around...non-disturbing.

"We shall now close our eyes and all the senses. You will discover that the thoughts surface and then fall back, almost like

84. आहारनिद्रा भयमैथुनञ्च सामान्यमेतत्पषुभिर्नराणाम् । बुद्धिर्हितिषामधिको विशेषो बुद्धिर्विहीनां पषुभिस्समानः ॥

the small wavelets on a river. Be attentive to your thoughts but at the same time, remember not to pay any special attention to any particular thought, if you do, you will flow and get involved." This time it was not all that easy, for before they became aware of any thought, their attention would go out and *seek* the objects of senses. Some of them did become aware of the thoughts but were carried away in the flow of connected thoughts and forgot to watch the thoughts! When they opened their eyes a little later one of the priests stood up and addressed the master:

"*Bhagawan*, I could not become aware of *any* thoughts, as the attention kept on listening to sounds and other sense objects. What should I do?" Bhagavadpāda responded:

"First of all let me assure you that this problem is common and almost everyone of us faces it. As we discussed earlier, when the senses and *Manas* are dominant they are active and strong, like the horses without any control. They act without any restraint or direction. It is like this. There is a car festival in this temple and thousands of people are moving about; added to this there is the noise of venders. Will you be able to listen to the person who is speaking in whispers and who perhaps is standing next to you? Because the gross sounds are dominant over the subtle voice of your neighbour! So the solution to this common obstacle to the *inner awareness* is to learn the art of quietening the senses and *Manas*, which demands courage and patience. Courage is needed for taking up the difficult task and patience, for not giving up the effort in spite of repeated failures. Tell me, how many of us have *never* fallen when we started to walk?"

"*Bhagawan*, none of us!" Almost everyone responded. *Ācārya* said affectionately.

"We are all children learning to walk within our own consciousness. Just as we never gave up in spite of falling repeatedly, we will learn to turn our gaze inwards, with patience!"

Sureśwara knew that if anyone could give real momentum to this great movement of rejuvenation of our culture it was his beloved *Guru*. As he gazed at that bright smiling face so much younger than him, he was overwhelmed by admiration, respect and affection for him. He realised the foolhardiness in his attempt to *defeat this great man who had changed his life permanently for the better*! Padmapāda, Śaṅkara's shadow got up and approached to whisper something in his ear. *Ācārya* smiled and said in good humour:

"My guardian tells me that it is time for my evening stroll!" They all laughed and stood up to make way for the master. Looking at the king *Ācārya* made a gesture to join him in his walk, which was gratefully accepted.

Both Bhagavadpāda and Kṛṣṇarāya were sitting on a rock which gave a panoramic view of the city below. They had climbed down half way through, behind them, a thousand feet above was the *Gopuram*—the tower of the temple. Kṛṣṇarāya did not disturb, noticing the contemplative mood of the master and sat silently feeling his presence. He heard master say:

"We are sitting in a spot that describes your position perfectly. *Behind* you is the Divine and in *front* of you, your kingdom. For being a just king you should maintain this always. You are a king *only* for your subjects, but are a servant of the Divine performing *His* work. If you attune yourself with the Divine, you will be able to get *His* guidance."

Kṛṣṇarāya was happy to note that he had been called by the master to help.him become a better human being. This advice coming from an enlightened master, at the spot that was most appropriate, touched his heart strings. He agreed fully to say:

"*Bhagawan*, how very right you are! I am concerned about the welfare of my subjects, and try to do as much as possible for them. But tell me, how I can *attune to the Divine*? But before telling me about the Divine, please guide me to get rid of my limitations."

Still looking at the city lit by the rays of the setting sun, Śaṅkara asked the king with the innocence of a child:

"What sort of limitations could you have?" The king smiled but he became grave as he started speaking.

"*Bhagawan*, my only problem and I feel this is *the* problem with all royalty, is this obstinate *indulgence*. Whatever comes in front of me as though beyond my control, I indulge—it may be food or music or senses. During the indulgence I am almost unconscious, knowing nothing else. But invariably, after I get the so-called satisfaction, I have regrets for being so impulsive. When you talked about the senses *going out to seek their objects*, I remembered my own helplessness in being under *their* power! I am aware of the Divine giving me this royal birth out of compassion, *without any eligibility on my part*. When I visit the temple—and that is not very often, not really due my duties as a king, but more predominantly my *indulgence* keeps me away from this sacred spot. Today I realise that it was *Viṣṇu who put the thought of summoning me, in the chief priest*! Otherwise I would not have had this great privilege of meeting you. I beg of you *Bhagawan*, please help me." Kṛṣṇarāya was in tears, and compassionate that *Ācārya* was, put his hand on his shoulder to console him with these reassuring words:

"Kṛṣṇarāya, first of all let me assure you that your problem is not as grave as you imagine! This is a universal problem faced by *all* seekers at one time or the other. The only thing is that the degree of its intensity differs from person to person. By understanding that *indulgence is not congenial for spiritual growth*, you have already put the first steps. Now we shall see the methods of reducing it and at a later stage eliminate it totally. Let me ask you something, when you are involved with your royal duties do you have any problem of lack of concentration?" The king thought for a while and said after a little deliberation:

"No *Bhagawan*, during my normal duties or when we are discussing the welfare of our subjects I never have any problems, and I am confident of discharging them to the best of my ability." *Ācārya* was satisfied. He asked further:

"What about other times, the times when you do not need any concentration, what happens then?" This time the king took longer to respond to the question. Clearly, he was trying to relive the moments.

"I think about the times when I enjoyed sensual indulgence and almost relive those moments! Now that you ask me, I think

I rather enjoy the sensual moments, whether it is food or music." Śaṅkara appreciated his frankness and said:

"A little while back in the *Satsaṅga* you talked about the *Śrīmadbhagavadgītā*. Do you read it often?" The king laughed and said gallantly:

"*Bhagawan*, I have only heard about it from our chief priest who also taught me state-craft. He used to quote extensively from the *Śrīmadbhagavadgītā.* He used to coax me to read it regularly, which I never did, except when my respected father once wanted to test me after giving me time to prepare! Oh I do not even want to remember that time!!" For which both of them laughed and *Ācārya* said affectionately:

"The priest was right in quoting the *Śrīmadbhagavadgītā*. It does not matter whether you have studied it or not. Why I asked you was that it has a solution to the task at hand. In the very second chapter Lord Kṛṣṇa gives the mechanism or the process of downfall in a human being: 'The man dwelling on sense-objects develops attachment for them; from attachment springs up desire, and from desire (unfulfilled) ensues anger. From anger arises infatuation, from infatuation, confusion of memory, loss of reason; and from loss of reason one goes to complete ruin.'[85] The beginning of this cycle of indulgence is *thinking about the objects of senses*. When one feels that *indulgence has become a problem, one should stop* ***thinking about them*** whenever there is no contact of the senses with their respective objects."

Ācārya observed that Kṛṣṇarāya was contemplating on what he heard, after a while with his eyes lit up, he expressed joyously:

"The analysis of desire is so complete and wonderful! Perhaps my obstinate nature needed you as my *Guru* to put into my dull head!" He stood up to touch master's feet. There were tears of gratefulness in his eyes. With an appealing look, he requested:

"*Bhagawan*, please guide me into the technique of stopping the thinking about the senses objects. I understand that it requires

85. ध्यायतो विषयान् पुंसः संगस्तेषूपजायते । संगात्संजायते कामः कमात्क्रोधोऽभिजायते ॥ श्रीमद्भगवद्गीता 2:62 ॥
क्रोधाद्भवति संमोहः संमोहात्स्मृतिविभ्रमः । स्मृतिविभ्रंशाद् बुद्धिनाशो बुद्धिनाशात्प्रणश्यति ॥ श्रीमद्भगवद्गीता 2:63 ॥

patience and great effort. But I am prepared to go to any extent to achieve self-control." *Ācārya* said compassionately:

"That was the reason why I asked you to join me in my stroll! Let us retrace our steps to the temple. Do you have time to be with us?" When he got an affirmative answer, he continued:

"After the evening worship of the *Viṣṇu*, we shall all sit together for some time. Now while walking back, we will maintain silence and try to concentrate totally on walking, by observing our steps, the breeze, the beauty of nature, by taking care to see that we do not judge any sensation as good or bad, pleasant or unpleasant. Just observe without any mental talk." By the time they reached the temple, there was a noticeable change on the face of the king. *Ācārya* knew that the king had put his first steps towards the process of *freedom from the impressions of senses*!

The night had set in when Śaṅkara Bhagavadpāda sat surrounded by his beloved disciples. As he guided them, and each one of them, felt that he was being instructed by the master personally. There was no visual distraction as it was dark. They could listen to his resonant voice that coaxed them and encouraged them helping them to change the direction of their consciousness:

"Let the senses come in contact with their objects, just be a *Sākṣi*—non-involved witness. Do not try to name any object, or give any adjective to it as good and bad, pleasant and unpleasant! You will observe that the sensation rises for a while, then sets. It is temporary and fleeting. Immediately, you may get another sensation when a sense comes in contact with its object. When you stop paying any attention to the sensations, you will start becoming aware of another function of the mind—*Manas*, with its *Cañcalatā*—randomness, due to its *curiosity* to *look for fresh sensations*. Again be a *Sākṣi*, let it wander all it wants."

Nearly an hour later, *Ācārya's* voice made them aware of the outside. In the pleasant orange light of an oil lamp, he saw that each one of them had had a glimpse into the wonderful world inside. They were refreshed as though they had a restful sleep, and yet they all had been alert and aware of the activity of their senses and *Manas*. They heard the master say:

"That was *Antarmukhatā*—the inner gaze." There was joy, a strange pride in his voice.

❐

15
Śravaṇa and Nididhyāsana

Dawn that followed the evening spent with the master was different than he had ever experienced. Though he had left the precincts of the temple rather reluctantly, his recent acquisition of the mood and the attitude had not left him when Kṛṣṇarāya had reached the palace. Bhagavadpāda had plucked a new string inside—unknown to him so far, that had started vibrating, creating ethereal music. Before he fell asleep, he once again started reliving every moment with his *Guru*, but realised that he was only repeating the same blunder he had been committing—reliving the past! Only, the object this time had nothing to do with any sense but was more subtle. With this sudden *remembrance* he became an uninvolved witness—*Sākṣi*, as it is called. The morning brought in a freshness he had never experienced in his adult life. He remembered, as a child it had been something like this which had kept on waning with the increasing awareness of *his being the crown prince and of the related responsibilities*! His mind was made up; he would never miss this opportunity of the presence of this enlightened Master. Hurriedly getting ready, he had called his principal minister and rattled of the instructions, most important of which being, not to disturb him as long as *Ācārya* Śaṅkara Bhagavadpāda was at Mahāsurapura! With a strange enthusiasm and energy, he reached the temple to be with the master.

"My salutations to Him who is awareness, all-pervasive, pure, non-dual, stainless and formless, who is attained through

Aumkāra, who is beyond the three *Guṇas,* imperceptible, the fourth, who is known as Supreme Brahman. I salute the immaculate, auspicious and tranquil, without beginning and end, life of the universe, not bound by time-space or matter, who is known through the *Vedas*."[86]

Having finished performing the *Pūjā* in the temple, Bhagavadpāda recited these verses in praise of All-Pervading Viṣṇu. A boy in his teenage was unable to restrain his curiosity to see the person reciting the *Stotra* on the Lord. He had never heard this before. Being responsible for collection of flowers and preparation of garlands, he loved his work. However, it had its limitations as he could neither perform *Pūjā*, nor even *think of learning it*! But he was content that his garlands would adorn all the gods in the temple. He had been left behind during a chariot festival of the temple when he had been of only three years. Kind-hearted chief priest had made arrangements for his upbringing, but as no one knew of his parentage, he could not be trained in the priest-craft. Everybody called him *Keśava*, some affectionately, some others for giving him work or finding faults in it, and those of his own age in envy or jealousy, as he was brighter with a sharper intellect and memory!

Keśava rushed towards the sanctum and stood behind the king and once in a while peeped over his shoulder! Though a few priests tried to warn him through their gestures, he either intentionally ignored them or his curiosity got better of him! But at the end of the recitation there were tears of joy flowing on his cheeks, his lips murmuring *Aum...Aum...Aum*. When it was over, everybody started joining the line to take the blessing of the saint, he realised his folly and withdrew to the back, embarrassment writ on his face. *Ācārya* had observed the boy and his sensitivity, and as the last one to take the dust of his feet left, he gestured the boy to come near. A priest whispered

---

86. चिदंशं विभुं निर्मलं निर्विकल्पं निरीहं निराकारमोंकारगम्यम् । गुणातीतमव्यक्तमेकं तुरीयं परं ब्रह्म यं वेद तस्मै नमोऽस्तु ॥ 1 ॥
विशुद्धं शिवं शान्तमाद्यन्तहीनं जगज्जीवनं ज्योतिरानन्दरूपम् । अदिग्देशकाल व्यवच्छेदनीयं त्रयीपंक्ति यं वेद तस्मै नमोऽस्तु ॥ 2 ॥
॥ श्री विष्णु भुजङ्गम् ॥

something in the ear of *Ācārya*, who only smiled and moved towards the boy, again gesturing him to stay where he was, Keśava obeyed.

Keeping his right hand on the shoulder of the boy, *Ācārya* came out. Boy was thrilled and at the same time afraid of the consequences. To put him at ease, Śaṅkara started talking to him:

"What is your name?" Feeling uncomfortable, he answered:

"*Bhagawan*, they call me Keśava. Please forgive my impertinence, I did not mean to disturb the sanctity of the shrine." Affectionately, Śaṅkara said:

"You have in no way disturbed anyone. But tell me why you are afraid?"

"I do not know my parentage! I cannot enter the sanctum." Seeing the king behind them, *Ācārya* addressed him, but actually to *everyone through him*!

"Do you know that one of my *Gurus* was a *Cāṇḍāla*? And I am convinced that but for his teaching, I would not have been eligible to even talk about *Advaita*." He sat facing south, leaning against a pillar. All of them, the disciples, the king and the priests, and the pilgrims sat around to behold the master and catch the gems coming from his mouth. Śaṅkara Bhagavadpāda made sure that Keśava sat near him and began talking.

"The castes were *not on the basis of either birth or parentage, but on the mental qualities, attitude and action*. Lord Kṛṣṇa says, 'The four orders of the society (*Brāhmaṇa*, *Kṣatriya*, *Vaiśya* and *Śūdra*) were created by me, classifying them according to their qualities and actions.'[87] How can a person who weaves beautiful garlands that adorn the deities of the temple be an untouchable? How can a boy who is enthusiastic and receptive to learn, be stopped from learning? Even if you stop him from entering your so-called sacred sanctums, will he not learn by listening to your recitations? Keśava, recite the *Puruṣa Sūktam*." Standing up Keśava turned in the direction of the sanctum, chanted the adoration on the Lord, flawlessly as well as effortlessly! Looking at the chief priest, *Ācārya* said:

---

87. चातुर्वर्ण्यं मया सृष्टं गुणकर्मविभागशः । तस्य कर्तारमपि मां विद्ध्यकर्तारमव्ययम् ॥ श्रीमद्भगवद्गीता 4:13 ॥

"You did well in bringing him up but did not pay proper attention to his upbringing! You could have treated him as your own offspring." There was regret in the eyes of the priest, but he asked hesitatingly:

"*Bhagawan*, but suppose his parents were from the lower caste?" *Ācārya* laughed and responded:

"But are you certain that they were from the lower strata? Even if they were, he has the qualities and attitude of a *Brāhmaṇa*. That was why we recollected that verse from the *Śrīmadbhagavadgītā*. In the absence of his parents, haven't you been his father, taking all the care in nourishing him with food and affection? No one knows of his parentage but everyone knows that but for your care the child who had lost his parents during the festival would be either dead or miserable. Extend your love for the child by allowing him to do what he loves most."

The priest had tears of repentance in his eyes, going near Keśava, he embraced him and the boy who was already moved by the kindness shown by the *Ācārya* became emotional, fell at the feet of his father! Looking at others *Ācārya* continued:

"Remember the more we divide the more distant we become to the Reality. What are we trying to achieve through all our spiritual or religious practices? We are trying to go near the *Iṣṭa*, God or Reality. The *Varṇa Dharma* was only meant to bring order in the society because there are only the four types of natures in the society. It was not for the division. However, I totally understand that it is difficult to eliminate these social notions, and as I said, even I had been a victim to the belief!" So saying he told the gathering about the Hunter on the bathing *Ghāṭ* of *Gaṅgā*.

"I am so grateful to that hunter, who he is my most revered *Guru*. It was he who shattered the mountain of my ignorance!" Śaṅkara's look was far, his voice had gratefulness in it. After a pause, he continued:

"Yesterday we discussed about *Antarmukhatā* and also tried to take the mind *inward*. It appears difficult initially *only because of the habit*, but with practice it can become quite effortless.

The episode of Keśava today has given us an opportunity to learn more about mind control. How? The mind has another quality, though *Manas*—the function of mind responsible for gathering information of the outside world is always restless, *Buddhi*—responsible for analysis and decision taking is always guarded in going against its *Saṁskāras*—the memories of earlier experiences and beliefs inherited from our ancestors. We feel most of you are good *listeners*. The difference between hearing and *listening* is that while hearing we are not with the speaker *totally* but also hear various sounds falling on our ears. But when we listen, there is nothing else but the speaker and you, this has been called as *Śravaṇa*. There is neither any sense object nor is there any thought, like either agreeing or disagreeing with what you listen. Let us do *Śravaṇa*."

Ācārya looked at Padmapāda, who said, understanding what his master wanted:

"You may be aware of the *Upaniṣads*, and many of you may have even studied them. Though they are *believed* to be only for recluses or *Sanyāsins*, they are actually meant for everyone in the society." As he uttered these words, the orthodox priests had protests on their brows! Padmapāda smiled and continued:

"It may sound blasphemous but *Bhagawan* has assured whoever he meets, that they are to be studied and understood by everyone in the society if we want the regeneration of our great culture. Please keep the conventional view aside for a while as I will explain you what they contain." Some of the elder priests were doubtful whether to listen to what this young *Sanyāsin* had to say! But soon as they beheld the youthful countenance of both *Guru* and his disciples, the burning aspiration for reviving our grand heritage, and the sincerity in their eyes, they remained seated. At least they could listen to what was being said out of courtesy if not curiosity! Padmapāda continued:

"There are innumerable *Upaniṣads*; some say one hundred and eight, others say less and some others say that there are many more! But all of them contain the description of Truth, Reality, God or *Paramātman* and of realising It. Now a question arises, 'if they all are giving the description of the same entity, why should there be so many *Upaniṣads*?' It is because they are the utterances of our ancient *Ṛṣis* in their highest states of consciousness, when they realised the Truth or Self. As the *Ṛṣis* were different individuals, they necessarily had experiences *from their point of view*." The listeners were totally with the speaker, but some of them wanted clarification.

As if to demonstrate what he wanted to say, Padmapāda moved to his right, stood there for some time and said:

"I shifted from the place where I was standing earlier. Now is the view same as before or different? Can you say that it is identical to the earlier view?"

"It is different." Everyone responded.

Padmapāda moved to his left, slightly turning towards his master. Once again he asked:

"Has the view changed now?"

"It has changed!"

"Not only has it changed due to my change of position, but even from *your position*, each one of you is seeing me from your unique perspective. And all the while, neither have I changed, nor have you as a seer, but only the perspective has changed! It is the same in the *Upaniṣads*, each *Ṛṣi* due to his nature and position *tries* to give us a description. I said *tries*, because *Brahman* or the Reality is beyond description. These different descriptions not only help us get a broader view of Reality, but help us move towards It from our position. We shall take a few examples for further clarification."

In the pause that followed, the audience tried to recollect the facts given by Padmapāda. Everyone liked his demonstration for explanation of *perspective*! Some of them remembered the story from *Hitopadeśa* about the five blind men's description of the elephant. Deep voice of the speaker recited a *Mantra* to bring them back to the present:

"'That from which all these beings are born; That in which they live having been born; That towards which they move and into which they merge. That is *Brahman*.'[88] The *Ṛṣi* is viewing

---

88. यतो वा इमानि भूतानि जायन्ते । येन जातानि जीवन्ति । यत्प्रयन्त्यभिसंविशन्ति ।तद्विजिज्ञासस्व । तद् ब्रह्मेति ॥ तैत्तिरीयोपनिषद् 3:1:1 ॥

the Reality from the perspective of *Sat*—existence. We can understand this through the simile of the ocean. The waves and froth, which are born in the ocean, live in the ocean and into the ocean they merge. The ocean remains undisturbed amidst all the hectic activity.

"'*Brahman* is Truth, Wisdom, and Infinite.'[89] Wisdom or knowing, as different from knowledge, which is only information, is the second perspective—they called as *Cit*, which is pure awareness, the very principle of wisdom. The third perspective, and *Bhagawan* says, the most important, is the *Ānaṅda*—bliss. 'He realised Bliss as *Brahman*. One, who has known the Bliss that is *Brahman*, is not subjected to fear'.[90] This bliss is different from *Sukham*—happiness which depends on a cause, while *Ānaṅda* is natural, causeless and hence eternal." Kṛṣṇarāya stood up and asked:

"How can one find out one's position and perspective? I am asking this because only after knowing one's own perspective can we start our journey towards realisation." Padmapāda smiled and replied:

"Maharaja, having come in contact with *Bhagawan*, each one of us has already started that journey! But the perspective is that which is predominant in the mind; thoughts which are somehow connected with existence—birth, life or death, or about *knowing* the Truth or about that happiness, which does not wane with time. What is one's aspiration—is it to exist eternally or *Jñāna* that is free from ignorance or is it that Bliss which is unalloyed with intermittent pain? The answer you get *inside your own mind* is your perspective."

Padmapāda returned to his seat. He had given sufficient fodder for the mind to think and experiment. The assembly was silent for quite some time. The resonant and sweet voice of *Ācārya* made them realise that he had been with them all along and yet his silence had made him unnoticeable to all!

---

89. सत्यं ज्ञानमनन्तं ब्रह्म ॥ तैत्तिरीयोपनिषद् 2:1:1 ॥

90. आनन्दो ब्रह्मेति व्यजानात् ॥ 3:6:1 ॥ आनन्दं ब्रह्मणो विद्वान् । न बिभेति कदाचनेति ॥ 2:4:1 ॥ तैत्तिरीयोपनिषद् ॥

"Padmapāda gave us certain facts and all of us not only heard but *listened*. We listened to certain truths that are in tune with our *Swabhāva*—our basic nature. So we shall discuss today about another tool of quietening the mind: *Nididhyāsana*—meditative contemplation.

Before we start doing *Nididhyāsana*, let us recall the process of *Antarmukhatā*—taking the mind inward which we had done last night, and only then shall we start analysing what we heard."

Most in the assembly reverted back to the practice of the previous evening, of listening to the sounds *without either labeling or judgment*. They just heard the sound, and passed on to the next. In a little while, their wandering minds became steady and to a great extent, silent. Keśava who had just joined the group just listened to the master's voice, following it as it rose from and merged into silence. The oneness with his master was so intense that Keśava became silent by the time *Ācārya* stopped speaking! In this collective silence everyone felt expansive and blissful. Once again, without disturbing the silence Bhagavadpāda spoke:

"This silence or expansiveness is not our destination, but only milestone! The silence we are experiencing now will help us to observe the deeper functions of the mind. Try to see *what is silent*? The senses and *Manas* are silent, which is observed by someone. Try to find out who is that." During a longer pause that followed, they felt the entity observing the silence to be discriminative and also decisive. They continued to observe further when they started noticing *Sphandana*—the rising of *Aham...Aham...Aham*.... The priests, Keśava or Kṛṣṇarāya had never experienced this! They were, to say the least, euphoric!

"That (*Brahman*) is Whole; this (the world) too is Whole. The Whole (the world) has come out of the Whole (*Brahman*). The Whole (*Brahman*) remains the same, even when the Whole (the world) comes out of the Whole (*Brahman*). Let the Peace descend on all the three planes. AUM."[91]

---

91. ॐ पूर्णमदः पूर्णमिदं पूर्णात्पूर्णमुदच्यते । पूर्णस्य पूर्णमादाय पूर्णमिवावशिष्यते । ॐ शान्तिः शान्तिः शान्तिः ॥ शुक्ल यजुर्वेदः ॥

As their minds started becoming conscious of the external with the resonant voice of *Ācārya*, they discovered a new freshness in the world. Everything appeared to be in its place, and apparently there was nothing to complain! Śaṅkara Bhagavadpāda looked at each one of them affectionately like a mother proud of the achievement of her off-spring! Amidst the milieu of contentment wanting to know their response and their experiences, he asked them to tell him individually. The first one to stand up was the chief priest:

"*Bhagawan*, how foolish I was to think that performing the ritualistic *Pūjā* was more than sufficient to attain *Mukti*! I now feel I have so much to learn and so little time." There was regret in his voice. Śaṅkara consoled him:

"For everything there is an allotted time, yours has come now. Don't squander it away with regret or repentance. Tell me how did you *feel*?" stressing the last word.

"I feel as if I was born only today! I notice that the world is beautiful as it is. How did this transformation occur?" There was wonder in the voice of the priest. *Ācārya* smiled and said:

"You have learnt how to keep away the *description of the world from your mind and to see it without any Upādhi—adjective* or *description*. If you ask me as to what stops us from being happy, I would say that it is *Upādhi*.[92] Every sensation, every interaction, why, even every moment our world is governed by *Upādhis*! But does it mean *Upādhi* is to be avoided totally? No! Like everything in this existence, it has its advantages and disadvantages! It is necessary for *Vyavahāra*—the transactions and activity in the world. But as far as the quietening of the mind is concerned it is a hindrance. For example, you are now sitting and do not need any activity in the legs. But if you keep on moving them, you will not be able to relax and the movement becomes a hindrance to your relaxation! *Upādhi* is the offspring of *Buddhi*, as it is judgmental, and judging is one of its functions; its other function is to analyse

92. J. Krishnamurti used to say that we should learn to see the world as it is. Normally, we see only the description of the world, through either past impression or opinion. Bhagavadpāda used the word *Upādhi*.

or to differentiate. Sākya Muni Gautama Buddha while talking of mind called it *minding*, to stress that it is an *activity*, like any other activity that can be stopped. *We should use the faculty but should not be used by it. We become the helpless slaves of the function, when we are unable to curtail if not stop that activity.*"

"*Bhagawan*, we have heard of *Śravaṇa*, *Manana* and *Nididhyāsana*. We did *Śravaṇa* and tired to do *Nididhyāsana*. Should we not do *Manana*?" It was Janārdana a disciple who had joined the group recently, who was an accomplished scholar of scriptures, but who was disillusioned with scholarship! Śaṅkarācārya looked at him curiously, and finding a genuine seeker in him said:

"Generally, the convention is in that order: First you listen; then you think out what you have listened, and then after getting convinced about what you have listened, do the *Nididhyāsana*. We did not need *Manana*, as we have learnt to silence the activity of senses and *Manas* to achieve *Antarmukhatā*—the inward gaze." Toṭaka stood up.

"*Bhagawan*, what is the procedure of *Nididhyāsana*, that is, what *we do*?"

"In the external gross world, to get something, effort is mandatory. We have to act or *do something* for getting something. But as and when we start moving from the gross to the subtle or to put it in other words, start our *inward journey*, the effort or any kind of activity starts reducing. That was why a few days back we had said that 'action is only meant for the purification of *Cittam* and *not for the realisation of Truth*'. Because realisation is *being what you already are*, while all action is effort *to become something which you are not*!"

Looking at the expression of most, Bhagavadpāda felt he had to offer further clarification. He knew this to be one more stubborn notion that is difficult to remove, and unless we eliminate it, realisation is really an up-hill task! He continued:

"The basic human need is happiness. Not just the kind of happiness that is temporary and passing, but *Nityam*—permanent and without break; *Pūrṇam*—which is not dependent on place; *Sarvātmakam*—it should be in everything and everyone, that is, we should be happy with any object or person; *Swataḥsiddham*—that it is available without much or preferably no effort! And most of all, the happiness should be *Aparokṣam*—that is, we want to be *directly aware of that happiness without any medium in between.*"

"*Bhagawan*, we understand that we seek permanent happiness that is independent of place and situation and of course, without effort! But can you please explain *Aparokṣa*?" It was Kṛṣṇarāya who sought clarification.

"We get connected to the world through *Dehātmabhāva*—identifying ourselves to our bodies; by identifying with *Manas*, we get carried away by our desires; when identified with *Buddhi*, we experience the dualities like right and wrong, good and bad, virtue and vice, etc. These intermediate activities like *Manas*, *Buddhi*, corrupt the happiness. Unconsciously, we seek *direct happiness* without anything to disturb it. Unfortunately, not understanding that we are really seeking such happiness with these characteristics, we go after materials or mental and intellectual objects, which are the mediums." There was a pause, in which they contemplated on what they had just listened. The master continued:

"Which is that entity that is *Nityam*, *Pūrṇam*, *Sarvātmakam*; *Swataḥsiddham* and *Aparokṣam*? I shall put it in other words: What is mandatory to *experience*, or to *know* the world, without which we cannot experience and know?"

"It is the 'I'!" There was enthusiasm in audience as they responded to the question. *Ācārya* smiled and continued:

"It is *Ātman* and not the 'I' or *Ahamkāra* which cannot be eternal, but is temporal as it comes and goes. Let me give you an example from our day-to-day experience: we go to sleep let us say, slumber or deep sleep, in which you are neither aware of the world outside, nor are you aware of your body, nor of your social status. There is an appropriate *Mantra* in the *Bṛhadāraṇyaka Upaniṣad* describing this: 'In this state, father has ceased to be the father; a mother is not mother; Gods are no longer Gods; thief is not a thief; killer of an embryo...; the austere no longer austere; they have all gone beyond the virtue and vice and have crossed over the miseries of the mind.'[93]

Some of us when we wake up, experience no objects, are unaware of the place or time, and may not even remember our name! The first *Sphuraṇa*—vibration is *'I'... 'I'... 'I'* which shows that even this 'I' was not when we were in deep sleep. But we declare that we have had a restful sleep, indicating that there was another entity which was witnessing the body in sleep, and the mind and *Ahamkāra* to be resting *during the sleep*!"

Almost all of them had this experience while some of them had always had this quality of sleep! Again in the silence they became attentive to their inner faculties, when they realised that they *remembered* having this experience, when they discovered that no other faculty was active except this activity of *remembrance*! Noting this, *Ācārya* continued in all joy:

"You have discovered another truth: *only one faculty is active at a particular time*! This is what we have been trying to know through experience, that body, senses, *Manas*, *Buddhi*, *Cittam* and *Ahamkāra* are all gross and function, one at a time! And there is another *entity*—as it is not an activity, but which is *Sākṣi*—a non-involved witness. This *Sākṣi* is *Nityam*—eternal, *Pūrṇam*—available at all times and all places, *Swataḥsiddham*—available without any effort, and is *Aparokṣam*—direct." The faces of the listeners glowed with understanding. And all that remained was to seek that *Entity* which had eluded them all the time! The resonant, soft and melodious voice of the master guided them to seek.

"Imagine a lamp that is spreading light all around, is covered with different layers of different materials. As the layers do not allow light to spread, there is darkness. But as we start removing the layers we will be able to know that there is a light source underneath. When we remove all the covering layers the light becomes evident. All the external activities like selfless action, *Upāsana*, *Prāṇāyāma*, *Pratyāhāra*, *Dhāraṇā*, etc., are all for the purpose of *Citta-Śuddhi*—purification of

---

93. अत्रपिताऽपिता भवति माताऽमाता...देवाऽदेवाः स्तेनोऽस्तेनो भवति भ्रूणहाऽभ्रूणहा...तापसोऽतापसः...अनन्वागतं पुण्येन अनन्वागतं पापन तीर्णो हि तदा सर्वान्शोकान्हृदयस्य भवति ॥ बृहदारण्यकोपनिषद् 4:3:22 ॥

Cittam, and once we achieve this, *Truth is realised. Just as you do not have to create the light on removing the layers, you do not have to become Ātman, you already are*! So all we have to do is, eliminate the layers of ignorance. We are aware that there are many approaches, and any approach is as valid as any other. There is nothing like *the best or the fastest approach*, because each person is unique and different and has a unique method to fit her or his nature!" There was a long pause, during which some tried to contemplate upon the truths they had listened; some others tried to intensify their inner gaze; while a few like Hastāmalaka and Sureśwara were able to *be*!

Gong of the bell announced the time for noon *Pūjā*. They had spent nearly three hours with the master. They all realised—especially the chief priest and the king that they had become wiser than they were, before sitting for the *Satsaṅga*. All of them got up in all gratefulness and proceeded to make preparations for the worship of *All-Pervasive Viṣṇu*!

❒

16
The Bridge of Knowing

At eighteen years of age, Lingayya could not think of *any reasons* for all those incidents which happened in life. His mother had died during his birth; his father had remarried and had two younger brothers and a sister; in spite of the fact that his father had worked honestly and sincerely as a farmhand in a landlord's property, he could barely support his family, which lived in utter penury. The children had spent most of their childhood near the temple of Viṣṇu, sustaining on the *Prasād*—the food offered to the deity. Though curious, he had never been able to learn either letters or skills. And yet Lingayya had nothing to complain about life, for the manager had allowed him to water the plants in the temple complex. Few years back he had been allowed to collect flowers for the gods. Being sensitive, he used to pluck the flowers and sacred leaves like *Tulasi*—Holy Basel, so tenderly, as not to hurt the mother plants! He had become quite close to Keśava, to whom he used to give the collected flowers for preparing garlands. They shared thoughts and feelings with each other. The previous day's event of the young *Guru, touching him*, and the chief priest's acceptance of Keśava as his son had kindled hope in Lingayya.

During the *Ācārya's* discourse previous evening, he had been unable to restrain his curiosity to know what was going on, as his dear friend too was in it. He had chosen to sit near the corridor wall of the temple, where the group sat, for he had dared not to go too close, he had felt some new energy flowing in his veins, as though some divine had taken possession of his being. Early next morning he had finished his work and was waiting for *Ācārya* to take his daily stroll. On seeing the youthful figure approaching him, Lingayya, fell prostrate. Śaṅkara Bhagavadpāda came near and placed his hand on his head saying:

"What is your name?" Lingayya was unable to restrain his emotions, with choked throat he managed to say:

"*Swāmi*, you have touched me!" Raising him up, *Ācārya* gestured to accompany him. Putting his hand on his shoulder Śaṅkara asked:

"I have seen you watering the plants and also gather flowers for the worship. You are doing God's work, so how could I *not touch you*?!" and again repeated his question.

"Swāmi, my name is Lingayya and Keśava is my friend. I do not know what happened to me last evening. Fearing that someone would discover me, I was sitting near the corridor, to listen to what was going on. Though I did not understand anything, I felt so happy, as though some divine light entered my being. Today I just wanted to pay my respects to you...." He continued to speak, as if the flood gates of his emotions had opened! Listening to him with all attention and compassion, *Ācārya* kept responding to him through gestures. On approaching the stream, Lingayya had exhausted whatever he had to speak. *Ācārya* said with a smile:

"Let me have my bath, you wait here." Lingayya was flabbergasted at the unassuming nature of this great man, who had not only *touched him*, but had heard what he had to say with much love and compassion. In silence, for he had become calm and composed after his chattering, he observed Swāmi wash his own clothes, spread them on a stone for drying, and take his bath. Having stepped out of water, he sat on the bank in meditation wearing only a loin cloth. After sometime, the *Ācārya* started chanting in his sonorous voice:

"Shaking off their body-centered ego, looking for *Ātman* in Self alone; who blissfully roam around in *Brahman* night and day, blessed are the loin-clothed ones. Content in their innate blissful state, controlling their minds by quietening their senses; remembering neither end, nor middle, nor the outer world, blessed are the loin-clothed ones. Uttering the sacred five-syllable *Mantra* (*Aum Namah Śivāya*), worshipping the Lord Maheśwara in their heart of hearts; roaming everywhere, being fed on alms, blessed are the loin-clothed ones."[94]

Lingayya did not understand the words, but the spirit of the recitation floated into his heart like fragrance of jasmine into nostrils. He was convinced that whatever Swāmi was chanting, rose from his heart, nay from his life. He was carried away in a flood of emotions for the master, and suddenly it crossed his mind that unless he spent the rest of his life in the service of this great personage, his life would be in vain! He jumped into the river to cleanse his body, and with wet clothes, he prostrated. With an appeal in his eyes, he entreated:

"Swāmi, please allow me to serve you! I noticed that you washed your own clothes, let me wash them for you, let me look after your needs." With infinite compassion, Śaṅkara said:

"Lingayya, though I have Toṭaka, my disciple to look after me, I like to be on my own for survival. Moreover," he continued with love oozing out, "You have the responsibility of your family, your younger brothers and sister. What will they do without you?" Lingayya was surprised to note that his background was known to Swāmi! He said with wonder in his tone:

"Swāmi, how did you know about my family?"

"Oh, Keśava told me all about you! Do not be worried, we shall meet in future, when you will be more ready for fulfillment." Bhagavadpāda said with a faraway look in his eyes.

"Swāmi, can I be your shadow as long as you are in Mahāsurapura?"

---

94. देहाभिमानं परिहृत्य दूरात् आत्मानमात्मन्यवलोकयन्तः ।अहर्निशं ब्रह्मणि ये रमन्तः कौपीनवन्तः खलु भाग्यवन्तः ॥ 3 ॥
स्वानन्दभावे परितुष्टिमन्तः स्वशान्तसर्वेन्द्रियवृत्तिमन्तः ।नान्तं न मध्यं न बहिः स्मरन्तः कौपीनवन्तः खलु भाग्यवन्तः ॥ 4 ॥
पञ्चाक्षरं पावनमुच्चरन्तः पतिं पशूनां हृदि भावयन्तः ।भिक्षाशना दिक्षु परिभ्रमन्तः कौपीनवन्तः खलु भाग्यवन्तः ॥ 5 ॥ कौपीनपञ्चकम् ॥

"You may, but we shall be leaving tomorrow." Bhagavadpāda said with a smile.

After the morning *Pūjā*, they all gathered in the eastern corridor of the temple. They had come to know that the entourage of Śaṅkara Bhagavadpāda was leaving for its pre-decided destination the next day. Though their mood was sombre, they were extremely receptive not to miss any word from the master. *Ācārya* chanted in his sweet resonant voice:

"May quietness descend upon my limbs, speech, breath, eyes and ears; May all senses wax clear and strong. Everything is *Brahman*, reveal the *Upaniṣads*. Never may I deny *Brahman*, nor *Brahman* ever deny me. I with Him and He with me, may we abide always together. May the Truth of the *Upaniṣads* be revealed to me. AUM! Peace! Peace!! Peace!!!"[95]

As he uttered *Peace* three times, it appeared as though the peace *had* descended on to them!

Lingayya sat near the wall as he had done the previous evening. There was some strange contentment in him. He had never experienced such love before, so much attention and yet, Swāmi appeared to be *distant*; overwhelming him with his concern and yet, there had been absolutely no *expectation*! He tried to listen but could not comprehend what was going on. He was however, feeling oneness with the group, as he too was receptive, aware and alert. But the group as such was unaware of his presence! *Ācārya* started talking to them:

"Since each one of us has a perspective, each one of us understands the world in his own unique way. Let me explain it. Suppose we enter a marketplace, with various shops selling many items. If one is hungry, he or she notices only those shops that sell eatables; someone else desirous of buying clothes notices those shops selling clothing; and similarly according to the need or desire the other shops are noticed. It is obvious that in spite of the shops selling variety of items, we *notice* only those which interest us! In a very similar manner, when we move

---

95. आप्यायन्तु ममाङ्गानिवाक्प्राणश्चक्षुः श्रोत्रतथो बलमिन्द्रियाणि च सर्वाणि । सर्वं ब्रह्मौपनिषदं माऽहं ब्रह्मनिराकुर्यां मा मा ब्रह्मनिराकरोदनिराकरणमस्तु अनिराकरणं मेऽस्तु ।तदात्मनि निरते य उपनिषत्सु धर्मास्ते मयि सन्तु ते मयि सन्तु ॥ ॐ शान्तिः शान्तिः शान्तिः ॥ साम वेदः ॥

into the *inner world* consisting of *senses*, *Manas*, *Buddhi*, *Citta* and *Ahamkāra*, we understand it from our perspective depending upon our *Saṁskāras*."

Listening to him, they recalled the last statement made by him the previous evening that *Sākṣi* is *Nityam, Pūrṇam*, *Sarvātmakam*, *Swataḥsiddham* and *Aparokṣam*. During the night they all had tried to discover their individual perspective and succeeded. A question arose in their receptive minds: 'how do I proceed now?' As if in response to this question *Ācārya* said:

"*Kaṭhopaniṣad* gives a hierarchy of functions in the body-mind complex, which is the *means for the quest*. 'The sense objects are subtler than their respective senses, *Manas* is subtler than the objects; *Buddhi* is subtler than *Manas*, *Mahānātma* subtler than *Buddhi*. *Avyakta*—non-manifest is subtler than *Mahānātma*, *Puruṣa* is subtler than *Avyakta;* there is nothing subtler than *Puruṣa*, Who is the ultimate Limit and State.'[96] Any experience is possible *only when there is awareness*. If there is pleasure or discomfort, we are aware of the body, senses, and their objects, depending upon the experience. This hierarchy gives us a great method to transcend the gross to enter subtler dimensions."

The close disciples of *Ācārya* especially Padmapāda, Sureśwara, Toṭaka and Hastāmalaka, knew that *Kaṭhopaniṣad* was one of the favourite *Upaniṣads* of *Ācārya*.[97] They had seen him go into raptures while discussing *Vedānta* through it, which had the lyrical beauty, the logical presentation of ideas and the practical hints for growth. But every time he spoke on it there was something new for them. To their pleasant surprise, they discovered that this discussion was taking them much deeper into the subject matter and more importantly, they were discovering more about their *Real Self*.

---

96. इन्द्रियेभ्यः परा ह्यर्था अर्थेभ्यश्च परं मनः ।मनसस्तु परा बुद्धिर्बुद्धेरात्मा महान्परः ॥ कठोपनिषद् 1:3:10 ॥ महतः परमव्यक्तमव्यक्तात्पुरुषः परः । पुरुषान्न परं किञ्चित्सा काष्ठा सा परा गतिः ॥ कठोपनिषद् 1:3:11 ॥

97. *Kaṭhopaniṣad* was also the favourite *Upaniṣad* of Swami Vivekananda; he picked up his well known call उत्तिष्ठत जाग्रत प्राप्य वरान्निबोधत ।क्षुरस्य धारा निशिता दुरत्यया दुर्गं पथस्तत्कवयो वदन्ति ॥ कठोपनिषद 1:3:14॥ "Arise, Awake, and stop not till the goal is reached!" He used the example of Naciketa to explain *Śraddhā*.

"Normally, we try to control our senses *at their level*. Let us say, that we are attracted to sound or form, which distracts us from meditation. What we do is we try to *replace* the sense object with our *Iṣṭa*. This is no doubt effective for normal transactions, but a seeker, who needs to *transcend* the senses it is not enough. Similarly, we try to *replace* the thought in the mind, which is though effective, is only a temporary solution. Instead, the *Maṅtra* from the *Upaniṣad* gives an effective method for transcendence."

A soft cool breeze started blowing from the east; on a nearby pillar, a pigeon was calling its companion; smell of smoke from the offerings made at *Yajña Śālā* was entering the nostrils. Amidst all these sense objects, the steady and soft voice of *Ācārya* dominated the consciousness of the listeners. *Ācārya* continued:

"Your predominant attention on my voice makes you unaware of the cool sensation of the breeze on your skin, the call of the pigeon on the pillar, and also the fragrance of the offerings from the *Yajña Śālā*. Any experience is possible only when there is awareness. When there is pleasure or discomfort we are aware of the body or senses and their objects, depending on the experience. Taking this great hint of awareness, it is possible to transcend the gross and enter the subtler dimensions. This technique of transcendence is given in one of the most eloquent *Maṅtras* in Vedāṅtic literature." So saying *Ācārya* closed his eyes, the listeners too closed their eyes and waited for the recitation with bated breath:

"Man of *Prajñā* merges speech (etc.) into *Manas*, which he merges into *Jñānātman*—enlightened *Buddhi*, which he merges into *Mahat*—pure activity, which in turn he merges into *Śānta-Ātman*—the peaceful State."[98] In the long pause everyone was trying to get the essence of the *Maṅtra*. Śaṅkara Bhagavadpāda continued:

"Our mind is crowded by innumerable thoughts. Each thought has words associated with it, and a verbal pattern.

---

98. यच्छेद्वाङ्मनसी प्राज्ञस्तद्यच्छेज्ज्ञान आत्मनि ।ज्ञानमात्मनि महति नियच्छेत्तद्यच्छेच्छान्त आत्मनि ॥ कठोपनिषद् 1:3:13 ॥

Speech is very intimately related to the process of thinking. These thoughts and words are gathered during its transactions with the world outside with every sense experience. Each experience, nay each contact of the sense with its object leaves an impression on the mind. Thus, '*Vāk*—speech in this *Mantra* represents all the senses.'[99] We are connected with the outside world through our senses, which gather external stimuli. The senses thus act as windows. But unless *Manas*—the faculty of mind responsible for gathering as well as sifting the sense stimuli—is connected with the senses, the senses in themselves are ineffective. That was why we saw that you were not aware of the cool sensation, or of the pigeon or of the fragrant smoke." They realised how well he had observed the human behaviour, and why he had talked about their not being attentive to different sensations! Kṛṣṇarāya stood up to ask a question:

"*Bhagawan*, can you please tell us more on the *sifting* function of *Manas*?"

"Hundreds of sensations are received, if all of them were attended to, then we would be in deep trouble, as they would disturb us all the time. The *Manas chooses only a few, and rejects most* according to one's nature, depending upon one's *Saṁskāras*! And the chosen sensations are passed on to the *Buddhi*. The word *Yacched* means *merge*. During the contact of senses with their objects if there is any judgment—good, bad, etc., or any reaction, like infatuation, hatred, etc., the experience has a conditioning effect. Sage Patañjali and later Buddha advised the seekers to develop the mood of *Upekṣā*—*indifference*, which helps in developing non-involvement. In turn, non-involvement helps us to be aware of the *grosser* activities of the body, senses, and *Manas*. This activity of *awareness* has been named by the *Upaniṣad* as *Jñānātman*. Non-involved awareness is effortful as there is a constant struggle between will and nature and if one relaxes the effort, one slides back to *involvement*!"

This is the *most common experience* of everyone. The faces of the listeners were lit up, when *Ācārya* told them this

99. वागत्रोपलक्षणार्था सर्वेन्द्रियाणाम् ॥ शंकरभाष्यम् 1:3:13 ॥

fact. They recalled their session in understanding *Antarmukhatā* when they had learnt to *witness* different senses in contact with their respective objects *without involvement*. It had been quite effortful, as initially they had either judged or reacted as the master had rightly observed! *Ācārya* did not allow them to dwell on the past for long as his voice brought them back to present!

"The *Maṅtra* asks us to merge *Jñānātman*—the effortful awareness *of doing*, into *Mahat*. As and when *Jñānātman* becomes natural and effortless one discovers that *all activity*—whether at the level of body, senses, *Manas* or *Buddhi* is just *pure awareness without any Upādhi*! There is neither any object nor any reaction, but just a *Sphuraṇa*—'I-am…I-am.' This has been called as *Mahat* by the *Ṛṣi* of this *Upaniṣad*. *Mahat* is very deep and subtle, and is something like a bridge between *Idam*—this or the perceivable, knowable and expressible dimension, and *Tat*—That, which transcends thought and speech. Being in this state, one is able to look both ways: the external as well as the internal. The *Maṅtra* suggests the seeker to continue to merge even the *Mahat* into the *Śāntātman—the peaceful Ātman*, which is the *no activity State*."

All those who were with the *Ācārya* had the feeling that they were being led by him into the inner world. The initial hesitation had been replaced by absolute trust in their *Guru*, who was slowly introducing them to their own inner layers and leading them to their true *Home*. They all were in that state of being which when turned their attention outside could see their body, senses, *Manas*, *Buddhi* and *Ahamkāra*, to be just restless activity. Before getting involved with what they saw, *Ācārya* gave them the final push:

"Look within, in the opposite direction. *Who is looking at that activity*?" Soon as they heard this grand affectionate yet powerful suggestion, they became *Aware*—of nothing in particular, but strange as it may seem, *everything came under the purview of That entity, Who did no action, but only witnessed*. And suddenly peace, expansiveness and bliss descended upon them, like the dew from the moonbeams, like the warmth from the rays of the rising sun!

"That is *Śāntātman*!" said Śaṅkara Bhagavadpāda. Though the gong announced the time for the noon worship, the disciples heard it not. But their lifelong habit did not allow them to continue to rest in *Self* and they opened their eyes reluctantly. Śaṅkara smiled!

That evening *Ācārya* went for his evening stroll with Keśava and Lingayya. He was convinced that these boys would be of help for his chosen mission of cultural regeneration. He had seen in them a very strong trust in our great heritage. They had been happy as two children, feeling privileged to be with *Bhagawan* on his last evening at Mahāsurapura. They both had a conviction that in joining him *they would be blessed*! They reached the temple, Kṛṣṇarāya awaiting the arrival of *Ācārya* came and prostrated. Blessing him, *Ācārya* said:

"I want you to do us a favour." Kṛṣṇarāya was too happy to do something in return for what he had learnt and *lived* in these past few days.

"Can you arrange for the education of Keśava and Lingayya? They will be under your care till we need them for our mission." Kṛṣṇarāya responded.

"*Bhagawan*, it will be my great privilege. I shall personally supervise their education. These two boys will be the contribution of Mahāsurapura towards the great mission you have undertaken."

All—the priests and the devotees, joined Śaṅkara Bhagavadpāda on the corridor. They had realised that this would be their last session with him. Keśava and Lingayya too sat with the group, for everybody had accepted them as co-pilgrims on the path of self-realisation. *Ācārya* began his discourse:

"Now that we have started on this inner journey, we have to remember a few things. Life is a combination of various faculties and their use. We have the capacity for *volition or action* or hand, we feel through our emotions or heart, and we understand through our head. We have been trying to *understand* the mechanism of knowledge in these past few days, through our *Buddhi*. Phenomenon of knowledge happens to be one of the deepest mysteries of existence. We can know everything, except the *knower*—the *one who knows*; because to know something implies, that the thing known has to be reduced to an object. The process of knowledge depends on the duality of the known—which is outside, and the knower—inside. The knower cannot possibly be known because it can never be kept outside as an object! Knower always remains a perpetual subject. This introduces us to a third entity, that is, the *unknowable*, because it can never be known through objective methodology." There was a pause when the words sank into the consciousness of the listeners. Śaṅkara observed that none of them was either agreeing or disagreeing with what he said, but they had become *pure listeners*. He continued with a lot of satisfaction:

"*Dharma* or Religion and *Adhyātma* or spirituality begin with an effort to probe into the unknowable. This effort can be called as *Knowing* to differentiate it from knowledge, in which the known is reduced to an object. All *Upaniṣads* are profound because they try to take us towards *subjectivity*. There, however, is one *Upaniṣad* which deals with the subjectivity in the most direct manner. It is *Kenopaniṣad*. *Kena* implies a question, meaning '*by whom*?' But this question arises in the mind when all the grosser urges have been *seen through and through*, as limited and repetitive interaction between the senses and their objects; when it is experienced that all knowledge leaves one shallow, as it does not help one to overcome the human weaknesses."

'What is that question which launches the seeker on that great adventure of consciousness?' was the question that crossed the mind of the listeners. Reading into the mind of listeners, *Ācārya* continued:

"'Willed by whom, does the mind alight on its objects? Impelled by whom, does *Prāṇa* proceed to its function? Directed by whom do men utter this speech? By whom is the speech willed that people utter? What *Deva* directs the eyes and the ears?'[100] While all knowledge gathered by the intellect is almost mandatory for the transactions in the world outside, it is not at all

---

100. 'केनेषितं पतति प्रेषितं मनः केन प्राणः प्रथमः प्रैति युक्तः ।केनेषितां वाचमिमां वदन्ति चक्षुः श्रोत्रं क उ देवो युनक्ति ॥ केनोपनिषद् 1:1 ॥

necessary for the search within. So, this is *not a question to be asked at the intellectual level.* We have to remember repeatedly that in our search, verbal knowledge has to be transcended for *being the Self*, even the scriptures! The deepest mystery as well as the limitation of human life is the involvement and identification with the external world."

Ācārya looked at each one of them with compassionate affection, understanding their problem. They all responded with an appeal in their eyes to guide them towards the great glimpse into *Self*! He continued:

"All *Upaniṣads* or for that matter, all scriptures try to suggest means and methods of overcoming this limitation. We stand near the window to look outside, but forget that we are separate from the window as well as the object of our curiosity. Instead we merge with the window as well as the object! We have so exaggerated the importance of the objective world, that we have totally ignored the inner dimension. We try to seek permanence in the objective world, which by its very nature is impermanent. We are trying to construct our home on sand. We are sowing bitter gourd in hope that it will yield sweet mangoes! Misery is imminent. The *Upaniṣads* keep repeating that being established in Self or the realisation of the Self, is the prime purpose of life. Out of many methodologies to be adopted, one is to reach the origin, which is possible only when one transcends the limitations of the objective world. This is evident from the reply given by the enlightened *Ṛṣi* to the question in *Kenopaniṣad*: 'It (the *Ātman*) is the ear of the ear, the mind of the mind, the speech of the speech, the *Prāṇa* of the *Prāṇa*, and the eye of the eye. Wise men separating the *Ātman* from these (sense functions), rise above sensual life to attain immortality.'"[101] The recitation of *Mantras* was so clear and sweet that the whole temple premises resounded in response. Some of the listeners were moved.

"The Master explains the disciple that the power behind the various functions of the body-mind is the *Ātman*. It

---

101. श्रोत्रस्य श्रोत्रं मनसो मनो यद्वाचो ह वाचं स उ प्राणस्य प्राणश्चक्षुषश्चक्षुरतिमुच्य धीराः प्रेत्यास्माल्लोकादमृता भवन्ति ॥ केनोपनिषद 1:2 ॥

is the *changeless subjectivity* behind the activities of the changing mind, senses and the ego. It is not just a concept or a philosophical statement, but the very principle of awareness which imparts meaning to all concepts and philosophies. As the Self, It can be realised. The methodology is by carefully separating It from the conglomeration of objects, senses and mind. The senses deal with the perishable things of the objective world, but the *Ātman* is the eternal subject, immortal and changeless. To go beyond the mortal—from the non-self to the Self, requires more than just intelligence and courage. While intelligence and courage are enough to achieve a very high degree of success in life, they are inadequate for the realisation of the Self. 'Without uncommon intellect (which is full of discrimination), it is not possible to give up the identification of the Self with the organs of hearing, seeing etc.'[102] *Uncommon intellect* is that, which has *outgrown the objective toys, and its total reliance on the objective experience*, common among the intellectuals. Normally, a raw individual as he is, normally wrongly identifies the *Ātman*—the Self, with the body and the senses; the more intelligent may identify the *Ātman* with the mind and the ego. The wise one alone knows that any of these are *not-Self*, including the ego, which are subject to change and destruction, while his *Ātman* is immortal and fearless. 'The dull-witted man thinks he is only the body; the book-learned man identifies himself with the mixture of the body and soul. The sage, possessed of realization through discrimination, looks upon the eternal *Ātman* as his Self and thinks *I am Brahman*, the Self of all.'[103] A seeker has to understand this and commence his journey from where *he is*—the level may be body, senses, *Manas* or *Buddhi.* We have learnt how to dissociate ourselves from the objective world. In this *Satsaṅga,* we shall try to seek That *Entity* which is *seeing, listening, tasting, smelling and feeling the sense of touch*. Let us all join our effort, and together we shall find Him—the effulgent One!"

---

102. न हि विशिष्टधीमत्त्वमन्तरेण श्रोत्राद्यात्मभावः शक्यः परित्यक्तुम् ...॥ शंकरभाष्यम् 1:2 ॥

103. देहोऽहमित्येव जडस्य बुद्धिर्देहे च जीवे विदुषस्त्वहंधीः । विवेकविज्ञानवतो महात्मनो ब्रह्माहमित्येव मतिः सदात्मनि ॥ विवेकचूडामणि 160 ॥

At that time, something wonderful was happening in the precincts of the temple of *Viṣṇu*—the All-pervasive! The group sitting with Bhagavadpāda, the nature around, the whole stone structure, why even the whole area appeared to be ready to *receive the Divine*! All they were aware of was the resonant voice coming out of *Ācārya*, which was like the nectar pouring from cosmos onto the existence!

"'*Annam*—Body, *Prāṇa*, eyes, ears, *Manas*, and speech are the aids for *knowing Brahman*'[104] proclaims *Taittirīya Upaniṣad*. Remember this great truth: *Everything can be taken as an aid to Be the Self which you already are. Every transaction, relationship is a potential reminder of our real nature.* Whatever you do is for clearing the *Āvaraṇa*—cover that makes us forget our real nature. Once you succeed in removing the *Āvaraṇa*, Y*ou Are*! Like the sun is not affected by the clouds, but when the clouds dissolve, sun can be seen in all his glory! Let us all *be together* as we start our *inner walk*. I am able to *feel* the body, which means I am separate from it. The senses are quiet at the moment, and I am able to feel that quietude, and so, I am not the senses but *Sākṣi*—an *uninvolved witness*." As and when the collective consciousness started moving *inward*, the group felt that the voice of Śaṅkara Bhagavadpāda was commanding from within!

The listeners and the speaker had merged into one mist of consciousness that had crossed over the obstacle of body-senses-mind-ego. The mist was ready to take that great plunge, that leap into the unknowable mystery of *Self*! Like an experienced guide Śaṅkara Bhagavadpāda stood at the edge of the *bridge of knowing*, beckoning his companions into his Cosmic Being, with a welcoming smile playing on his lips, full of love and care. And needless to mention, they successfully entered!

❒

---

104. अन्नं प्राणं चक्षुः श्रोत्रं मनोवाचमिति ॥ तैत्तिरीयोपनिषद् 3:1:1 ॥

17
Basking in Self

With much effort the entourage had reached the top of the mountain range that separated the valley of Kashmir from the rest of the country. All the strain and struggle vanished as they beheld the most wondrous glimpse of nature. It appeared as though the Reality had taken great care to create this place! It was a plateau at the height of six to eight thousand feet, surrounded by sky reaching mountains. Each peak adorning a crown of snow as though they all were gods, not only guarding the nature, but also ready and waiting to bear witness to an event that would change course of history. It had snowed recently—the last snow of the season, for spring was knocking at the doors of the valley, which was slipping to the ground through the pine needles of coniferous trees. Tender leaf-shoots were appearing on the Cedar—*Safedā* and Maple—*Chinār* as called by the local people. The earth below had been cleared of the snow by the warmth of the sun, which was approaching western horizon illuminating the snow peaks with his golden luminance. Smoke from the hearths rose to the sky as if in veneration of the divine! The small streams of crystal-clear water flowed making excited gurgle. The disciples had not seen anything like this before! Śaṅkara Bhagavadpāda stood on a shoulder of the mountain absorbing Divine everywhere. He had experienced this feeling earlier but this was different in the sense that there was neither *otherness* within nor without. He was the nature and nature was him, so much so, that the disciples received these vibrations of bliss and for no reason they were euphoric!

The journey to this heaven on earth was being taken when the flag of *Advaita—No-Otherness* had started fluttering in the four directions of South, East, West and North. *Ācārya* met the leaders of the quarreling factions of various systems and practices. *Ācārya* with his disciples transformed them to the higher vision of unity as proclaimed by the *Upaniṣads*. The commanding respect of these factions made him bring them together for the noble purpose of revival of our culture. In his farsighted wisdom, Bhagavadpāda grouped all such spiritual leaders under categories, calling them *Daśanāmis*,[105]and put them under the allegiance of the four *Maṭhs* or the *seats of wisdom* established in four directions. *Sanyāsins* and *Brahmacārins*[106] belonging to the *Maṭhs* were to look after the spiritual .welfare of the whole country. Bhagavadpāda was very clear that those who had dedicated their lives to the mission had to study all the scriptural literature in general. Apart from this, they were enjoined to make special study of one of the four Vedas. The *Mahāvākya*—the great statement, contained in the particular Veda would be for them, the subject of deeper contemplation and meditation.

The first *Maṭh* at Jagannātha Puri in the east and Padmapāda, who was incidentally the first disciple, was made the first *Ācārya*. The inmates of the *Maṭh* were to make special study of *Ṛg Veda*, the first *Veda* and the most ancient of the scriptures. The meditation would be on the *Mahāvākya* "*Prajñanam Brahma*"—Awareness is Brahman, which occurs in *Aitareya Upaniṣad*.[107]

The journey of life that has spiritual growth as its goal begins with awareness! The whole plan is so well thought of that it not only represents the human growth but also that of the human race. *Vana* and *Araṇya* are the titles of *Sanyāsins* and *Prakāśa* is the title of the *Brahmacārins* associated with it. This *Maṭh* is called the *Govardhan Maṭh*, *Tīrtha* or the sacred water-

---

105. *Saraswati, Bhārati, Puri, Tīrtha, Āśrama, Giri, Parvata, Sāgara, Vana and Araṇya.*
106. *Caitanya, Swarūpa, Ānanda and Prakāśa.*
107. सर्वं तत्प्रज्ञानेत्रम् प्रज्ञाने प्रतिष्ठितं प्रज्ञानेत्रो लोकः प्रज्ञा प्रतिष्ठा प्रज्ञानं ब्रह्म ॥ ऐतरेय उपनिषद् 3:1:2 ॥

body is *Mahodadhi* (Bay of Bengal). The Divine is worshipped here as Lord Viṣṇu—*Jagannātha*. His *Śakti*—power is *Vīmala*—which means *Pure*!

Śringeri, the second such centre, headed by *Ācārya* Sureśwara was to look after the spiritual welfare of the country in South. *Yajur Veda* was the scripture with its *Mahāvākya*, "*Aham Brahmāsmi*"[108]—I am *Brahman*. This centre is famous as *Śārada Maṭh* and *Tīrtha* is *Tungabhadra*. The *Sanyāsins* associated with this institution are *Saraswati*, *Bhārati* and *Puri*, while the *Brahmacārins* have the title *Caitanya*. The Divine is worshipped here is *Candramauḷīśwara—Śiva,* with His *Śakti* as *Śri Śārada*. This centre has a special significance as it was here that Śaṅkara had decided to have a centre for the propagation, on his way to the banks of Narmadā to meet his *Guru* Goviṅda Bhagavadpāda.

The western *Maṭh* was established in Dwārakā on the shores of the western sea, and Hastāmalaka was to be the first *Ācārya*. The *Sanyāsins* owing allegiance to this *Maṭh* are *Tīrtha* and *Āśrama*, and the *Brahmacārins* have the title *Swarūpa*. They are enjoined to make special study of *Sāma Veda* and the *Mahāvākya* to be meditated upon is "*Tat-Twam-Asi*"—That-Thou-Are.[109] This is called as *Kālikā Maṭh* and river Gomati is the *Tīrtha*. *Siddheśwara* with his *Śakti Bhadra Kāli* are worshipped here.

For the spiritual welfare of northern region a *Maṭh* was established at *Jyotirdhām* in the Himalayas, about thirty kilometers from the famous pilgrim centre of *Badrināth*, with Toṭaka as its first *Ācārya*. The titles of *Giri*, *Parvata* and *Sāgara* are given to the *Sanyāsins* belonging to this *Maṭh* and the *Brahmacārins* have the title *Ānanda*. They are expected to make special studies of *Atharva Veda* and to meditate on the *Mahāvākya* "*Ayam Ātmā Brahma*"—All This Is *Brahman*.[110] This *Maṭh* is called as *Jyotir Maṭh, Alakanandā* its *Tīrtha*. *Nārāyaṇa* is worshipped here as the Divine, along with His *Śakti Pūrṇagiri*.

---

108. ब्रह्म वा इदमग्र आसीत्, तदात्मानमेवावेत्, अहं ब्रह्मास्मीति ।....॥ बृहदारण्यकोपनिषद् 1:4:10 ॥
109. स य एषोऽणिमैतदात्म्यमिदं सर्वं तत्सत्यं स आत्मा तत्त्वमसि श्वेतकेतो ॥ छान्दोग्योपनिषद् 6:8:7 ॥
110. सर्वं ह्येतद् ब्रह्म अयमत्मा ब्रह्म ॥ माण्डुक्योपनिषद् 2 ॥

Kānci is one of the seven cities held sacred in our country, others being *Ayodhyā, Mathurā, Māyā* (*Haridwār*), *Kāśi, Avanti* (*Ujjain*) and *Dwārakā*. Of these three are considered to be sacred to Śiva and three to *Viṣṇu*. *Kānci* is sacred to both. During his travel in south, Śaṅkara Bhagavadpāda found many patrons in the Royalty of the kingdoms. Like King Kṛṣṇarāya in Mahāsurapura, King Rājasena who ruled the kingdom of Kānci, became an ardent disciple. Looking into the sincerity and pure intentions of Rājasena, *Ācārya* agreed to give the plan for the renovation and reconstruction of the town. A geometrical pattern in the form of *Śrī Cakra*[111] was adopted for this purpose. The temple and image of *Kāmākṣi* were placed in the *Bindu*—centre and all other temples were made to face this temple. *Ācārya* had predicted that this city would be the centre of learning and composite culture. Sureśwarācārya was entrusted to guide this centre personally and also to depute his worthy disciples to continue this sacred tradition.

True to the tradition of catholicity of *Sanātana Dharma*, Śaṅkara Bhagavadpāda did not look down upon or negate any tradition or belief, but accepted them all as aids to the spiritual journey every being has to take, for the final fulfillment of existence. A synthesis to include all beings into the fold of *Advaita* was what he developed. He declared that the *journey has to begin from where one is*; the *understanding has to dawn from the level in which one presently is* and not unlike the Buddha, coaxed them to take that first step in the journey!

It was during his visit to the great temple city of *Cidambaram* that he had the vision of Kṛṣṇa Dvaipāyana Vyāsa. *Ācārya* was coming out after propitiating the *Ākāśa Lingam*—the symbol of Śiva in Space, when he found Vyāsa sitting leaning against a pillar of the great temple. After prostrating and offering his gratitude, Vyāsa said in all affection and appreciation:

"*Sādhu*! You have succeeded in reviving the all inclusiveness of *Sanātana Dharma*! It is true that our culture has faced great challenges in the past, not only faced them head on,

111. A geometrical and mystic symbolic representation of *Śiva* in union with his *Śakti* used in *Tāntric* worship.

but has grown stronger by accepting the strength of those very challenges. And that is the reason why, *Sanātana Dharma* is not any religion, *but a Way of Life*. It shows the way to understand the meaning and goal of existence in general and human life in particular. Human mind as such has myriad expressions and perceptions. No two minds can ever be the same, why I even feel that even one mind never remains the same! It needs many props and aids to quieten. *Sanātana Dharma* accepts action, emotion, will and intellect as the means to achieve *Pūrṇatva*—wholeness and fulfillment of life. Your life will remain exemplary for understanding and emulating the true spirit our grand culture." His eyes were beholding the future as he continued:

"Śaṅkara my child, you are more than ready to take up a task now. In Kaṣhmir, there is a temple of *Śāradā*—the Goddess of learning having a gate each in four directions. This temple is called as *Sarvajña Pīṭham*, the seat of Omniscience. In the past, the enlightened scholars from North, East and West had opened the three respective entrances. Till now there has been no one from South. We want you to go there to open that gate." Śaṅkara said in all sweetness that was at his command:

"Revered *Bhagawan*, my life is dedicated to our culture, I am its servant. I shall do your bidding. With the blessings of persons like you, that gate will be opened, and true to its name the temple shall receive wisdom to spread it in all four directions!" So saying Śaṅkara fell at the feet of the great sage, who withdrew after blessing the *Ācārya*.

The journey from south to Kashmir had been eventful when entourage of *Ācārya* Śaṅkara met people belonging to various groups advocating multifarious beliefs and practices, each considering itself as exclusive custodian of our culture! Some were easily convinced of the ultimate goal of *Advaita*, where all paths have to reach, others resisted with all the power at their disposal! Whenever *Ācārya* met or interacted with people, it was *never* from a higher level, but from *no-otherness*, as a result, there was loving compassion and deep sympathy which in turn won the hearts. They were more than convinced that their practice, *Iṣṭa* as well as philosophy led them to *Advaita* and the others who believed in a different system *were not in any way inimical or contrary, but reaching the peak of Advaita from a different path.*[112] They visited Venkatācalam,[113] Kāśi, Prayāg, Ujjain, Girnār, Somnāth, Dwāraka, and Prabhāsa Tīrtha where Lord Kṛṣṇa had given up his body. Moving through Gurjara they reached Puṣkara and worshipped in the only temple dedicated to Brahma, the Creator. They crossed Thār the Great Indian Desert, to reach Sindhu Saṅgama—where river Indus meets the ocean. Moving up the river, they entered Puruṣapura, in the kingdom of Gandhāra.[114] Traveling on, they reached the kingdom of Kashmir. And so it was that they were in the heaven on earth.

The entourage of *Ācārya* consisted of all his four principal disciples, a few other disciples with *Brahmacārins,* three kings, Keśava and Lingayya who had joined him. They were elated to be a part of his group, as every moment with their beloved *Guru* had been enlightening and memorable; each word an aid for meditation and each gesture door-way to ecstasy!

The king of Kashmir made arrangement for their stay; while they rested after the physically exhausting journey, the scholars of the region came in a group to meet the *Ācārya.* They said that unless he defeated the learned persons of *Śārada Pīṭham* there, they would not accept the supremacy of *Advaita.* The custom was to place the most learned man on this seat and crown him as *Sarvajña*—the All Knowing. Obviously that man alone could adorn the seat who was a master of all branches of knowledge both sacred and secular. Padmapāda and other disciples requested the master to accept the challenge. Śaṅkara Bhagavadpāda consented and reached the temple of *Śāradā.*

Remembering the decree of Veda Vyāsa, he smiled and remembered his *Guru Parampara*—the illustrious lineage of masters and offered his salutations mentally. He wished to enter the temple through the southern gate with his disciples, but was stopped reverentially by a group of pundits who challenged him

112. Paramahaṅsa Śri Ramakrishna used to say '*as many mat—opinions, so many paths to reach God*'.

113. Present Tirumala-Tirupati.

114. Modern Peshawar and Afghanistan.

to a discussion on *Nyāya* and *Vaiśeśika* systems. He answered their questions to the satisfaction of all, and they allowed the group to encounter a second assembly of scholars well versed in *Sāṅkya* and *Yoga*. Śaṅkara satisfied them with his experiential understanding of the two systems. He was challenged by the third assembly of scholars who were the masters of Jain and Buddhist philosophy. They were silenced by his brilliant arguments which they found to be from his inner experience. The last group was that of *Pūrva Mīmāṅsa*. Sureśwarācārya smiled as he remembered the time when *he* had challenged his *Guru* into a bout of argument and was grateful that *he was defeated*! Without any effort on his part, Bhagavadpāda easily convinced them of *Advaita* which is the effortless and spontaneous nature of the *Self*.

It was not just his tremendous intellectual capacity or the brilliance of his arguments that made him win over his opponents. He was a *Śrotriyam*—one who lives the truths enshrined in the scriptures and *Brahmaniṣtham*—was established in *Brahman*. His so-called arguments were quite simple: that *Self is the basis of all perception, of all imagination and of all understanding*; *that the world outside is just a wave on the consciousness and it dissolves and appears with time*; *and the only reality which is eternal is the Self*. He declared that the perception of the world, the understanding and the memory of the experience *rise and fall* as waves of consciousness, the *One Who perceives, experiences, understands and remembers IS, even when there is neither perception, experience, understanding or memory*. The greatest stroke of the Master was when he said that *all systems of thought and belief are the gateways for eliminating the ignorance, and that no one can deny the existence of 'I'—the experiencer, actor and knower.* When he gave these truths, he was not just verbalizing, but was speaking through his continual experience that could be felt by his opponents. In one stroke he had embraced all the systems and all the practices, by declaring that *they all helped in achieving Citta-Śuddhi—purification of mind*!

Then Śaṅkara Bhagavadpāda walked towards the decorated *Sarvajña Pīṭham* amidst cheers of victory. He was stopped by a female voice. When he looked in the direction he saw a lady with a bright countenance and a knowing smile on her face, who asked:

"How can you sit on the throne of Omniscience, with impurity in your being?"

With childlike innocence Śaṅkara responded:

"Mother, it was in a discussion that I was asked by another mother certain questions on the *Kusumāstra Śāstram* that I had ventured to learn. But let me assure this august assembly that this body is pure and not contaminated by sense indulgence." But the lady, smilingly countered:

"The contamination is not of the body alone, is also of the mind, and *Ahamkāra*!"

Without any hesitation whatsoever, Śaṅkara replied:

"Very true, but by body, I meant body-mind-ego. Even before the *Parakāya Praveśa,* I had detached my Self from it and had identified with *Sākṣi*—the pure witness. By the time the episode was over *Idam*—all this was only *Draśyam*—the perceived and separate from *Me*—the *Sākṣi. It has been so ever since.*" Listening to the response of Bhagavadpāda, the venerable lady smiled and commented:

"My child, I know it. And when you came here it became evident that even the duality of *Draśyam* and *Dṛg* has merged into *Advaita*—No-Otherness! Adorn the throne, it is all yours!"

Everyone looked at *Ācārya* Śaṅkara with veneration and respect, but as they brought back their eyes on the spot where that lady had stood, she was not there! However, they all stood and gave a standing ovation.

Bhagavadpāda held the hand of Padmapāda who was on his left, and that of Sureśwara who was on his right. He was followed by Hastāmalaka and Toṭaka closely behind him as he ascended the Throne of Wisdom. When asked as to why he had held the hands of his disciples, he said with that ethereal smile of his:

"It is not an individual's victory, but the victory and glory of our culture. Those who held my hand were not individuals but represent the directions and the four Vedas!"

The king of Kashmir present in the assembly of luminaries was moved by the victory of this young *Sanyāsin* who had fascinated him even on his first meeting. He prostrated in all appreciation, and requested him with folded hands:

"*Bhagawan*, though I have so many scholars in all branches of knowledge, I had not seen any underlying connection amongst them. Only today while you were *talking*—as I did not see any eagerness in you *to prove your point*, to these scholars who were all out to defeat you, did I realise that you are the person who has seen and lived that harmony. What is that which you have known, by knowing which everything is known?[115] Will you please enlighten us on this subject?" The assembly was silent, alert, waiting to listen and receptive like a fisherman sensitive to that tug on the line! Śaṅkara Bhagavadpāda smiled and glancing at them in all compassion, the looking at the king said:

"O king, patron and worshipper of wisdom, you have asked that very question which was asked by the seeker *Śounaka*. As a reply to this question, the *Ṛṣi* had responded and I would like to repeat that very response, which I hope will appease your thirst."

"The Mother who stopped me by the comment about my being impure is the Goddess Śārada whom you all worship. Her comment helped in my response which explains the query you have asked. There are two types of *Vidyā*: *Aparā Vidyā* or secular knowledge and *Parā Vidyā*. He dares to include even the sacred *Vedas* and *Vedāṅgas*[116] under *Apara Vidyā*. If we understand the process of gathering knowledge we can appreciate this division of *Vidyās*. The senses perceive something *outside* and the impressions are passed on to *Manas* which in turn transfers it *Buddhi* which comprehends. This experience is *remembered* by the *Cittam*. The whole process

115. कस्मिन्नु भगवो विज्ञाते सर्वमिदं विज्ञाते भवति ॥ मुण्डकोपपिषद् 1:1:3 ॥

116. *Śikṣā*—pronunciation, *Kalpa*—application of *Maṅtras*, *Vyākaraṇa*—grammar, *Nirukta*—origin of words, *Chanda*—science of meters and *Jyotiṣām*—science of time, are aids to the knowledge of Vedas.

of knowing is supervised by *Ahamkāra*, and knowledge is an object and separate from the *knower*. In fact, the knower is able to know because he is separate from the known! In *Aparā Vidyā*, stress is given to the *known* and unfortunately during the process of gathering external knowledge, the inner being, the *Sākṣi* who sees both the world *as well as the lack of it*, who witnesses both knowledge *as well as the lack of it*, is lost! And what remains is only a body of words!"

The whole assembly was with the *Ācārya* listening to him in rapt attention, nay the very words coming out of his being had started transforming them! He continued:

"The *Ṛṣi* then makes a very bold statement '*Parā Vidyā* is that through which one *realises Akṣaram*—the Eternal'.[117] This search for the Eternal, the indestructible, the *Pūrṇam* is called as the *Parā Vidyā*. Our culture has discovered the means and methods to seek the *Pūrṇam* and be one with it. All the systems of philosophy, beliefs, faiths and paths are all paths to realise It. Anyone who *knows this Principle and identifies with It, becomes a Sarvajña, Not because he knows everything, but because he knows the Principle which is the Basis of all knowledge, all experience and all action*! The providence chose me as its vehicle, and the grace of the sages brought me to the feet of my master *Guru* Govinda Bhagavadpāda, who in his compassion led me through! Friends, fellow seekers and companions, with this understanding, let us all *bask in Self*, become *Its* instruments. Let *It* handle our life and guide us to do as *It* wills and let *It* take care of the world!"

❐

117. अथ परा यया तदक्षरमधिगम्यते ॥ मुण्डकोपपिषद् 1:1:5 ॥

18
No Other

Silence reigned supreme in the valley of *Kedār*. The surrounding snow peaks reflected crimson-gold, greeting the morning sun. Into this celestial cup flowed *Mandākini*, a thousand feet below carrying with her the molten snow from the peaks. There was no gurgle but only the rapid movement, it was as though she did not want to disturb the prevalent silence. Coniferous trees stood rooted on the slopes like the ascetics established in their *Tapas*. Everything was in its place, every being in perfect harmony. It was as though the existence was receptive, waiting for an important event about to happen. The whole valley as well as the surrounding mountains had become divine, a grand temple, a place of worship. Padmapāda beheld this sight from the cave in which the Master and his four intimate disciples were staying.

Śaṅkara Bhagavadpāda had brought them there for giving them the final benediction, his eternal message to the world. Sage Vyāsa had told him that his mission would be over when his body would turn thirty-two years of age and that was to be soon, very soon. Though the *four directions* as he had called his disciples were aware of this fact, they had started personifying *Prajñānam—awareness,* for they were totally aware within and without as they had started living *Advaita*. They had identified with the infinite nature without, and the grandeur of the eternal, unchanging Spirit within. Their life was dedicated to the world, for alleviating the darkness due to ignorance. Śaṅkara wanted to ascertain that these last days on this planet, be used to allocate responsibilities to his beloved disciples so that the work that was set in motion could continue in the millennia to come.

It was on the morning after their arrival at Kedār that they had gathered on the shoulder of the mountain. The disciples were awaiting the reason for their being in such a beatific place, for they knew that their *Guru* always chose time and place to teach them. Their implicit trust that the master had something very important to bestow on them, and they were patient to wait for eternity if needed be! When Bhagavadpāda started speaking it felt as if the Himalayas were speaking through him, such was the enormity of his being.

"It may be that you are wondering about the reason for this pilgrimage, when so much remains to be done; that after identifying with the eternal, unchanging principle, whether any pilgrimage is necessary at all; and that whatever the purpose, could it not be fulfilled at the places of action allotted to each one of you. *It is possible*! It was not at all necessary to come here to have the clear vision of the Self. But we want to have *clearer vision,* and be *Brahma Niṣtham—established in Brahman*, and I felt this place would be ideal. You are to be the flag bearers of our culture, and necessarily must live it through thought, word and deed. All of you are more than eligible to play the roles decided by the Providence."

During the pause, he looked at each of the disciple by turn. There was so much of love and benediction in that look, that the disciples felt privileged and blissful to be *his* disciples.

"He is the *Guru*, who is well versed in scriptures, guileless, un-afflicted by desires, is the knower of *Brahman*, who is calm as the fire that has burnt up its fuel, who is a boundless ocean of mercy that needs no cause for its expression and who is an intimate friend of those who have approached him for support and have surrendered to him."[118]

As he recited this spontaneous verse, they knew that the qualities mentioned therein, were those of the preceptors who

---

118. श्रोत्रियोऽवृजिनोऽकामहतो यो ब्रह्मवित्तमः ब्रह्मण्युपरतः शान्तो निरिन्धन इवानलः ।
अहेतुकदयासिन्धुर्बन्धुरानमतां सताम् ॥ विवेकचूडामणि 33 ॥

were to be world teachers. Before they thought of the content, their master started speaking:

"You have all these characteristics and the eligibility to be *Gurus*. I can see a small doubt floating in your consciousness—*self doubt*! You have to eradicate even this doubt, however small, before starting your mission. It is a normal experience, that each one of us appears different, in spite of having the same eyes, nose, mouth and ears! More so is the mind that has myriad of variety with infinite possibilities and combinations, with likes and dislikes, past experiences and the milieu in which one is brought up. Accordingly, one has her or his perspective and preference. We have been together, learnt from events and people and have tried to teach some persons. Most importantly, we have learnt from one another. Toṭaka, how do we learn?" The disciple was about to stand, but the master gestured him to sit.

"*Bhagawan*, it is by observing the world outside, and also the world within."

"Let us take our specific group. Hastāmalaka will you tell the qualities of one of this group?" As was his wont Hastāmalaka replied with much deliberation:

"*Bhagawan*, Padmapāda is able to *feel*, he has a very strong alley in his heart. He has infinite *Śraddhā*, not only in his *Guru* and scriptures, but also in *Himself*."

"Good!" responded the master, and looked at Padmapāda, who responded:

"*Bhagawan*, Sureṣwara has a very strong reason and is precise in his thought and expression. He takes time to accept, but once having accepted, he remains unshaken in his wisdom." It was Sureśwara who joined in:

"*Bhagawan*, Hastāmalaka *lives Advaita*. Through every thought, word and deed he permeates *Brahman*. Just by being with him one can learn. He need not speak!" *Ācārya* spoke with appreciation:

"Toṭaka has surrendered his *Kartṛtva*—doer-ship and so, in spite of the fact that he is active all the time, action does not bind him. Your responsibilities were allotted depending upon your natures, aptitude and attitude." Padmapāda interjected:

"*Bhagawan*, can you please clarify our responsibilities?" *Ācārya* responded with a smile:

"Padmapāda is given the responsibility of *Govardhan Maṭh* at Jagannātha Puri in the East. It is called *Govardhan* because it is meant to enhance our *capacity to feel. Ṛg Veda* is in adoration of nature, man's relationship with it. When you observe the world or the nature outside, you use your senses. The senses collect the details of *Draśyam*—the scene and pass on the *impression* to *Manas*, which is nothing but a wave, either big or small on the ocean of consciousness; this *impression* is analysed by *Buddhi*—intellect, and understood by it, which again is an *impression*, is remembered by *Cittam*, again an *impression* on the consciousness. So the whole process of *feeling or* experience results in *Jñāna*—wisdom. The *Mahāvākya, 'Prajñānam Brahma'—Consciousness is Brahman* is meant to have this experiential wisdom."

The master continued:

"This centre will spread through the purified emotions like sensitivity and selfless love that will result in *Jñāna*. *We must always remember that Vedānta aims at understanding the unity behind the universe, like the recognizing the thread that ties all flowers in a garland.* We can very easily see the colourful flowers, but not the thread. Emotions, feelings and love get evoked in the consciousness, are sustained in the consciousness, and finally merge into the consciousness. Being aware of *this* consciousness is *Prajñānam*. Padmapāda is accomplished in *Upāsanā*. He started his journey with *Bhakti* and is now established in *Jñāna,* he will spread *Bhakti which culminates in Jñāna.*"

Listening to the master made them aware of the profundity of the allotment of their actions and responsibilities. They felt fortunate and privileged to be a part of such a grand scheme for the resurgence of our culture. Śaṅkara Bhagavadpāda continued:

"Sureśwara will be looking after *Śārada Maṭh* at Śringeri. *Śāradā* is the *Vīṇā*[119] and this centre will *vibrate* with the

119. *Vīṇā* is a stringed instrument in the hands of Saraswati—the goddess of learning, which can vibrate wonderful music in the dexterous fingers of an artist.

sanctity of purified action. Every action—big or insignificant, will purify the mind, and thereby will sanctify the society. Sureśwara has had a very sound foundation in *Karma* under the guidance of great Kumarila Bhaṭṭa, who sacrificed his life for the revival of our *Vedas*. He will use his experience and wisdom to help people understand that *though the action in any form is temporal, the one who sees the action without involvement is the peaceful Self—the 'I'*, which is identical with *Brahman*. That is why *Yajur Veda* is chosen as the main scripture of *Śārada Pīṭham* and the *Mahā Vākya* is '*Aham Brahmāsmi*'—'*I am Brahman*'." It evoked a sense of awe and wonder in the disciples. They wondered how all these small little details were thought of while planning these centres. As though in response to this thought *Ācārya* continued:

"When you have totally dedicated your life for a cause, you become an ideal instrument in the hands of Providence. The very idea of setting up centres came from It, along with all the relevant details! All we have to do is to drop *Bhoktṛtva*—experiencership, *Kartṛtva*—doership and *Jñātṛtva*—knowership. We should also remember one more important thing that these centres are not *only* for the recluses and *Sanyāsins*, *but more for the common mass of people*, innocent and simple. We should never frighten them with our intellectual scholarship! We should reach out to them at their level and offer them methods and means of overcoming their day-to-day problems of life."

The long pause that followed this intimate talk made them retrospect and finally come to a firm understanding that without the support of the common people the work ahead would be partial and incomplete. Because the *Sanyāsins* as well as the recluses came from the society! They took a firm decision never to forget this fact in all their future actions. A man in the society understands only those instructions which guide him to *do something*, to follow some *rules and regulations*, and to recite some verses in praise of the deities known to him. The youth can be inspired to engage in some activities that relate them to the society, which will not only help in the reconstruction of the society, but also broaden their hearts, purify their minds and ultimately help them understand and *experience the divine within*.

Hastāmalaka broke the silence with his soft voice:

"*Bhagawan*, will you please elaborate on the other two centres in West and North?" *Ācārya* gazed at Hastāmalaka for a while and said:

"You are looking after the western *Maṭh* at Dwārakā. You were a born *Siddha*, already established in Truth. This centre will spread the vibrations of peace and bliss. All music originates in the *Sāma Veda*. When we listen to the music, we do not seek any explanations, but only merge with it. How will we achieve this, *just by being the Reality and allowing it to spread*! A realised person inspires others to emulate him just by his very presence; he does not have to *do anything*! Just as, when you are far away from home and see another from your native village, you are happy and become his friend instantly, when you are in the presence of an enlightened person, you see your own possibility of being in *that state*! This *Maṭh* is named after *Kālikā*—the destructive power of the divine. This centre will eliminate ignorance and to take the aspirants to *Siddheśwara—the Lord of Siddhis*. It will keep *reminding* the aspirants of their potential divinity through the *Mahāvākya 'Tat Twam Asi'—That (Reality) You Are*!"

The bright rays of the sun had silently entered the cave, eager to be a part of this great benediction! The rays were spreading sweet warmth into the disciples, who had become very sensitive to receive the spiritual warmth from their beloved master. A bird with its coloured plumes came in and sat on the boulder by the entrance as if joining the music made by the *Ācārya*:

"Our national spiritual odyssey commenced and fructified in the Himalayas—the home of the Divine. *Jyotirmaṭh* located near Badrinath in Himalayas, is meant to spread the light of *Jñāna*. *Toṭaka* is looking after this, by totally eradicating his self-identity he has identified with the great mountain. Without any trace of *Kartṛtva*, or *Bhoktṛtva* or even *Jñātṛtva*, he is just being with Self—*Satyam Jñānam Anaṅtam Brahma.*[120] We came here a few days back and ever since, all of us without exception are going into meditation by just looking around. The grandeur, the expansiveness of the snow peaked giants and the nature around have such soothing effect on us, that our ego has gone into insignificance! We have this experience not only in the Himalayas, but also in front a vast ocean, or when we just look up into the night sky. We identify ourselves with them as *everyone and everything is only a part of this* ***Anaṅtam—*** *Infinite*, and this Infiniteness is our *Swabhāva*—the real nature."

As they all listened to *Ācārya* they could *feel* the light of the truth behind his words, for they had come from his realisation. Though they had glimpses whenever they were with their beloved master of heard him, this time the expansive luminosity of their beings started overflowing the cave as though a new celestial river had descended to flow into the plains, into the waiting hearts of the receptive. The affectionate voice of Śaṅkara was like its enlightening gurgle!

"***Ayam Ātma Brahma***—This Self Is Brahman."

There was a full pause, as they all *lived* the essence of the *Mahāvākya* of *Jyotirmaṭh*!

As the master spoke, the voice not only carried the words and syllables, but the experience of millennia of that search carried out by our ancient *Ṛṣis*, which acted like the nectar to rejuvenate our culture, to fill with all the confidence needed to face any onslaughts from without and within. Identified as they were with the soul of our great nation, it filled them with enthusiastic joy.

"My dear companions, this is our last time together. Providence has chosen us to be the comrades at arms for this divine *Yajña*. This cave has been sanctified by the *Tapas* of innumerable seekers and *Siddhas*. They are witness to what is happening today. Close your eyes to feel that *Being,* Who fills the entire existence."

---

120. सत्यं ज्ञानमनन्तं ब्रह्म ॥ तैत्तिरीयोपनिषद् 2:1:1 ॥

This short suggestion overflowing from Bhagavadpāda, worked as a diving board to plunge within. They realised, that their minds were no more individual, but the collective *activity in the consciousness*; as they plunged deeper within, the intellect was just *another activity* of the consciousness; similarly the ego was but a *tiny wave*! The differences dissolved, and so did the *habitual individuality*, because it was only *Bheda Vāsanā*—the habit of differentiation[121] that is the cause for all trouble! With the elimination of *Bheda Vāsanā*, there was *no other*, and what remained could not be called even as *one*! The ready consciousness of the disciples got ignited to become a steady flame for enveloping the whole of the existence. All that was left for them was to vibrate as the strings of the *Divine Vīṇā*, in *His* fingers!

Pilgrims negotiated the winding paths, invigorated by the mountain air, enthused by their aspiration to reach the destination. Amongst wayfarers were Keśava and Lingayya who had left their places of action on receiving the news of Bhagavadpāda. Both of them had been initiated into *Sanyāsa* by Sureśwarācārya. The hurry in the steps failed to hide their eagerness and restlessness at the prospect of meeting their beloved—how should he be addressed, savior or friend or mentor or all these and more? All through the difficult journey, all they had talked of was on their beloved *Swāmi*. With minimal stops on way, they had covered the distance and were now looking forward to be with *Him*! As they entered Kedār, they could *feel* His consciousness welcoming them. *Ācārya*, who was attuned to them, sent Toṭaka to guide them to the cave.

The two youth reached this sacred place after bathing, and were in the presence of Śaṅkara Bhagavadpāda. The very sight of *Swami* made them emotional. There had been no change in his youthful handsome face, only they *felt* a strange aura around him radiating concern, care and love for the whole of existence. His smile welcomed them and put them at a great comfort level. They thought that the news of the impending departure of *Swami* was after all only misplaced news!

---

121. Refer *Hues of Devotion*, for more details.

"Come! It was good you came here in such a short time! The others too will be here shortly. If you have any clarifications to seek, we will discuss them later. But now let us all sit *together* in silence." Keśava and Lingayya sat, eyes closed absorbing the radiance of the *Five*. In that *togetherness* their individuality dropped on its own. They all *felt* that the cave had been sanctified by many *Ṛṣis* and seekers through *Tapas*, as mentioned by Śaṅkara Bhagavadpāda. Now, it was *their turn* to contribute to its sanctity with their *being*!

The three kings of Mahāsurapura, Kānci and Kashmir with their companion seekers reached Kedār shortly. There was a peculiar restlessness in their beings, as they knew that they had very little time left, to be with *Ācārya*. But as they wanted to make the most of the time left, they *ignored the concern for the future*. The seekers had joined their entourage with a hope of meeting the enlightened sage in person and may be receive the light he was lavishing on the existence!

"*Bhagawan*, we have been listening to you and your disciples, and are convinced of the great value your teachings have on leading sane and healthy life of harmony. We are trying to live what we have learnt through various spiritual practices that involve the action, emotions and will.[122] I am unable to grasp the method of *Jñāna*, and especially *Advaita*."

It was Kṛṣṇarāya, the king of Mahāsurapura. Most of the audience had this doubt lurking in their minds. They could understand when they were asked to *do something* but what could one *do* if someone told them *to be, just be*?! All eyes were fixed on the master who gave his beatific smile and then spoke slowly and deliberately:

"They are *not my teachings but our cultural treasure, our greatest inheritance*! To claim them, you have to be innocent and simple. Keep aside all your previous knowledge and try to *listen to me totally*! Let me ask you one small question: 'How do you perceive the world?'"

---

122. *Karma Yoga, Bhakti Yoga and Rāja Yoga.*

They all realised that it was not an academic question, but a practical one. So they started looking within for an answer. After a while Rājasena of Kānci spoke:

"*Bhagawan*, we perceive the world through our senses. We see with our eyes, hear with the ears, smell with the nose, touch with the skin and taste with our tongue."

"Introspect on this question: "What or who *initiates the perception*?" Observing that it had evoked a blank, *Ācārya* continued, "Do the objects start the process of perception, or the senses, or the mind?"

The question evoked an insight in the listeners, who all responded spontaneously:

"The mind initiates the perception, when there is a *Kalpa*—thought in it, in the form of a curiosity or a desire to perceive!"

"Good, now we shall go deeper on this subject. When you perceive, what happens to the object that you perceive? Does it change in any way?" Once again the group continued to contemplate with eyes closed. It was Keśava who responded:

"There is no change in the perceived object, but there is an *impression* on the mind which *perceives* the object." *Ācārya* noted that everyone nodded to this observation. He was in a mood to extract the solutions to their own queries from the listeners! He asked:

"*Sādhu*! Now let us understand this *impression*—as you mention rightly. Does it in any way *change the mind*?" There was again silence before Keśava responded:

"No *Bhagawan*, this impression of perception rises and after sometime, merges back into the consciousness!"

"With such wave-like behaviour of rising and falling, does the mind which you refer to as the consciousness, change?" This time it was Rājasena, the king of Kānci who responded.

"*Bhagawan*, no there is no change in the consciousness, only an activity which begins and ends." *Ācārya* was quite satisfied that this group was totally with him, for they had started treading the path of *Vicāra*. He probed in deeper.

"Let us now go further deep into ourselves. Who initiates this whole process of perception?" It appeared as though they did not understand the question. *Ācārya* clarified:

"Do the objects influence your mind, or is it the mind that *becomes attentive* to the objects?" This time it was a new seeker who had accompanied the group:

"*Bhagawan*, it is the mind which initiates the process of perception, because without its attention, we do not respond to the objects of senses. For instance, there may be many sounds that are falling on our ears, but we are not *aware of them*, as *we are attentive* to you and the discussion that is taking place and not the other sounds." Śaṅkara Bhagavadpāda was visibly happy! They all sat in silence to absorb the truth of the conclusions. *Ācārya* struck when the iron was hot!

"Now let us go further. If the mind alone initiates the perception process, what is the field of impressions where the *impressions* in the form of *resultant reactions of pleasure-pain, good-bad, happiness-misery, emotions, analysis, decisions and all that we consider important in life*?"

"*Bhagawan*, it is consciousness alone. In fact, the consciousness *functions as Manas, Buddhi, Cittam and Ahamkāra,* which proves beyond any doubt whatsoever, that without the *Prajñā*—awareness or the *attention* the world is not!" It was Toṭaka who used to be mostly silent during such discussions! As Bhagavadpāda continued to probe, there was a trace of blissful pride in his voice.

"*Sādhu*, *Sādhu*! Now if we agree that the perception happens *within*, what about the responses and the reactions to the external perceptions, where do they get generated, where are they sustained, and ultimately, where do they all dissolve?" There was a spontaneous outburst from the disciples:

"It is within!" With love oozing out of his being, *Ācārya* added another question for taking them to the deeper recesses of their being:

"By these perceptions, responses and reactions is there any change in the mind?" Knowing that it was a difficult question, he clarified, "By change I mean, is there any quantitative change in the mind, because you have *added the perceptions of the external world, you have evoked responses and provoked reactions*! Is there any *basic change* in your mind? To understand this we should probe into what happens after the passage of time."

"We normally forget the perception, our response or even reaction to it, with the passage of time, as the perception is generated, sustained and dissolved by and in the mind." It was the king of Kashmir. Nodding approvingly, *Ācārya* continued:

"There is neither quantitative change, nor *qualitative* change. When one stands in front of a mirror, his image gets reflected in it. An elephant passes by and its image too gets reflected. Just as there is no change whatsoever in the mirror, our consciousness too reflects, responses and reacts. The only difference is that for a mirror the object is external, but for the mind or the consciousness *everything is internal*! The tendency to project the change in consciousness on *Self* is *Adhyāsa.*[123] *Actually the Self is only witnessing the change without any involvement whatsoever*! Let me explain it further. Like *Jāgrat Awastha*—the wakeful state, we have two more *Awasthas*, *Swapna* or the dream state and *Suṣupti* or the deep sleep state. What you dream does not remain and you require lot of effort to remember your dream. In deep sleep, you are totally *unaware*. After waking up, all you do is *declare that you slept nicely and that the sleep refreshed you!* Though you do not remember what had happened *during your dream or sleep* you *were* during the sleep and continue to *be* after waking up! The only reality is the *Sākṣi—pure* witness. Everything else is only a perception."

All of them experienced an insight, much like the persons moving through a dark tunnel see a hint of light when they approach the end of the tunnel. Bhagavadpāda resumed:

"The perception, response, emotions, reactions, analysis and the *Ahamkāra* are but waves of the same consciousness and this consciousness is changeless, immutable, infinite and eternal.

---

123. अन्यस्मिन् अन्यावभासः; अतस्मिंतद् बुद्धिः अध्यासः । The perception of the *other* in the *other*; perceiving that which is *not* is *Adhyāsa*.

Only *IT IS* and the *Dvaita—otherness* is only apparent, like the waves are *no-other* than the ocean. We are those waves, who have been brought together by Providence. Let us plunge into the ocean *Brahman* to merge with IT."

Knowing that they were with him all along, the wave Śaṅkara Bhagavadpāda enveloped the other waves and gave that final benediction:

"Oh how wonderful! I am the infinite ocean and all the creation with all its creatures is but my waves that naturally rise, grow, play and enter me!"[124]

Down below, some of the pilgrims *felt* that the mountain range was spreading light. When they pointed it to others, the others saw it not! How could they, for they were *nurturing otherness*. Most of even those who had perceived the light felt that it was only an apparition of the mind! But two of them were seekers, made bold to climb the mountain to trace the source of light. They did not regret it, for they saw the group consisting of persons from different strata—monks, recluses, householders, as well as kings sitting without being conscious of their status, absorbing holiness which was enveloping the region. The very sight humbled them. They sat and involuntarily closed their eyes to join the feast!

Snow peaks of Himalaya were bathed in the amber light of the sun on its journey towards the western horizon. The solar day was at its conclusion, but another day had just begun, the day when the sun of *Advaita* had risen never to set again. It was not that *Advaita* was not, in the earlier ages. It had been the experience of all those spiritual scientists—our ancestors, whom we call *Ṛṣis*. Śaṅkara Bhagavadpāda had been chosen by the Providence to revive it and to remind our nation of its inherent greatness and its all-encompassing culture.

As the group opened their eyes, they beheld their beloved *Guru* who was more like a friend, and a caring parent, smiling affectionately and giving benediction to each one of them. They too shared *his fulfillment, his Being and His enlightenment* in that moment. They heard his sweet melodious voice reciting:

---

124. मय्यनन्तमहाम्भोधौ आश्चर्यं जीववीचयः । उद्यन्ति घ्नन्ति खेलन्ति प्रविशन्ति स्वभावतः ॥ अष्टावक्र गीता 22:25 ॥

"I am neither the mind, nor the intellect, nor the ego, nor the mind-stuff;

I am neither the body, nor the changes in the body;

I am neither the senses of hearing, taste, smell, or sight,

Nor am I the ether, the earth, the fire, the air;

I am Existence Absolute, Knowledge Absolute, Bliss Absolute—I am He,

I am He. (*Śivo'ham, Śivo'ham*).

I am neither the *Prāṇa*, nor the five vital airs;

I am neither the seven materials of the body, nor the five sheaths;

Neither am I the organs of action, nor objects of senses;

I am Existence Absolute, Knowledge Absolute, Bliss Absolute—I am He,

I am He. (*Śivo'ham, Śivo'ham*).

I am neither aversion, nor attachment, neither greed nor delusion;

Neither egotism nor envy, neither *Dharma* nor *Mokṣa*;

I am neither desire nor the objects of desire;

I am Existence Absolute, Knowledge Absolute, Bliss Absolute—I am He,

I am He. (*Śivo'ham, Śivo'ham*).

I am neither sin nor virtue, neither pleasure nor pain;

Nor temple nor worship, nor pilgrimage nor scriptures;

Neither act of enjoying, the enjoyable nor the enjoyer;

I am Existence Absolute, Knowledge Absolute, Bliss Absolute—I am He,

I am He. (*Śivo'ham, Śivo'ham*).

I have neither death nor fear of death, nor caste;

Nor was I ever born, nor had I parents, friends and relations;

I have neither *Guru*, nor disciple;

I am Existence Absolute, Knowledge Absolute, Bliss Absolute—I am He,

I am He. (*Śivo'ham, Śivo'ham*).

I am untouched by senses, I am neither *Mukti* nor knowable;

I am without form, without limit, beyond space and time;

I am everything, I am the basis of the universe, everywhere am I;

I am Existence Absolute, Knowledge Absolute, Bliss Absolute—I am He,

I am He. (*Śivo'ham, Śivo'ham*). I am Existence Absolute, Knowledge Absolute, Bliss

Absolute—I am He,

I am He. (*Śivo'ham, Śivo'ham*)."[125]

When the disciples and the devotees opened their eyes, they did not see the physical form of Śaṅkara Bhagavadpāda, but the refrain of *Śivo'ham, Śivo'ham, Śivo'ham, Śivo'ham, Śivo'ham, Śivo'ham...* continued to reverberate from the cave, its resonance spreading in the valley, on to the mountains and re-echoing throughout the Existence. They knew that their beloved *Guru* IS—*NO-OTHER*!

❐

---

125. *Nirvāṇaṣaṭkam* translated by Swami Vivekananda (*Complete Works*, Vol. IV, pp. 391-92. Advaita Ashrama, Calcutta, 1997).

मनो बुद्ध्यहंकार चित्तानि नाऽहं न च श्रोत्रजिह्वे न च घ्राण नेत्रे ।न च व्योमभूमिर्न तेजो न वायुः चिदानन्दरूपः शिवोऽहं शिवोऽहम् ॥ 1 ॥

न च प्राणसंज्ञो न वै पञ्चवायुः न वा सप्तधातु र्न वा पञ्चकोशः ।न वाक्पाणिपादं न चोपस्थपायु चिदानन्दरूपः शिवोऽहं शिवोऽहम् ॥ 2 ॥

न मे द्वेषरागौ न मे लोभमेहौ न मे वै मदो नैव मात्सर्यभावः ।न धर्मो न चार्थो न कामो न मोक्षः चिदानन्दरूपः शिवोऽहं शिवोऽहम् ॥ 3 ॥

न पुण्यं न पापं न सौख्यं न दुःखं न मन्त्रो न तीर्थं न वेदा न यज्ञ ।अहं भोजनं नैव भोज्यं न भोक्ता चिदानन्दरूपः शिवोऽहं शिवोऽहम् ॥ 4 ॥

न मे मृत्युशंका न मे जातिभेदः पिता नैव मे नैव माता न जन्मः ।न बन्धुर्न मित्रं गुरुर्नैव शिष्यः चिदानन्दरूपः शिवोऽहं शिवोऽहम् ॥ 5 ॥

अहं निर्विकल्पो निराकार रूपो विभुत्वाच सर्वत्र सर्वेन्द्रियाणाम् ।न चा सङ्गतं नैव मुक्तिर्न मेयः चिदानन्दरूपः शिवोऽहं शिवोऽहम् ॥ 6 ॥

॥ निर्वाणषटकम् ॥

Śankara—No-Other (Epilogue)

Clouds meandered on shoulders of the snow peaks while a blanket of mist covered the valley. The coniferous sentinels played hide and seek with the eyes of the beholders. The river flowed below negotiating the boulders and rocks, discovering her path. Having bid farewell to *Bhagawan* Śaṅkara Bhagavadpāda in the physical dimension all the devotees had moved to *Jyotirmaṭh*. All they thought and spoke was about their beloved *Guru* whose benign person had brought them all together. It was he who had instilled in them the sense of love and pride in our culture; it was due to him that an atmosphere of receptivity had been created in the length and breadth of Bhārat. The *four directions* as *Bhagawan* had addressed them had taken on the responsibility as guides to the devotees. They continued to *be* in *Advaita*, though their transactions with one another and the world *appeared* normal! Realising that the task their beloved master had for them would not allow them to be with one another anymore, they wanted to make the best of the time they had with one another.

Each day they would sit with the devotees and the initiates and have *Satsaṅga*. They would reminisce of their times with Bhagavadpāda, when they had learnt to live the truths enshrined in our scriptures. While these sessions made their bond for one another stronger, also strengthening their commitment to the *Guru Paramparā* in particular and our culture in general. It all began one day when Kṛṣṇarāya asked Padmapādācārya:

"*Ācārya*, will you please tell us how did *Bhagawān* Śaṅkara Bhagavadpāda influence your life?" The assembly was all ears when Padmapādācārya started speaking.

"How can a drop dare to describe the infinite ocean?" As he uttered these words, there were tears of gratefulness flowing from his eyes. Recovering he continued with a smile: "I am basically an emotional person reacting spontaneously to the situations. But I was not aware of my nature. It was our *Guru*, who made me aware of it while guiding me to use it to my advantage. When I came in search of knowledge to *Vārāṇasi*—the city of light, I met many seekers and saints, learnt a few things while forgetting others! But one evening I heard a sonorous musical voice which enchanted me. Attracted I went in the direction to find our beloved Master reciting *Annapūrṇāṣṭakam.* Perhaps his mood or his being or the way in which he had identified with mother *Annapūrṇā*, I forgot everything else and sat lost, tears flowing down my eyes and just happy. I came to my senses when Master patted me, and that first touch made me *his* forever!"

In that pause, everyone recalled their first meeting. Though it had been different for every one of them, the effect had always been the same, He had conquered their hearts! The steady voice of Padmapādācārya brought them back into present.

"'Your nature is *Bhāva Pradhāna*,' he had pointed out, 'You forget yourself while in *Bhāva*.' I had realised then that I always flowed with my emotions! Master had explained that normally, we all flow with our emotions[126] and that our emotions can be used for our growth.

He had then advised me to direct the emotions to my *Iṣṭa*. But as and when I started identifying with my Master, I discovered that the emotions are only the manifestations of thoughts and that 'I' can be *Sākṣi*—a non-involved witness."

The listeners recalled that Padmapādācārya had identified with the Master to the extent that he transcended even the physical barriers so as to come walking on water at the beck

126. Derived from the Latin word '*emotus*' which means to *move* or to *flow out*.

of *Bhagawān* that had earned him his name! King of Kashmir interposed:

"*Ācārya*, can you please elaborate on this, because most of us *are* emotional and it will be of great help to our growth."

"All emotions flow towards someone with whom there is a relationship—mother, father, friend, master, beloved or the enemy. The first five evoke positive emotions while the last evokes negative emotions. It is safer to relate oneself with the *Iṣṭa* positively, though there are examples in our *Itihāsa* who accepted the Lord as their enemy![127] Initially, I used to relate myself as the servant, but as and when my identification with the Master grew, Master became my *Iṣṭa*; He was related to me in every possible way. During the last few days, in the cave when I was alone with him...." There was silence as he relived those moments. Every one became all ears. After a pause *Ācārya* continued with his eyes lustrous, his being luminous:

"There was a sudden shift in my being. I sat facing Him and it was not the Master that I saw. Instead, it was an expansive ocean of light without beginning or end. My heart welled up with thoughts and emotions, and they just merged with the ocean. Mind, Intellect, Ego...were just wavelets of that ocean. To my awe, I became the ocean of awareness and ever since, I continue to *be*!"[128]

The group had a small glimpse of the *Being* of Padmapādācārya. They heard a full laughter, which had bliss as well as humour in it! When the eyes turned in the direction it was Sureśwarācārya, who was laughing at *himself*!

"Forgive me, brothers, I am laughing at my ignorant impudence when I first beheld him, young, fresh as a blossoming lotus in the morning, pure and innocent. I now know that it was my jealousy. How an inexperienced youth can understand anything in the scriptures, I had wondered! It was as though

---

127. Hiraṇyakaśipu-Hiraṇyākṣa, Rāvaṇa-Kumbhakarṇa, and Dantavakra-Śiśupāla were the door-keepers of Viṣṇu had to either choose ten incarnations as devotees or three as the Lord's enemies. They chose to be His enemies!

128. This is the realisation of the *Mahāvākya—Prajñānam Brahma*.

the death itself had appeared in *his form*! I did die, as Maṇḍana the scholar, to be born as an humble disciple of the Master. He guided me slowly to make me realise that *all activity is meant to purify the mind*; that pure mind is mandatory to behold the Truth; and that the Truth is never *outside but ever within*!"

"*Ācārya*, is there any specific method to purify the mind?" It was Rājasena of Kānci. Sureśwarācārya responded.

"There is nothing like a specific activity because each one of us is unique! The joy lies in *discovering* that path which suits the individual. 'That path alone, by following which a person becomes grounded in real *I-principle*, is the right path for him. There is no one single path which suits all alike.'[129] That does not however mean that one should wait till the suitable path is discovered. And that is where our *Śāstras* help us by offering so many options at the body, senses, mind, intellect and *Ahamkāra*."

Eyes half closed, Sureśwarācārya was reliving the moments he had learnt to really *live*! When he resumed, there was humility and pride; humility due to the grace of providence on him, and pride for his being a disciple of *Bhagawan* Śaṅkara Bhagavadpāda.

"It was His genius to keep me engaged in such activity that would not only purify my mind, but also would make my *Ahamkāra* expansive and *all inclusive.* His directive to write a *Vārtika* of his commentary on the *Brahmasūtras* was not really to test my understanding of *Advaita*, but to test my *living Advaita* day-to-day! I am now certain that it was *His* conspiracy to create a situation of jealousy and the subsequent command not to write the *Vārtika* but to venture on an independent work! Initially, I felt that all the activity was performed by *Him*, through me; gradually I started experiencing that *He too was an instrument of something More Expansive and Greater*. This brought about a great change that made every action effort free! It was in the cave that day when there was sudden change in consciousness, an indescribable awareness that 'my puny *I* is *no other* than

---

129. यया यया भवेत्पुंसां व्युत्पत्तिः प्रत्यगात्मनि । सा सैव प्रक्रिया साध्वी ज्ञेया सा चानवस्थिता ॥ सुरेश्वराचार्य उपनिषद् वार्तिका ॥

Brahman!'[130] The whole gross universe as well as the subtle *creation* of the mind, intellect and ego, appears and disappears like a dream, while the only reality is *Brahman*!"

Experiential words coming out Sureśwarācārya further helped the devotees to get into their being to savour bliss therein. If someone not acquainted with spirituality would say that the whole group consisted of persons who were not really sane! And how mistaken would they be, for all of them personified sanity!

The group of devotees felt the whole place charging with the peaceful benevolence, warmth, and an unmistakable bond of love. It was as though it was spreading and holding all of them in its invisible arms! Everyone merged in that grand *Bhāva*—mood, to partake the nectar. It was quite some time when they started coming back to their so-called normal consciousness. Padmapādācārya was smiling and looking at Hastāmalakācārya with respect and adoration. He said:

"Brothers, Hastāmalakācārya did not want to *say anything*! He gifted us a glimpse into his natural state of being. He is a man of very few words!" The devotees were filled with awe and reverence for him. But Keśava did not give up, he approached the *Ācārya* and prostrated. He asked in al humility:

"*Ācārya*, the other day I did not dare to disturb *Bhagawan* with my doubt for we all wanted *Him* to speak. But He made a passing reference to *Adhyāsa*. You are the right person to tell us about it." Hastāmalakācārya smiled and cleared his throat:

"Brother, the experience you all had is a natural and perpetual state of being. Our involvement with mind and intellect, and indulgence with the gross matter however, cover the state and gradually we forget it. Just like our involvement makes the dream *apparently real*, because the entity that dreams is forgotten. Whatever we see in a dream is nothing but the mind itself, but it *appears* real *during the dream*! *Avidyā,* the forgetfulness of the Self, is the cause for being involved with the *impression of perception* of ever changing and temporary world of objects. The objects as such are *only impressions* and

130. Aham Brahmāsmi—I am Brahman.

temporary waves of consciousness! We take them to be *real* and forget the *Self*, the substratum of experience. This is *Adhyāsa.*"

They all had an insight into the truth contained in the statement of Hastāmalakācārya. The world outside was real *only when the Self perceived it*, and *never otherwise*! And the perception no matter big or small *never affected the consciousness*! This understanding took them further into the infinite dimension of Self. For a long time, in fact none of them were aware of any time or space as such, but got absorbed in the revelation of No-Otherness. After a while returning to the so-called normal consciousness, they realised that there was one more *direction* sitting with them incognito. They all looked at Toṭakācārya with affection and appeal in their eyes to talk to them. There was a smile and a feeling of intimacy radiating from his being. He spoke:

"I came to *Bhagawan* attracted by his smile! His ever smiling eyes preceded all his actions. I fell at his feet and confided that I did not have any education, and I desperately wanted to be with him. In all compassion he asked me to be his attendant. I started following him everywhere like a shadow. I found that his words and deeds always matched, nay they were identical. How could such a person miss to behold the Truth? He became my ideal and my Truth! Then commenced my journey, as I was with the group everywhere and every-when! During the journey, after meeting a vast variety of people of regions and languages, I started noting that each individual is unique having a perspective that is unique to that individual. Though two persons were looking at the same object or discussing the same topic, each perceived it in his own unique way! This was due to the individual position, nature and conditioning. But as Master always understood and accepted the differences, he helped them to shift their attention from gross to the subtle. That was why, whoever came to him, joined the band of soldiers of our culture. Due to my identification with the master, slowly and steadily, my vision became expansive and almost all inclusive. One day, when we were in Kashmir, just after His ascension to the *Sarvajña Pīṭham* he called me…" Toṭakācārya fell silent for a pause. The group was totally receptive and waiting with a baited breath. He continued:

"*Bhagawan* asked me to sit in front of him. All my attention rested on his gentle face. He then looked into my eyes in all compassion. In those pools of eyes, I saw myself, my own eyes and to my utter amazement, those very eyes contained the whole of creation, without beginning or end. Yes, words fail me and any speech can only be a *description*! Yet I shall only try."

While all the four *directions* had merged to become *Ākāśa*—space, the rest of the group had become ready receptacles to behold the essence of the words contained in the speech of Toṭakācārya:

"The eyes contained the creation of past, present and also the future, the universe in all its splendour and magnificence. A voice declared '*All This verily is Ātman, This Ātman is Brahman.*'[131] By this act of compassion *Bhagawan* assures all of us that in spite of all limitations, Truth is the birthright of each one of us."

It was as though the assurance came from Śaṅkara Bhagavadpāda through his beloved disciples, the *four directions*! The group got pushed into a silent benevolence and expansion. All of them had become recipient to the benevolence of *Śankara—No-Other*. So can we!

❐

131. Ayam Ātmā Brahma—This Self is Brahman.

Index

R

S

T

U

V

Y

❑❑❑